EDNA E GAMMON

A Fatal pickup

THE BRUTAL WARTIME MURDER THAT SHOCKED TWO NATIONS

EDNA E GAMMON

A fatal pickup

THE BRUTAL WARTIME MURDER THAT SHOCKED TWO NATIONS

MEREO
Cirencester

Mereo Books

1A The Wool Market Dyer Street Cirencester Gloucestershire GL7 2PR
An imprint of Memoirs Publishing www.mereobooks.com

A FATAL PICKUP: 978-1-86151-400-4

First published in Great Britain in 2015
by Mereo Books, an imprint of Memoirs Publishing

Copyright ©2015

Edna E Gammon has asserted her right under the Copyright Designs and Patents Act 1988 to be identified as the author of this work.

A CIP catalogue record for this book is available from the British Library.

This book is sold subject to the condition that it shall not by way of trade or otherwise be lent, resold, hired out or otherwise circulated without the publisher's prior consent in any form of binding or cover, other than that in which it is published and without a similar condition, including this condition being imposed on the subsequent purchaser.

The address for Memoirs Publishing Group Limited can be found at
www.memoirspublishing.com

The Memoirs Publishing Group Ltd Reg. No. 7834348

The Memoirs Publishing Group supports both The Forest Stewardship Council® (FSC®) and the PEFC® leading international forest-certification organisations. Our books carrying both the FSC label and the PEFC® and are printed on FSC®-certified paper. FSC® is the only forest-certification scheme supported by the leading environmental organisations including Greenpeace. Our paper procurement policy can be found at
www.memoirspublishing.com/environment

Typeset in 10/15pt Bembo
by Wiltshire Associates Publisher Services Ltd. Printed and bound in Great Britain by Printondemand-Worldwide, Peterborough PE2 6XD

ACKNOWLEDGEMENTS

My grateful thanks to Rodger Hull, a researcher at the Liverpool Library and Record Office, whose help with this case was valued in writing this book.

My thanks also to Topfoto, who provided me with images which at one time I thought I would never obtain.

A special thanks to my husband for the long hours he spent sifting through British, American and Australian newspaper archives relating to this case. The information he discovered and his support and devotion have been amazing.

Many thanks to Stockholm City Archives for supplying the parentage of Karl Gustav Hulten.

Very special thanks must go to Theresa Fitzgerald, the Archivist at The National Military Personnel Records Centre at St Louis, MO 63138-102 USA. Her help and guidance on this case have been second to none and I shall never be able to thank her enough. With her help I was able to purchase a copy of the trial transcript and In *The Court Of Criminal Appeal*.

PREFACE

I was a young girl in 1944 when the brutal killing of a London cab driver took place. Karl Gustav Hulten, an American GI based in this country in preparation for D-Day, and his accomplice, Elizabeth Maude Jones, were convicted of the crime. There was shock and anger across this country, and even more so in America.

At the time an older sister of mine, Manda, was going out with 'Strat', an American GI, who was stationed just outside Warrington. Before this murder took place my late mother was subjected to much ill feeling in the neighbourhood because of Strat and my sister. When the news of this murder was made known, this bad feeling became much worse. I think Strat knew what was going on in the neighbourhood, but he never said a word about it, or the murder. My feelings at the time were that he had great respect for our family, especially my mother. Strat, who came from Chicago, was posted back to America, I believe in 1945. He proposed several times to my sister, but she did not have the same feelings for him.

Sadly Manda has gone, and I imagine so has Strat, and also many of the people I once knew during those difficult years. Writing this book takes me back to that time in my life.

Contents

Introduction

Chapter 1	The GI and the girl from South Wales	P. 1
Chapter 2	London – city of dreams and disappointment	P. 4
Chapter 3	A deadly partnership	P. 9
Chapter 4	Death of a cab driver	P. 13
Chapter 5	A tissue of lies	P. 18
Chapter 6	The trial - first day	P. 24
Chapter 7	The trial – second day	P. 70
Chapter 8	The trial - third day	P. 178
Chapter 9	The trial - fourth day	P. 273
Chapter 10	The trial - fifth day	P. 378
Chapter 11	The trial - sixth day	P. 417
Chapter 12	The verdict	P. 421
Chapter 13	Aftermath	P. 429

Introduction

In January 1945, during the closing days of the Second World War, 22-year-old Karl Gustav Hulten, an American GI based in England in preparation for D-Day, and Elizabeth Maude Jones, a so-called striptease dancer, were found guilty of the brutal murder of George Edward Heath, a London hire car driver.

The case was a sensation from the start, and dominated the newspaper headlines on the home front, in America and across the world. Both were sentenced to hang, but at the eleventh hour Jones was reprieved, which caused widespread anger across the country, especially in her home town of Neath in South Wales. The Prime Minister at the time, Winston Churchill, told the Home Secretary, Herbert Morrison, that his decision to grant Jones a reprieve was in his view wrong.

Hulten was hanged on the 8th March 1945, aged 23. Jones served nine years in prison and was released on licence in 1954. There were several reports as to what happened to her after that, but it seems she disappeared into the ashbin of history.

This all happened not long after the historic D-Day landings in Normandy by the Allies, on the 6th June 1944, and Hulten was hanged just before Germany's final surrender in May 1945. Thanks to its potential for stirring up Anglo-American animosity, the propaganda value of the case was claimed by the Germans to be worth a military division in the field.

CHAPTER ONE

THE GI AND THE GIRL FROM SOUTH WALES

Karl Gustav Hulten was born in Stockholm to Swedish parents on the 3rd March 1922. His father was Gustaf Adolf Hulten, born on 2nd November 1876 at 9 Rosenbad in Karlstad; his mother was Signe Maria Hulten (nee Jansson) born 22nd January 1895 at 4 Hjarnegatan Kungsholmen, Stockholm. Karl was baptised on the 5th September 1922 at Kristinehamn.

While Hulten was still a baby, his parents separated. In 1923 his mother emigrated with her baby son to America in the hope of a better life. Mrs Hulten found work in Boston, Massachusetts, as a domestic worker in a wealthy American household.

On leaving school Hulten took a job as a grocer's clerk, then a lorry driver for the Salvation Army and finally a driver for a car rental company. This was the start of his great passion for motorcars. His mother always claimed he was a good son and never gave her any cause for concern.

Hulten also went to the Farm And Trade School at Thompson's Island, Boston. The headmaster at the time was William M. Meacham, who said Hulten had an IQ of 96, slightly below average.

On an evening out with friends, Hulten met dark-haired Rita Pero and fell in love with her; they married after a brief courtship. The marriage produced a baby daughter, who they named Jean.

After the bombing of Pearl Harbour which brought the United States into the war, Hulten was inducted into the Army on the 7th May 1942 and sent to Fort Benning, Georgia, for training as a paratrooper. Reports say his Army record in America was satisfactory, but it was claimed he had a weak character and was easily led and careless with money. He was never short of girlfriends.

Hulten's unit sailed for England in January 1944 in preparation for D-Day. Little did he know it was the last time he would see America and his family.

Elizabeth Maude Baker was born on the 5th July 1926 at Brynbedw, Lonlas, Skewen, Neath, South Wales, to Arthur Thomas Baker and Nellie Baker. Arthur Baker worked as a labourer in an oil refinery. She had an elder sister, Gwladys, who was a semi-invalid, and Baker would always claim her parents lavished all their love and attention on her.

Baker became wilful and rebellious at an early age and eventually her parents were unable to control her. Several times she ran away from her home and was found by the police roaming the streets of Swansea. Her parents had no choice but to seek the help of the Juvenile Court, who without hesitation sent her to an approved school in Sale, Cheshire.

For a short time Baker responded to the strict rules of the school, but again her rebellious nature surfaced and she ran away back to her distressed parents. They were not prepared to cope with their wayward daughter, and she was taken back to the approved school.

Nearing the age of fifteen, Baker became interested in dancing, and the school encouraged this as they hoped it would take her mind off trying to run away. It became an obsession with her and she dreamed of being a star in London's nightlife. She enticed another girl at the school to run away with her to London. One night they stole clothes and money and left the school. Together they went from one London dance hall to the next, dazzled by the music and the crowded dance floors, and Baker was truly hooked.

The police discovered them sleeping rough and they were taken back to the school under escort. For the next few months Baker behaved herself, but she was unable to forget the glittering world of London's nightlife.

The school decided soon after her sixteenth birthday to send her home for a short holiday as a test of her behaviour. During this holiday she met a young man who her parents had known for some time, Stanley Jones, a Corporal Gunner in the Airborne Forces. In the cunning mind of Baker, Jones was going to be the means to get her away from the life she was leading and from the approved school.

Jones was attracted to her and was surprised when she agreed to marry him at sixteen. Her parents were alarmed when Baker told them, as they did not consider her fit to marry at such an early age, but Baker made it clear that she would never go back to the approved school and would leave Neath if she had to. Her parents knew they had to give in, so the couple were married at Neath Registry Office in November 1942.

This sixteen-year-old's plan was now in motion, and furthermore she had an Army allowance to sustain her. Reports say the marriage was never consummated and a few days following their wedding she quite coolly told Stanley Jones she was leaving both him and Neath, and there was nothing he could do about it. Her new life was about to start - and what a life it was going to be.

CHAPTER TWO

LONDON – CITY OF DREAMS AND DISAPPOINTMENT

Elizabeth Jones, as she now was, arrived at Paddington Station, London, on 25th January 1943 with two small suitcases and no place to go. She had no job, but she had her Army allowance of £1-12 shillings a week. At this point in time there was nothing glamorous about her. She was shabbily dressed, her hair a dull brown and she wore cheap make-up, but she was going to change all that.

She was still obsessed with dancing, but she had the good sense to realise that she needed more money than her Army allowance for this. Jobs she took on included working as a waitress, a barmaid and a cinema usherette. She then began to do the rounds of the London nightclubs in the hope of finding other work, but without success.

At a dance hall she met a musician, who arranged for her to have an audition at a Knightsbridge club. She told the manager she was a striptease dancer, but he was not very impressed with her first performance in private. Her knowledge of the art of undressing alluringly was slight, to say the least. However, he decided to give her a chance.

On her first night in the spotlight of the club, Jones was as hopeless as he had feared. Her clumsy efforts to undress in a sexy way were pathetic, and eventually she was booed off the floor. She blamed the band for not playing in the right tempo.

This experience dealt a blow to Jones' ambitions to be a stripper. This young, foolish teenager had obviously been under the illusion that all she had to do was to walk on to the stage floor and while the band played, remove her clothes. In fact this type of performance requires a great deal of training and time to reach perfection. The legendary Gypsy Rose Lee was considered second to none as a striptease artiste and actress, and her whole life revolved around perfecting every performance.

Jones went to live in Lexham Mews, Kensington. She dyed her hair peroxide blonde and wore cheap, flashy jewellery and all the things she thought would make her look glamorous. She found work as a hostess at a sleazy nightclub and drinking haunt mainly frequented by Americans based in England, who were fleeced by being sold cheap booze at high prices.

From her small room, still in the hope of a stage career, she constantly wrote letters to famous personalities. One of these letters was sent to Jack Buchanan, the entertainer and actor.

Back in Neath her parents were worried about what was going to happen to their daughter. They constantly wrote to her asking her to return to Stanley, her husband, but the thought of going back to Neath and her boring husband repelled her. She lived a life of idleness, staying in bed until midday, lazing the afternoon away and then later preparing for the American officers she was going to entertain in the evening.

For some reason she lost her job as a hostess at the nightclub. She became depressed and careless about her appearance and totally dissatisfied with her lifestyle. During any short-lived acquaintance she had with one of the Americans she would tell them fantastic stories, such as telling them her career as a striptease dancer was on hold, as she was considering a possible offer of a stage job. Reports say at this point in time she was living on her Army allowance and her savings.

The bombing of London disturbed her to the extent that she went to stay in Cardiff, but the lure of the glittering nightlife was so intense that she soon returned to London.

In August 1944 Jones returned, with a girlfriend, to her parents, laden with goods they had been given by their American boyfriends. Her parents would say later that their daughter was like a stranger to them. While she was in Neath Jones met her husband for a short time, and it appeared they had become reconciled, but reports said the marriage was still not consummated.

Stanley was eventually recalled to his unit and Jones, after many frequent rows with her parents, left Neath. The next time she would see her parents would be in Holloway Prison – on a murder charge.

★ ★ ★

When Hulten landed in England in January 1944, Jones was doing the rounds of London's nightlife. The odds that these two would meet at that time seemed long. Hulten, it was said, was a happily married man with a baby daughter. He was training for D-Day, and his army record up to this point was claimed to be satisfactory. But fate had other plans.

Their future victim, George Edward Heath, was a 34-year-old private hire cab driver who was married with two sons, Tony and Arthur. At the start of World War Two, Heath had been a war reserve constable, then a driver for the Royal Army Service Corps. He ended up in France. At the time of the Dunkirk evacuations in 1940, he managed to get back to Britain with what was left of the British Army, but he was left a broken and sick man.

In September 1940, while he was recovering, a bomb fell near his house. Heath and his family escaped with minor injuries, but his health suffered a complete breakdown. He was sent to a mental hospital at

Epsom in Surrey and his family was evacuated to Worcester. On his discharge from the hospital the family returned home and they found another house in Ewell in Surrey.

When Heath's health improved he was offered a job as a hire car driver, which he accepted, and from there on life for the family was good. The dark days seemed to have passed. But as time went on Heath's life began to change dramatically. He was described as a 'wide boy' who was apparently heavily involved in horse race betting and the black market.

Later on his wife, Winifred Ivy, would say in her statement that their marriage was not a happy one. George liked to have plenty of money, and he had a quick temper. He also liked going out with different women. In the autumn of 1943 he left her. After leaving his wife he was involved in a fight in a public house and subsequently charged with an assault on the publican. But by the time the court appearance was due to take place, Heath was dead.

★ ★ ★

In the summer of 1944 with Hulten in his camp, Jones living in Hammersmith and Heath driving his hire car, the separate destinies of these three individuals were rushing towards each other with relentless speed.

At the end of August 1944 Hulten left his unit. He always insisted he had gone absent without leave. To desert meant one had no intention of going back to the unit, while absent without leave meant your intention was to return to your unit at some time. Hulten's unit was based near Reading and he became troublesome to the military police and left the camp on more than one occasion. However, reports say that because of the preparations for D-Day, little notice was taken of this.

At the beginning of August 1944, Hulten's unit crossed the Channel to join in the battle for France. Hulten was left behind to look after the motor transport pool.

On the 28 September 1944, a Private J B Patterson left his USA army truck No 4544863-S outside Reading railway station to use the toilet. When he returned after a few minutes the truck was gone. By all the evidence presented, this was the Army truck Hulten took and used. Private Patterson said in his statement that he never saw the vehicle again until the 16th October 1944.

On or about 10th September 1944, Hulten stole from Staff Sergeant Irving, who was based on the same station, a .45 calibre pistol. For weeks he lived the life of a gangster, sleeping in his truck, while under the cover of the blackout he robbed shops, taking money and goods. It would seem he revelled in this new life.

CHAPTER THREE

A DEADLY PARTNERSHIP

Hulten was wearing a stolen American officer's uniform when he walked into a café in Hammersmith on the Tuesday 3rd October 1944 and met Jones for the first time. She was sitting at a table with a man named Leonard Bexley, who Hulten knew slightly, and it was Bexley who introduced them. Jones gave her dancer's name, Georgina Grayson, and Hulten gave his name as Ricky Allen. It was by these names that the pair were to know each other throughout their partnership.

Hulten had no trouble in persuading Jones to go for a drive almost at midnight that same night. What these two discussed during the drive will never be known, but according to Jones in her statements later, Hulten told her that the truck they were riding in was a stolen Army vehicle. He then went on to tell her that back in Chicago he had been a big-time gangster and he was building up a gang in London. She also claimed that he showed her an automatic pistol at this time. How much of this is true we will never know, but it has to be remembered what type of character Jones was. In any event she was obviously impressed. Up to now her acquaintance with American gangsters had been confined to films and magazines, and now with Ricky her dreams of being a gangster's moll might become a reality.

Hulten would claim later that she responded with enthusiasm to all his suggestions and went on to say she wanted to do something dangerous, like flying over Germany in a bomber. Their six days of crime, and eventually murder, were about to start.

On Wednesday 4th October 1944, as the couple were driving towards Reading on a lonely country road, they saw a young girl riding home on her bicycle. Jones claimed that Hulten turned to her and said, 'Watch this!' He then swerved to one side, knocking the girl off her bicycle. She also claimed that he robbed her. They then drove off, leaving the girl dazed on the roadside.

There was some contradiction in the newspapers at that time as to whether this young girl was killed or not and regarding her identity. On this particular occasion, going by Jones' version of what happened that night, Hulten's second statement would dispute this. It will be noted that this second statement to Lieutenant De Mott was not put as evidence at the trial by the prosecution, but this will be explained later in the book.

On Thursday 5th October 1944, Hulten and Jones went to the pictures, and after a meal they drove off in the direction of Reading. According to Jones, Hulten planned to rob again, and on the way he pulled into a hotel car park, but he quickly drove off, saying they were being watched, and they headed back to London.

Hulten said that Jones suggested they hold up and rob a taxi driver. He then followed a cab going in the direction of Cricklewood. Having forced the cab to stop, he approached the driver, waving his gun at him, and demanded money. John Strangeway, the driver, said he had no money, as this was his first fare of the night. Hulten then looked in the back of the cab and saw there was a passenger. It was an American officer, Lieutenant George McMillan-Reeves, age 22 years, No 0866084 of 18a Weather Squadron, 367 Detachment, APO 639 USA. Forces. Hulten was badly shaken. He fled back to the truck and drove off to London's West End. John Strangeway said in his statement that this happened about 2.10 am on the 6th October. The American officer had just taken his lady friend home to Neasden.

Driving along the Edgware Road, Hulten and Jones saw a young girl with a large suitcase walking towards Paddington Station. Her name was Violet May Hodge, she was eighteen years and three months old and she lived at 8 Cowdray Road, Filwood Park, Knowle, Bristol. On Wednesday 27th September 1944, as a result of a quarrel with her mother, she had left home and gone to stay with her aunt, Mrs Kathleen Chapman, who had two rooms above Hornby's Dairy in Bristol. After spending some time in Bristol she borrowed a case from her aunt and went to London, arriving on Thursday 5th October 1944. She found there was no suitable place for her stay in London and made the decision to go back home to Bristol.

Later Hulten claimed it was Jones who insisted on giving Violet a lift, telling the young girl they were on the way to Reading and she could catch the train to Bristol from there. Violet got into the truck and sat between Hulten and Jones. No doubt a murderous plan was in their minds.

What exactly took place is based on what the police believe may have happened and the story that Jones told them to her own advantage. However Violet Hodge's own statement, taken at 2 pm 6th October 1944 at Windsor emergency hospital, differs in some of the details.

Suddenly Hulten stopped the truck, saying something was wrong with the wheel. Both girls got out. Jones stayed near the truck door and Violet, concerned over missing her train, walked to the back of the truck. Hulten came from behind and struck her on the head with a block of wood. He then hit her again with his fist and she fell to the ground unconscious.

During all this Jones stood by watching. Hulten shouted to her to help him to go through her handbag and suitcase, but all they ended up with was a few shillings. Jones took Violet's coat off and put it on, and they then carried her across a field and threw her into the river Thames. The rest of the girl's belongings were taken back to Jones' room, where Jones and Hulten happily spent what was left of the night together.

By some miracle Violet Hodge survived her ordeal. Reports said that the cold water of the Thames might have helped to revive her enough to drag herself out of the water and onto the bank, where she lay for some time. She managed to stagger across the field, where her cries for help were heard by the occupants of a house that was close by and she was taken inside.

The address was Beaumont Lodge, Old Windsor, Berks, the home of Ada Selina Mills and her two sons, Peter and John. The police were contacted and Violet was taken by car to the emergency hospital at Old Windsor. She was treated for severe head injuries and haemorrhage of the left eye.

On Friday 6th October Hulten spent most of the day at Jones lodgings. They were both very moody over the failure of their first taxi hold-up. Hulten would later claim Jones talked of nothing else but a further hold-up of a taxi. Hulten spent some hours cleaning his automatic pistol. Later he left her lodgings, calling back at about 11.30 pm, when they both got into the truck and drove off into a cold and wet night.

CHAPTER FOUR

DEATH OF A CAB DRIVER

On that same evening, Friday 6th October, George Heath was leaving for work in his Ford V8 saloon, registration number RD 8955. At 7 pm he called on a Mrs Violet Fleisig, a lady friend who lived at 43 Cumberland Street, Pimlico, SW1, and they agreed that he would pick her up at 8 am the following morning for a day's outing together. Before he left she lent him a fountain pen, a silver propelling pencil and a small polo cigarette lighter. He was wearing his own silver wristwatch on a leather strap and had a black leather wallet containing a photo of Mrs Fleisig in his inside jacket pocket.

Heath's destination that evening was Maidenhead, where he was to collect a party of Americans and bring them back to London. On his way he called into a garage for petrol. He then checked his watch and found he was running ahead of time, so he drove slowly.

As he was passing Hammersmith Broadway, a young girl came out of nowhere and hailed him down. Because she was almost standing in front of his cab, he had no choice but to stop.

'Are you a taxi?' she asked. 'No miss,' Heath replied, 'I am a private hire car, where do want to go?'

She replied, 'My home at King Street, Hammersmith'.

Heath was a little reluctant, thinking of his other fare waiting in Maidenhead. He checked his watch again for time. He could do it, but it was going to cost her.

The girl went to a doorway and reappeared with an American soldier. Heath had not bargained for a second passenger and told them it would cost them ten shillings, and they agreed. The pair got into the back seat of the cab and Heath turned the car around and headed back to Broadway, Hammersmith. Jones was sitting on the left side and Hulten was sitting directly behind Heath with the gun concealed in his right hand and the safety catch off.

When Heath arrived in King Street he started to slow down. Hulten leaned forward, saying 'It's a little further yet'. As they reached the Great West Road, Heath asked, 'How much further?' Hulten replied 'We are almost there'.

Then Heath pulled up, saying 'I can't take you any further, I have to drive to Maidenhead to collect another fare'. Hulten said 'OK, how much do we owe you? Heath then reached over to open the passenger door for Jones, and as he did so Hulten's gun fired.

In such an enclosed space it must have sounded like a bomb going off. The bullet went through the seat into Heath's body, and his cry terrified Jones as he slumped down moaning.

According to Jones, Hulten then got into the driver's seat and told the injured Heath to move over or he would give him another dose. During the drive Jones went through Heath's pockets. He was still breathing and later Jones would say that Hulten had ordered her to do this, saying that if she refused he would turn the gun on her. She removed his wristwatch, wallet, cigarette lighter and a fountain pen. Her hands were now covered with Heath's blood.

Hulten stopped the car at Knowle Green, near Staines, and with the help of Jones he threw Heath's helpless body into a ditch. It was now the early hours of Saturday 7th October 1944, and they headed back towards Jones lodgings.

On this same day Hulten sold the items that had been stolen from

Heath. That afternoon they went with a friend to the White City dog track and both won several pounds. In the evening they went out for a meal, followed by a visit to the cinema.

Sunday 8th October 1944 found this murderous pair planning more robberies. Jones was getting very ambitious as to what she would like to wear, and an expensive fur coat was in her mind. Hulten promised that if that was what she wanted, he would get one for her.

Later in the evening they went back to where they had left Heath's car, then drove to the West End, Jones telling Hulten to stop at one of the best hotels and wait. They stopped at the side entrance of the Berkeley Hotel near Piccadilly, and Jones' eyes lit up with excitement as she watched and waited. Several women appeared wearing fur coats, but Jones was not impressed. Then a woman wearing a beautiful white ermine came into view. She was only slightly built, so Hulten thought he would have no trouble. He rushed towards the woman, pulling off the fur coat, but her screams attracted a nearby policeman, who quickly came to her aid. Hulten dropped the coat, fled back to the car and drove away like a madman.

If Jones was disappointed by this setback, she tried not to show it. She wrote a letter to her father saying what a nice time she was having and that she had won some money at the races. 'I will close now as I'm going to a dance with an American officer,' she said.

★ ★ ★

On Monday 9th October 1944 Hulten and Jones parted; the reason for this is unknown. Hulten got into Heath's car and went to see another young girlfriend, Joyce Cook, aged 16, who lived at 159 Fulham Palace Road. He parked Heath's car in Lurgen Avenue on the corner of Fulham Palace Road.

Heath's body had been found early in the morning of Saturday the

7th October, the day after he was killed. Police inquiries showed he had earned his living as a private car hire driver, and they were now looking for the Ford V8 registered number RD 8955. A description was sent out to all police stations, and it was not long before a constable on his beat saw the car parked outside a house in Lurgen Avenue. In a short time Detective Inspector Tarr and Detective Inspector Read, who was leading the hunt, were alerted.

With reinforcements, the two officers went to Lurgen Avenue. As it was getting dark spotlights were trained on the parked car, ready to be switched on when the order was given.

It was some time before Hulten walked out of a house and got into the car. The spotlights were immediately turned on and several police officers rushed forward and pulled Hulten out of the car, pinning him up against a wall. He was asked if the car was his and said 'No'. A loaded automatic pistol was taken from his hip pocket, and he was then handcuffed and taken to Hammersmith police station.

In relation to an agreement made in 1942 between Britain and the USA, one of first things the British police were required to do in such circumstances was to contact the US Army authorities. No criminal proceedings were to be taken by a British court against a member of the American armed forces. If such a person was arrested for an offence, they were to be handed over to their own police for questioning and trial.

Lieutenant Robert De Mott of the American Army Criminal Investigation Department went to Hammersmith Police Station on the 10th October to question Hulten. De Mott cautioned him the American way, saying 'It is your privilege to remain silent and you do not have to make a statement, however if you choose to make a statement it may be used for or against you in the event of this investigation resulting in a trial'.

De Mott asked Hulten if he understood his rights, and Hulten just nodded his head and said 'Yes sir'. De Mott then proceeded, 'You are Karl Gustav Hulten, age twenty-two years, and you have been absent without leave from your unit for several weeks. When you left your base you stole a ten-wheel truck and a loaded automatic gun, is all this correct?'

Hulten replied, 'Yes sir, that is correct'.

De Mott then asked about the Ford V8 car. Hulten said he had found it abandoned in Newbury and went on to say that when Heath was shot on the night of the 6th October he had been sleeping in the truck near Newbury. De Mott had good reason to doubt what Hulten had told him.

Later in the day of Tuesday 10th October De Mott again questioned Hulten at the American CID Headquarters near Piccadilly. Hulten now changed his story, saying he had stolen the car from a car park in Hammersmith and had spent Friday night, 6th October, with a girlfriend. Hulten then remained under arrest at the United States Guard House. The following morning, Wednesday 11th October, he agreed to show De Mott where his girlfriend lived in King Street, Hammersmith.

The British police were notified, and without delay went to Jones' lodgings, arriving about midday to find her still in bed. She was taken to the police station, where she agreed to make a statement.

CHAPTER FIVE

LIES AND MORE LIES

On Wednesday 11th October 1944, Jones made her first statement. She gave her name as Elizabeth Maude Jones, born in Neath, Wales and eighteen years old. She went on to say that she was married and her husband was in the Army on active service, but she had been informed he was missing presumed dead. She went on: "I occupy one flat at 311 King Street Hammersmith and I have lived there about four weeks. I am a striptease dancer and the last engagements were in the Panama Club in Knightsbridge and the Blue Lagoon Club in Carnaby Street W1. That was five months ago and I have not had any engagements since."

She said that on Tuesday 3rd October she had met 'Ricky' in a café in Hammersmith; at the time she was sitting at a table with a Leonard Bexley, who Ricky new slightly. He introduced them as Georgina Grayson and Ricky; she agreed to go for a ride with him later that night. On the night of the murder, Friday 6th October, they went to the cinema. Ricky then left her for about three hours. He then returned, spending the night in her room. The next day, Saturday 7th October, was spent at the White City dog track. Jones duly signed her first statement, witnessed by Albert Tansill, Detective Inspector 'F' Division. The police decided at this time that there was no reason to detain her and she was allowed to leave the police station.

A FATAL PICKUP

At this point Hulten was making a further statement to De Mott saying that on the night of Friday the 6th October he had taken Joyce Cook to the movies. 'We returned to her house where I stayed until about eleven o'clock' he said. 'Afterwards I went back to see Georgina and we went for a walk. We had tea and a sandwich at an all-night café in Fulham Palace Road and left there about one o'clock in the morning. We returned to Georgina's lodgings where I spent the night.'

Hulten then said to De Mott in a frustrated manner, 'I do not know a George Heath. I have never met him, though I did see his picture in the newspaper. I swear I had nothing to do with his murder and I found the Ford V8 in a car park on Monday the 9th October'.

Hulten and Jones statements did not agree at certain points. The British police were in a difficult situation; how much truth was there in Jones' statement, and had Hulten shot George Heath, or was he innocent? However, to the advantage of the police, all this was going to change in the next few hours.

On her way home from the police station Jones met a war reserve policeman who she knew by the name of Henry Kimberly. He noticed she seemed to be in a dazed state and asked her if anything was wrong. Jones replied to say she had just made a statement at the police station in connection with the murder of George Heath. She told him that the man they had inside had been with her all that Friday night and then when on to say 'If you had seen somebody do what I have seen done you would not be able to sleep at night'. The war reserve policeman was astonished at what Jones was saying, and he immediately reported the encounter to Inspector Tansill, who had interviewed Jones only a few hours before.

Without delay Inspector Tansill and Kimberly went to see Jones at her lodgings. She told him she had lied when he had first questioned her and now she wanted to tell the truth. Inspector Tansill then took

Jones back to the police station; she was cautioned before making a further statement. Her second statement was made the same day, the 11th October 1944.

'I was in the car when Ricky shot Heath' she said. She then went on to tell of her six-day friendship with Ricky and the other crimes that had taken place. She said that on the night of Wednesday 4th October, while driving towards Reading, Ricky had knocked a young girl off her bicycle with the truck and robbed her. Jones became very distressed when describing what happened to Violet Hodge and how Ricky had struck her over the head with a block of wood, then hit her with his fist and thrown her body into the River Thames. She explained how the journey in Heath's cab had ended at the beginning of the Great West Road, and how Heath stopped the car and leaned over to open the passenger door for her, and Ricky had shot him. He had then got into the driving seat, ordering Heath to move over or he would give him another dose. Jones strongly claimed that Ricky had told her to go through all Heath's pockets, which she had done.

A few minutes later Ricky had stopped the car, dragged Heath's body out and dumped it in a ditch. They had driven back to her lodgings, where she had told Ricky 'It was cold-blooded murder' and he had replied 'I haven't had time to think about it'. Jones then duly signed her statement, witnessed by Wilfred Tarr, Detective Inspector, and written down by Albert Tansill, Detective Inspector, both of 'T' Division Metropolitan Police. This time Jones was held in custody.

The British police informed De Mott of the signed statement made by Jones, and the following day De Mott drove with Hulten to Hammersmith Police station. De Mott, after thoroughly absorbing Jones' statement, set about putting Hulten through an extensive examination in the presence of Inspector Tarr and Inspector Tansill.

Hulten readily admitted that only some of Jones' statement was in fact true. He viciously attacked her for trying to play down her part in the crimes that had taken place during those six days. Hulten alleged that Jones had been a willing partner to everything that had happened. He strongly denied that he intended to shoot Heath and rob him, claiming it was an accident and saying, 'I intended to fire the gun through the car. As I did Heath leaned over to open the passenger door and the gun went off.' Hulten went on to say that Jones had helped him to carry Heath's body to the ditch.

Hulten remained in De Mott's charge and Jones was formally charged in connection with Heath's murder. She was then sent to Holloway Prison on remand. While she was at Holloway, she convinced herself that at the end of the trial at the Old Bailey she would walk away a free woman; it was Hulten who had shot and killed Heath, not her!

Jones then decided to write to Inspector Tarr, who went to Holloway Prison in response to her letter. What she told him was obviously going to be her defence. Jones said she had been terrified of Hulten throughout this dreadful affair. Whatever she had done, it was because she had been in fear of her life after what she had seen what Hulten was capable of.

Inspector Tarr's report was that Jones had never said anything like this in her previous statements.

★ ★ ★

At this point, the America Presidential Election had just finished. It was now that the United States Government waived its rights under the Visiting Forces Act of 1942 and allowed Hulten to be tried by a British court. Hulten was taken from American custody by Inspector Tarr and driven to the magistrates' court at Staines. Both Hulten and Jones were committed for trial at the Old Bailey. The date for the start of the trial was set for Tuesday 16th January 1945, and they were given legal aid at public expense.

While awaiting trial, Hulten was kept in Brixton Prison and Jones in Holloway Prison, which obviously gave them both plenty of time to think things over. Jones was still completely convinced that she was going to walk away from the trial a free woman. It probably did not sink in that the prosecution would prove that she had played a willing part in Heath's murder by robbing him while he was dying and helping Hulten to dispose of his body in a ditch, and that she would therefore be convicted of murder.

Reports say Jones had nothing but contempt for the other female prisoners, but she was more than happy to discuss the forthcoming trial with them.

In Brixton Prison, Hulten remained a quiet prisoner from the onset and had adopted an unemotional frame of mind. He wrote a few letters to his wife and mother in America.

Some time before the trial the British Government appointed the following:

Mr L. A. Byrne and Mr Gerald Howard, for the prosecution.

Mr John Maude KC and Mr T. K. Eadie, defence for Hulten.

Mr J. D. Casswell KC and Mrs Lloyd Lane, Defence for Jones.

Later it was announced that Mr Justice Ernest Bruce Charles was to be the presiding judge.

The time was now drawing near for Hulten and Jones to be tried for the murder of George Edward Heath. On the morning of Tuesday 16th January 1945, the start of the trial, crowds had begun to gather outside the Old Bailey hoping to get a seat. It had been many years since a trial at the Old Bailey had created so much public interest. The morning and evening newspapers continued to build the case of an American GI, a striptease dancer and a murdered man with a cleft chin.

Public interest in America was also being aroused, and correspondents were sent over to report the trial from the press benches. One bench in the court was fully occupied by American

Army Officers. Reports say that one newspaper paid the travelling expenses for Jones' parents to enable them to be in court.

The crowds outside the Old Bailey had little hope of getting a seat in the court. By 10.30 am it was completely full and the doors were shut and guarded.

CHAPTER SIX

THE TRIAL - FIRST DAY

TUESDAY 16TH JANUARY 1945

On the stroke of 11 am in No 1 court at the Old Bailey, all rose and Mr Justice Charles made his entrance, followed by the jury of nine men and three women. The clerk of the court then addressed Hulten and Jones:

'Elizabeth Maude Jones and Karl Gustav Hulten, you are charged with the murder of George Edward Heath on Saturday 7th October 1944. Elizabeth Maude Jones, are you guilty or not guilty?'

Prisoner Jones – 'Not guilty'.

'Karl Gustav Hulten, are you guilty or not guilty?'

Prisoner Hulten – 'Not guilty'.

Jones' face was pallid and her eyes were downcast, and the dark brown roots were showing through her peroxide hair. Hulten looked confident, unworried and clean-shaven.

Mr Byrne, prosecution for the Crown, then rose to address the judge and members of the jury, saying the United States had waived its rights under the Visiting Forces Act of 1942 and now the British court would try for murder a member of the United States Armed Forces. The victim was George Edward Heath, age 34 years, married with two sons and a private hire cab driver. His motorcar was a grey Ford V8 saloon, registration number RD 8955. This motorcar he had obtained on hire with an option of buying it from a Mr Hawkins, a garage proprietor in Sunningdale.

In the early hours of Saturday 7th October 1944 a night watchman by the name of Mr Hollis, employed by Hudsons' Motors on the Great West Road, reported that he had heard a sound like a gun going off.

'When all the evidence is heard in this case there can be no doubt that the sound that Mr Hollis heard was the shot killing George Edward Heath' said Mr Byrne. He went on to say that on Saturday 7th October several articles strewn on a grass verge were found by a Mr John Anthony Kerrison Jones, who was on his way to work along the Great West Road. He had taken them to the local police station. There was a wallet, an identity card showing the name of George Edward Heath, a driving licence with the same name and a chequebook.

The discovery of Heath's body was made by a Mr Robert Balding, a fireman making his way home from work at Knowle Green near Staines. He saw the body lying in the ditch and immediately contacted the local police.

A Dr Teare carried out a post mortem on Heath's body. He found that a bullet had entered Heath's body, grazing his spine and damaging one of his lungs, causing severe haemorrhage. The bullet had made its exit out through his chest. Doctor Teare said that in his medical opinion Heath would have been paralysed within seconds and died about ten to fifteen minutes later.

Examination of the car found dents on the nearside front door and dashboard and from an experiment carried out by Dr Teare, his view was that it was caused by a bullet fired from the back seat of the car going through Heath's body, striking the door and ricocheting off the cubbyhole in the dashboard.

'The question is, who killed George Heath?' he went on. 'Therefore I will now tell members of the jury more about these two prisoners.

'On Tuesday 3rd October 1944 the prisoner Hulten went into a café in Hammersmith and saw the prisoner Jones sitting at a table with a man he knew slightly as Leonard Bexley. It was this man who introduced them, Jones as Georgina Grayson and Hulten as Ricky.

'At this point in time Jones was living in a room 311 Kings Street Hammersmith. Mrs Evans, her landlady, knew she was seeing an American soldier. On the night of Friday 6th October 1944 Hulten called for Jones and she rushed out to meet him. Mrs Evans could not say whether or not Jones returned home that night.

'On Saturday 7th October 1944 Hulten went to a barbershop in Hammersmith and sold Heath's watch to an employee named Maurice Levene for five pounds, telling him that it was an American watch. Levene was busy in the barbershop and put the watch straight in his pocket. Later when he examined it he found it was not in fact an America watch.

'In the afternoon of that same day Hulten met Bexley and sold him Heath's fountain pen and pencil. At this time Hulten showed him the automatic pistol and offered to give him a lesson on how to use it. Jones, Hulten and Bexley then went to the dog track at the White City Stadium.

'Members of the jury, the prisoner Jones has claimed that at the White City dog track she made bets with her own money. The evidence will show as this case unfolds that the eight pounds she robbed from Heath's body was used to make those bets, and furthermore she won several pounds with it.

'We now go to Monday 9th October 1944. Police Constable Waters on his evening round passing through a road called Lurgen Avenue. He saw the wanted grey Ford V8 saloon with the number plate RD 8955 parked outside one of the houses. He immediately informed his police station.

Officers arrived and waited for the prisoner Hulten to appear.

Some time elapsed before Hulten walked out of a house and into the car. The police officers dragged him out of the car, he was stood up against a wall and his loaded gun was removed. He was then handcuffed and taken to the police station.

'Members of the jury, when the prisoner's gun was examined it was found to have six rounds of ammunition. The safety catch was back and so was the hammer, therefore this weapon could have been fired at once.

'This prisoner Hulten on his way to Staines to be charged said to the police 'I would not be here in this mess except for that girl. I just wanted to go for a walk but she didn't. We stood in a shop doorway, then she started yelling for a cab and Heath stopped his car and we both got in. Had it not been for her I would never have shot Heath'.

'On the morning of Tuesday 10th October 1944 the prisoner Hulten was seen by a military police criminal investigation officer, Lieutenant Robert De Mott, in the presence of two British police officers, Inspector Tarr and Inspector Tansill. He was cautioned and his rights were made clear to him.

'The prisoner Hulten was then asked to explain how he came in possession of the car. He claimed he found the Ford V8 saloon in a wood near his base. On the afternoon of the Monday 9th October, after filling it up with gas, he drove to see another girlfriend, Joyce Cook. Members of the jury, you will recall that the prisoner Hulten was eventually arrested outside her house in Lurgen Avenue off Fulham Palace Road. Hulten told De Mott that he left Joyce Cook's house at about 9pm that evening.

'De Mott then asked Hulten to account for his movements on the Friday 6th October. Hulten said he had slept in a truck just outside Newbury and made it quite clear he was not in London on that Friday night, 6th October.

'Members of the jury, on the same day, Tuesday 10th October in the afternoon, De Mott saw the prisoner Hulten again. He then changed his story as to where he had found Ford V8 saloon car. He had spent the Friday night with Georgina Grayson and had found the car in a Hammersmith car park on Monday 9th October.

'On Wednesday 11th October the prisoner Hulten offered to show De Mott where Georgina Grayson lived. Following this Inspector Tarr and Inspector Tansill went to 311 King Street Hammersmith, where the prisoner Jones lived. They arrived about midday to find her still in bed. She was asked if she knew an American soldier and Jones replied 'yes, his name is Ricky, he stayed with me several nights'.

The officers took Jones to Hammersmith police station, where she made a statement: 'My name is Elizabeth Maude Jones, I am eighteen years old and was born in Neath, Wales. I am married but I do not live with my husband. On the Tuesday 3rd October 1944 I was in a café at Broadway Hammersmith where I was introduced to an American soldier wearing an officer's uniform, he said his name was Ricky Allen.

'Later that night about 11.30 pm I went for a ride with him in a big American truck around London and he stayed at my lodgings a few nights. On Friday 6th October he asked me to go to Hammersmith Metropolitan Railway Station to collect a travelling bag. When I got back Ricky changed, we left my room about 4.30 pm and we went to the Broadway cinema in Hammersmith. On leaving there about 8.30 pm Ricky left me, saying he would see me later at 11.30 pm. He came back and slept with me that night.

'On Saturday 7th October we went to the dog track at White City Stadium with a friend name Bexley. I saw Ricky twice since then, on Sunday the 8th October and for a short time on Monday 9th October and during that time I did not see him with any car. This statement has been read to me and it is true.'

Having made that statement, Jones was allowed to leave the police station. On that same afternoon she met a war reserve policeman named Kimberley who she had known in the past. He was surprised to see how pale and tired she looked and asked if she was all right, and Jones told him that she had just come from the police station having made a statement in connection with the murder of the cab driver.

Kimberley said that if she had nothing to do with the murder then there was no need for her to worry. Jones replied, 'I know the man they have inside, he was with me all that Friday night so he could not have anything to do with the murder'. Kimberley told Jones to go home and get some rest, but then she said to him, 'If you had seen someone do what I have seen done you would not be able to sleep at night'. Then Kimberley told her the best thing she could do would be to go back to the police station and tell the truth.

Kimberley was disturbed at what Jones had said and he immediately informed Inspector Tansill, who went with Inspector Tarr to see the prisoner Jones at her lodgings. Inspector Tarr said to her, 'I understand you want to tell me something'.

Jones said that she had lied in her previous statement. 'I was in the car when Heath was shot' she said. Inspector Tansill stopped her and then went on to caution her. Jones then made a further written statement. Jones was advised of her rights by Inspector Tarr and told that she need not say anything if she so wished, but anything she did say would be taken down in writing and might be given in evidence.

Jones then went on to tell about her six-day association with Hulten. She said she had first met him in a café in Hammersmith on Tuesday 3rd October; they were introduced by a man named Bexley. They had gone for a drive that night at about 11.30 pm and driven around Reading, then gone back to London.

Jones went on to say that before she had left Hulten she had given him her address:

'On Thursday the 5th October he called for me at my lodgings, we had a meal out and then went to the Gaumont cinema in

Hammersmith. Then on Friday 6th October we stayed in bed until about 10 am, he gave me a railway cloakroom ticket to collect a travelling bag from Hammersmith Metropolitan Station. When I got back he changed and we went out about 4.30 pm. He came back at about 11.30 pm and said 'Come on, let's go and get a taxi'.

'We walked along the Hammersmith road and stood in a doorway I then saw a car coming from the direction from Broadway Hammersmith. I stepped out of the doorway and hailed it down. 'Are you a taxi?' I asked. 'No, private hire miss, where do you want to go?' 'Kings Street' I replied. I called Ricky and the driver watched him come out of the doorway. He said it would cost ten shillings and we agreed. We got into the back seat of the car and Ricky sat directly behind the driver.

'As we approached Kings Street, Ricky told him to go on a bit further and he would pay the extra. When we reached the Great West Road the driver said he could not take us any further because of another fare waiting in Maidenhead. The driver stopped the car and leaned over to open the passenger door for me.

'There was a sudden flash and a loud bang and the driver slumped over sideways, moaning. Ricky then got into the driver's seat with the gun still in his hand, saying to the driver 'move over or I will give you another dose'. As we drove off he told me to go through the driver's pockets and as I was doing this I could hear him gasping for breath. I think I took everything from his pockets.

'Ricky told me to look on the floor for the bullet, but I could not find it. He then turned the car of the main road into a field, he got out and dragged the driver's body from the car and I saw him roll the body into a ditch.

'We drove off and Ricky told me again to look for the bullet and with a torch that was in the car I found it on the floor by the nearside door and I gave it to Ricky. As we got to the roundabout on the Great

West Road I asked him where he had dumped the driver's body and he replied it was a place near Staines.

'We left the car in the Gaumont cinema parking lot in Hammersmith and we attempted to wipe the car inside and outside with our handkerchiefs.

'We went to a café to have a meal, then we went back to my lodgings. I was very upset and said 'The driver is dead isn't he, it was cold-blooded murder, why did you do it?' Ricky's reply was 'I haven't had time to think about it'. We then looked at what we had taken from the driver's pockets and then went to bed.

'On Saturday 7th October Ricky went out and sold the driver's watch to a barber he knew. We then went with Bexley to the White City dog track. At the races Bexley lit up a cigarette with a lighter that I knew was the one that I had taken from the cab driver's pocket. We left the races and Bexley and we went for a meal and then to the cinema. Ricky saw me home at about 10.30 pm, but he could not stay because my landlady was going to be home the next day, Sunday the 8th October.

'I stayed in all day on Sunday the 8th October until 8.30 pm, then I went out and walked to a public house next to the Metropolitan Railway Station. There I saw an RAF man and I spoke to him and he suggested we went for a drink together at another public house.

'We had a few drinks, then he walked me home at about 10 pm. I took him up to my room and I told him all about the murder. He asked me what the motive was and I said robbery. He then asked me if I wanted him to go to the police and I said no. He then gave me his name and address, saying to contact him if I needed help.

'Ricky then arrived and I told Mac he was the man that shot the cab driver. Mac then left. Afterwards Ricky and I went to the car park where we had left the Ford V8. On seeing the car Ricky said there was no need to worry, there were no reports in the newspapers and they obviously had not found the body yet. We were both reassured and drove to Reading. Afterwards we returned to the same car park and Ricky stole two five-gallon tins of petrol from an American truck parked nearby.

'On Monday 9th October we got back to Wood Lane, Shepherds Bush and went to a café for a meal. He then drove me home and parked the car behind an air raid shelter and we then went back to my lodgings and slept in bed until about two in the afternoon. Ricky then left and said he would be back about 5.30 pm. I saw him drive off in the car and that was the last time I saw Ricky.

'This statement has been read back to me and it is true.'

'Members of the jury, this statement as it stands made by the prisoner Jones is not evidence against the man Hulten. The statement made under these circumstances is evidence against the person who makes it, not to anyone who is referred to in that statement. It is only right that I make you aware of this.

'Mr Maude, who appears for the prisoner Hulten, has made it clear he will propose some legal objection to the admissibility of this statement, so therefore I will say no more to the members of the jury about the contents of this statement.

'On Saturday 14th October Hulten and Jones were taken to Staines Police Station, where they were both charged with being concerned with the murder of George Edward Heath on Saturday 7th October 1944.

'Members of the jury, the prisoner Jones when the facts are established subject to my lords ruling, although hers was not the hand that fired the shot killing Heath, she is as guilty as the person who did fire the shot, as she was aiding and helping the prisoner Hulten in that felony. Members of the jury, that is all I have to say in opening this case to you.'

The prosecutor, Mr Byrne, had been speaking for well over an hour. He obviously must have considered that here was a straightforward case of deliberate coldblooded murder and robbery of an innocent man and it demanded justice.

The case against Hulten and Jones was without doubt clear enough, but what line of defence were they going to take? After reading the statements, Mr Byrne knew there was going to be a grim battle between these two prisoners in their efforts to accuse each other to save themselves from the gallows.

Hulten and Jones were the only persons who knew what happened in that car on the Saturday 7th October and therefore they could dispute any story the prosecution put to them.

Mr Byrne: I will now, with the assistance with my learned friend Mr Gerald Howard, call the evidence before you.

Mr HOWARD for the PROSECUTION examined THOMAS WALTON, sworn.

Q. Is your name Thomas Walton?

A. Yes.

Q. You are Police Constable 807 of the 'T' division stationed at Staines?

A. Yes.

Q. On the 7th October 1944 did you go to Knowle Green Staines?

A. Yes.

Q. In the presence of Detective Inspector Tarr and Inspector Tansill?

A. Yes.

Q. Did you take measurements of a section of the road crossing Knowle Green?

A. Yes.

Q. Is that road a gravel road?

A. Yes.

Q. Were there any wheel marks on this gravel road?

A. There were no visible signs of wheels marks on the service of the road, but there were wheel marks on the grass on both sides of the road and tufts of grass had been disturbed suggesting they had come in contact with the undercarriage of a vehicle.

Mr CASSWELL for the Defence. Prisoner Jones, no questions.
Cross-examined by Mr MAUDE, Defence Prisoner Hulten.

Q. Is the grass on either side of the road long or short?

A. Fairly short.

Q. I want to know because you are the only person who has looked. Were there any marks found anywhere, as of a body being dragged?

A. No.

Q. There was no marks for instance such as heel marks or the wiping down of the grass? A. No I did not see any marks like that.

Mr HOWARD for the PROSECUTION examined HENRY CARTER, sworn.

Q. Your name is Henry Carter?

A. Yes

Q. You are a Detective Constable in the photographic department of Scotland Yard?

A. Yes.

Q. On the 10th November 1944 did you take a photograph of the inside of a Ford V8 motorcar registered number RD 8955?

A. I did.

Q. Is this the photograph?

A. Yes.

Mr Howard: May I hand this to the jury my lord?
Mr Justice Charles: Yes, by all means.
Mr Howard: Looking at the photograph there is a mark upon the metalwork of the door just below the window and another mark near the cubbyhole near the dash is this correct?

A. Yes.

Cross-examined by Mr Maude, defence for Hulten.

Q. Constable Carter, I want to ask you about the photograph: were you instructed to take any measurements of the inside of the car?

A. No.

Q. And you didn't do so?

A. I did not.

Mr Maude pointed out to the jury that the photograph they had in front of them represented perhaps only what the human eye could see.

Q. Is it different in some way?

A. It is exactly what you would see from back of the car. No measurements were taken of the inside of the car, as the police officer was not instructed to do so. The photograph was taken with the camera mounted on a tripod from the back seat. The police officer was given instructions to take it from exactly that position by Inspector Tarr.

Mr BYRNE for the PROSECUTION examined KNOWLAND HARRY HAWKINS, sworn.

Q. Your name is Knowland Harry Hawkins?

A. Yes.

Q. Are you a garage proprietor?

A. I am.

Q. You have five hire service cars?

A. I have.

Q. Is one of them a grey Ford V8, registered number RD 8955?

A. Yes.

Q. George Edward Heath – did you know this man?

A. Yes.

Q. On the 26th September 1944 did he hire the Ford V8 from you?

A. Yes.

Q. With the option to purchase the car?

A. Yes.

Q. When was he to return it to you?

A. It was left open more or less.

Q. Well, he didn't return it to you?

A. He did not.

Q. Ultimately you were shown that motorcar by the police at the police station?

A. Yes.

Q. When you looked at it, did you notice a mark on the inside of the nearside front door?

A. I did.

Q. And also another mark on the lid of a box, the cubbyhole?

A. Yes I did.

Q. Had any of those marks been on the car at the time you let Heath have it?

A. Most certainly not.

Mr HOWARD for the PROSECUTION examined ARTHUR CECIL GREEN, sworn.

Q. Arthur Cecil Green, is that your name?

A. That's right.

Q. Are you employed by Godfrey Davis Ltd, of Eccleston Square, SW1?

A. Yes and it's Eccleston Street.

Q. Do they carry on a motorcar hire business?

A. They do.

Q. Did you know George Heath?

A. I did.

Q. How long had you known him?

A. Fourteen years.

Q. Was he at one time a driver for Godfrey Davis?

A. He was.

Q. After that did he work for a Mr Collins?

A. He did.

Q. Did you sometimes pass on jobs that Godfrey Davis could not do, to Heath?

A. I did.

Q. Did you see Heath on Friday 6th October 1944?

A. At night I did.

Q. About what time?

A. Approximately between 11 and 11.15 pm.

Q. Had you seen him earlier?

A. Yes at eight o'clock.

Q. What, had you seen him about then?

A. He came into my office. He used to come in every night.

Q. Was there any job for him to do?

A. There was not at the time.

Q. On the last time he came what time was it?

A. About five minutes past eleven.

Q. On that last time he came in, did he show you anything?

A. Yes he pulled his wallet out and asked me for some change.

Q. He asked for some change?

A. That's right.

Q. Did you notice whether there was any money in his wallet?

A. Yes, I would say about eight pounds.

Q. About what time would it be when he left you?

A. Approximately I should say twenty past eleven.

Mr MAUDE: No question, my lord.

A FATAL PICKUP

Mr BYRNE for the PROSECUTION examined WILLIAM HOLLIS, sworn.

Q. Is your name William Hollis?

A. Yes

Q. Are you a night watchman employed by Hudson Motors?

A. Yes.

Q. Their factory is at Great West Road Chiswick, is it?

A. Yes

Q. Is it part of your duty to tour the works during the night?

A. Yes.

Q. When you do that, do you punch the time clock, which I suppose is a check upon your movements?

A. Yes.

Q. Do you recollect the early hours of Saturday the 7th October punching the clock in the early hours of that morning?

A. Yes.

Q. What time was it when you punched?

A. 2.30.

Q. Did you hear something just after you punched the clock?

A. Yes I heard the sound of a gunshot going off, it came from the London end of the Great West Road.

Q. What kind of weapon did you believe it to be that made that sound?

A. It had a muffled sound as though it was fired in a confined space and sounded like a heavy calibre revolver.

Q. Fired in a confined space?
A. Yes.

Cross-examined by Mr CASSWELL, DEFENCE for prisoner JONES.

Q. I'm afraid I do not know this part of the road, are there other factories in this immediate area.
A. No, Hudson Motors runs along the Great West Road from a bridge.
Q. What is the nearest factory to Hudson Motors?
A. Smiths Crisps over the other side of the bridge, and a railway line runs between us.
Q. Were you inside or outside the factory?
A. I was inside the factory.
Q. Were the windows open or shut?
A. The windows would be shut.
Q. How far do you suppose you were from the Great West Road?
A. Roughly about seventy to a hundred yards.
Q. And you could hear quite distinctly this shot?
A. Quite distinctly, because everything was dead quiet.

MR MAUDE: *No questions.*

Mr HOWARD for the PROSECUTION examined JOHN ANTHONY KERRISON JONES, sworn.

Q. Is your name John Anthony Kerrison Jones?
A. That's correct.

Q. In October of last year were you working as an electrician's apprentice with a firm who had a contract near Feltham?

A. That's correct.

Q. On the morning of Saturday 7th October were you walking along the Great West Road on your way to work?

A. Yes.

Q. About what time in the morning?

A. Possibly eight o'clock.

Q. Does the Great South West Road run from the Great West Road to Staines?

A. That's right.

Q. In which direction were you going?

A. Towards Staines.

Q. Did you notice anything on the grass verge?

A. Yes I did.

Q. Just look at this, did you see this?

A. That's right.

Mr JUSTICE CHARLES: That is the wallet, is it?
Mr Howard: Yes, my lord
(To the witness) Did you find that?

A. That's correct.

Q. And an identity card in the name of George Heath?

A. Yes.

Q. Did you find this also, a driver's licence in the name of George Heath?

A. That's right.

Q. And a chequebook?

A. That's correct.

Q. Which grass verge did you find those on which side of the road?

A. The east side of the road on the left hand side going towards Staines.

Mr CASSWELL: No questions.

Mr MAUDE: No questions.

Mr BYRNE for the PROSECUTION Examined ROBERT BALDING, sworn.

Q. Is your name Robert Balding?

A. Yes.

Q. Are you a fireman attached to the National Fire Service?

A. Yes.

Q. At the Ship Garage, London Road?

A. Yes.

Q. When you finished your work shift at 9 am on the morning of Saturday the 7th October 1944, did you take a short cut home across Knowle Green near Staines?

A. Yes.

Q. Which meant you left the roadway?

A. Yes, leaving the road a few feet.

Q. Did you pass close to a ditch, that would be the ditch on your right hand side? A. Yes.

Q. As you walked along did you see a man's body lying in this ditch?

A. Yes.

Q. Was he lying on his right side?

A. Yes.

Q. Was he wearing a blue overcoat with the collar pulled up over his head, hiding his face?

A. Yes.

Q. I think you took it that he was asleep when you first saw him?

A. I thought he had taken ill and I stooped down to see if I could help him.

Q. Did you shake him?

A. I shook him and he did not respond.

Q. Then did you realise that he was dead?

A. Yes.

Q. Having come to that conclusion did you send for the police?

A. Yes.

Cross-examined by Mr CASWELL Defence for Prisoner JONES.

Q. What was the grass like round the ditch, did you notice? In October was it fairly long?

A. I should say about three or four inches long, Yes.

Q. You did not look for any marks on the grass?

A. I did not, no.

MR MAUDE: No questions.

ADJOURNED FOR A SHORT TIME - THE JURY RETIRED

Mr BYRNE for the PROSECUTION Examined LIEUTENANT ROBERT EARL DE MOTT, sworn.

Q. Is your name Robert Earl De Mott?

A. Yes.

Q. Are you a First Lieutenant in the United States Army?

A. I am.

Q. Are you in charge of the 8th Military Police Criminal Investigation Section?

A. I am.

Q. As a matter of fact, in civil life you are an attorney-at-law are you?

A. Yes.

Q. And a member of the Bar of the State of Colorado?

A. I am.

Mr BYRNE: I am only going to deal with the written statements my lord, for the purpose of this argument. *(to the witness)* On the 11th October, did you see the prisoner Hulten at your office at half past ten in the morning?

A. I did.

Q. I think I can lead to this. Did he offer to show you where he had found the car and also where Georgina Grayson lived?

A. He did.

Q. I think you took him to Hammersmith Police Station and then went with him and two police inspectors and he pointed out the house and also the car park?

A. Yes.

Q. After that did you take him back to your office?

A. I did.

Q. When he arrived back at your office, what did you say to him?

A. I warned him of his rights and asked him if he would care to make a statement.

Q. Just tell me this before I pass to the details: was that the first time you had warned him of his rights?

A. No.

Q. When you say you warned him of his rights, what form of words did you use? Can you recollect?

A. Yes. 'It is your privilege to remain silent. You need make no statement whatsoever. Any statement you do choose to make may be used either for or against you in the event that this investigation results in a trial. Do you thoroughly understand your rights?'.

Mr JUSTICE CHARLES: What did he say to that?

A. Yes.

Mr BYRNE: Is that form of warning in accordance with American legal procedure?

A. It is.

Q. What happened then?

A. I then took a statement from him, which was reduced to writing and which he swore to before me.

Q. Would you be good enough to look at the statement, so that you will know which one we are talking about, Exhibit 15, is that the statement?

A. The statement I am looking at is a copy of that statement.

Q. A copy of the original statement?

A. Yes.

Q. Is that the original (Handed).

A. This is the original.

Q. Before he made the body of the statement, if you see what I mean, did he first of all sign that top piece of paper which begins 'Private Karl G Hulten, it is my duty to inform you of your rights at this time'? Do you see that?

A. Yes.

Q, Did you make any kind of inducement to him to make that statement to you?

A. I offered no inducement whatsoever.

Q. Did you make any kind of threat?

A. No threat.

Mr JUSTICE CHARLES: Did he become so exhausted that he could not understand the sort of answers that he was giving?

A. I am certain he did not, sir.

Q. When he signed it, was he in a perfectly fit condition?

A. In my opinion he was, sir.

Mr BYRNE: How long did he take to make the statement?

A. I don't know exactly, but I would say probably two to two and half hours.

Q. Perhaps I should have asked you this. When the statement was completed, did he read through it or was it read through to him?

A. He read it through.

Q. Did he make any alterations?

A. He did.

Q. They appear in the document?

A. They do.

Q. Now I think I can deal with the second statement much quicker. On Thursday, 12th October, at eight o'clock in the evening, did you go with the prisoner Hulten to Hammersmith Police Station?

A. I did.

Q. If you will, look at Exhibit 16 (Handed). Tell me if that is the statement.

A. It is.

Q. Once again it begins with the signed caution, does it not?

A. It does.

Q. Did he read that over after it had been taken, or was it read over to him?

A. He read it over.

Q. Did he make alterations in that?

A. Yes.

Mr JUSTICE CHARLES: He read it over and made alterations and signed it at the bottom of every page?

A. Yes my lord.

Mr JUSTICE CHARLES: I'm only looking at it to see whether the signatures show any sign of exhaustion.

Mr BYRNE: How long did it take to obtain that statement from him, about?

A. I should say about three hours.

Q. Were two English police inspectors present, Inspectors Tarr and Tansill?

A. Yes.

Q. Once again did you ask him questions?

A. I did.

Q. Did he do anything while he was answering your questions and making the statement? Did you notice him doing anything?

A. Nothing, only 'doodling' as we call it.

Q. That is what I meant – what you call doodling?

A. Yes.

Q. Did you keep the results of his doodling?

A. I did not.

Q. See if you would recognise them if I hand them to you. Just look at that piece of paper and tell me if you recognise his handiwork. (handed)

A. Yes I do.

Mr JUSTICE CHARLES: Let me have a look. Do you want to see it, Mr Maude?

Mr MAUDE: Yes, my lord and the statements. I should like to see everything.

Cross-examined by Mr MAUDE, Defence for prisoner HULTEN.

Q. Were you at the criminal Bar in Colorado?

A. No. Only a member.

Q. How long were you at the Bar?

A. I have been a member of the Bar since September 1942.

Q. Since 1942. You were called then?

A. Yes.

Q. How old are you?

A. I am twenty-seven.

Q. When did you go into the Army?

A. In October 1943.

Q. In the interval did you practise as a lawyer?

A. I did.

Q. In Colorado?

A. In Colorado, yes.

Q. That is a large place. Where?

A. In Denver.

Q. These drawings obviously are, now I see them, tanks, trucks, aeroplanes and so on. When do you say these were made?

A. They were made while I was taking the second statement.

Q. Did you have any assistance from the British officers?

A. I had no assistance at all.

Q. None at all?

A. No.

Q. They remained completely silent?

A. Completely silent.

Q. They never said a word?

A. They never said a word.

Q. Was he in your custody?

A. He was in my custody, yes.

Q. Why were these officers there, do you know?

A. They were there primarily at my request.

Q. You wanted them there?

A. I wanted them there.

Q. Why?

A. It was a matter of importance, and I did not want them to feel that there was any possibility of any irregularity.

Q. Then you start to ask the man who has agreed to be questioned any questions?

A. Pertinent questions.

Q. Any pertinent questions, material questions, of course. Would I be right in suggesting to you that clearly what you did in this case was to ask him questions off the prisoner Jones's statement she made?

A. That would be incorrect, actually.

Q. Have you got it in your possession?

A. I had it previously, but I did not have it at the time.

Q. What have you done with it?

A. It was in my office.

Q. Had you had it copied?

A. No, not at that time.

Q. You had got a copy?

A. I had seen a copy.

Q. It is a long statement, isn't it?

A. Yes.

Q. You went down to question this man without a copy of Jones's statement?

A. I did; I had read it.

Q. WHAT?

A. I had read her statement.

Q. Yes, you had read it. Had you left it behind on purpose?

A. No, I had not left it behind on purpose; I didn't think it necessary to bring it.

Q. Could you give me the exact times when you started these various interrogations of this man? Did you take a note?

A. I took no notes whatsoever.

Q. Do you ever put the times on the top when you start to take statements?

A. No, never.

Q. Would you give my lord an estimate?

A. I would say it was approximately eight o'clock in the evening when I started the second statement.

Q. I am putting it to you that it was something like three in the morning when you finished; is that right?

A. I should think it was not that late, but I am not certain.

Q. One or two?

A. Approximately midnight, I would think; I'm not positive.

Q. I want you to be as positive as you possibly can. It was certainly past midnight, wasn't it?

A. I should say somewhere in the neighbourhood of twelve.

Q. From eight to twelve?

A. From eight to twelve.

Q. Continuously?

A. In the meantime we had coffee and sandwiches and, as we say, we took a break.

Mr JUSTICE CHARLES: Just wait a minute, did the prisoner Hulten have coffee and sandwiches?

A. He did my lord.

Mr MAUDE: How long was the break?

A. At the time it did not occur to me that it was important, a matter of minutes I'm not sure.

Q. Roughly?

A. Probably forty-five minutes.

Q. Three quarters of an hour you four men sat together having coffee?

A. And talking, yes.

Q. Without doing anything?

A. Without doing anything material as far as the statement was concerned.

Q. What were you doing? Let me put it straight to you, as a policeman of two years standing, that you never sat for three quarters of hour in the middle of an interrogation doing nothing except eating sandwiches and drinking coffee.

A. Sir, you are questioning my integrity, and I am telling you to my best of my ability exactly what I did.

Q. May we cut it down gradually? May it have been…

Mr JUSTICE CHARLES: No that is not quite right. 'May we cut it down gradually'? He has already said, 'I cannot say how long it was. I attached no importance to it; I suppose it might be about forty-five minutes'; and then you press him and say it might be about thirty.

Mr MAUDE: That is a most astonishing time, forty-five minutes.

Mr JUSTICE CHARLES: But he attached no importance to it.

Mr MAUDE: I dare say he didn't, but I attach great importance to it.

Mr JUSTICE CHARLES: I know, but he says he didn't, how can you tie a man to time? Supposing I ask you something you did the other day? You would say, 'I never looked at the time'. I should not care to have my integrity attacked, and nor would you.

Mr MAUDE: No, my lord, but I should not have pressed it if I hadn't been told it was three quarters of an hour.

Mr JUSTICE CHARLES: No, he did not say that; 'about'.

Mr MAUDE: Did you have a lot of coffee?

A. I only had a cup of tea, that is all I had I recall.

Q. And during that time, three quarters of an hour or whatever it may have been, was he drawing any of these pictures?

A. I don't recall that.

Q. May he have been?

A. He may have been, but I think he was eating.

Mr MAUDE: My Lord, for what it is worth, he says he may have been drawing the pictures. (To the witness) The statement is in typescript?

A. Yes.

Q. Who was doing the typing?

A. I was.

Q. When it was finished, Mr De Mott, it was not read over to him, was it?

A. No, he read it over himself.

Q. Is that the usual practice?

A. It is our usual practice, yes.

Q. You never read statements over to these people?

A. Not if they are capable of reading.

Q. If you decide they are capable you hand it to them?

A. Yes.

Mr JUSTICE CHARLES: You had seen him sign his name at the beginning of it?

A. I did, my lord.

Mr JUSTICE CHARLES: It is not the writing of an uneducated man at all.

Mr MAUDE: So far as this is concerned, your Lordship will see and have seen where the correction and alterations are. (To the witness) Otherwise it is not taken down straight from his words, is it?

A. As nearly as possible.

Q. Who decides on the form of words? Do you?

A. I do.

Q. Did you first discourage the man from making any statement at all?

A. I merely warned him of his rights; as we say, I cautioned the man.

Mr JUSTICE CHARLES: I didn't catch that.

A. Counsel asked me if I had discouraged him from making a statement and I told him 'No'. I had cautioned him and warn him of his rights before.

Mr MAUDE: What I am instructed and have to put is this: that on Monday 9th October, you were present at the police station when the British police wanted to take a statement from him?

A. I was present on Tuesday morning the 10th October. I was not present on Monday the 9th.

Q. Perhaps I may be wrongly instructed as to the date, but were you there when the British police wanted to take a statement from him?

A. I was present.

Q. Do you remember Mr Tarr saying, 'Well if it's the truth then there's no harm in you making a statement about it'? Do you remember that?

A. Words to that effect.

Q. And at that moment did you shake your head to Hulten?

A. I did not.

Q. I must ask you: do you swear that?

A. I swear.

Q. No indication at all to him not to make a statement?

A. Not to make a statement?

Q. Not to the British police?

A. Not to the British police.

Q. Mr Tarr having said something to the effect that I put to you, what was the next thing that happened?

A. Would you repeat your question, please?

Q. Yes. What I put to you was that Mr Tarr had said to him 'Well if it's the truth there is no harm in your making a statement about it'. You say he said something to that effect.

A. Yes, that is quite correct.

Q. What is the next thing that happened, if you did not shake your head at him?

A. I did not.

Q. What did happen?

A. Shortly after we were all in the room together and I was preparing to leave with Mr Riddle, an assistant from my office, Private Hulten asked if he might see me. I told him 'yes'.

Q. Alone, you mean?

A. He asked if he might see me alone, yes.

Q. Did you advise him then under no circumstances to make a statement?

A. I did not.

Q. To the British?

A. I did not.

Q. Nothing like that at all?

A. Nothing like it at all.

Q. What did he want to see you about?

A. He asked me if he would be questioned further after I had gone and I told him no, that he would not be, and if he was he did not need to answer any questions until I returned.

Q. What did he say to that?

A. He seemed satisfied with that and I left.

Q. Just going back to the two statements, Exhibits 15 and 16, the written ones; was it difficult to get them from him?

A. Not at all.

Q. Quite prompt in answering your questions?

A. Quite prompt.

Q. I see it is quite a long statement, but as it goes straight down on the typewriter I'm suggesting to you it was quite a long time?

A. No, it hardly goes straight down on the typewriter. As I explained to you before, each sentence in that statement is a result of a question. I explained to the man as I went along, but the questions do not probably come just like that, one right after the other. It may be I was slower than I needed to be and perhaps he might, in spite of his willingness, have had to give some deliberation to his answer.

Q. Did you suggest any answers to him at all?

A. I suggested no answers to him at all.

Q. You know what I mean by cross-examination?

A. I know exactly what you mean by cross-examination.

Mr JUSTICE CHARLES: You say you did not cross-examine him?

A. I was examining directly, my lord.

Mr MAUDE: Did anybody take a note of these two interviews?

A. Not to my knowledge.

Q. Nobody else was taking a shorthand note?

A. No, definitely not.

Q. Who were the persons present? Inspectors Tarr and Tansill? Was Inspector Tansill there?

A. Inspector Tansill was there and a gentleman from my office, Mr Riddle.

Q. Was any of then taking a note at all?

A. Not to my knowledge, no.

Mr JUSTICE CHARLES: That will do sir, I am obliged to you. Now, Mr Maude, do you desire to call the accused? If you desire to call him I will hear his evidence.

Mr MAUDE: Yes my lord, I think he should go into the box.

Mr MAUDE for the defence examined KARL GUSTAV HULTEN, sworn.

Q. Hulten, so far as these two statements are concerned that you know we call Exhibits 15 and 16, the written ones that Mr De Mott took from you, I want you to deal with the second one you made, the final one. Do you remember?

A. Yes.

Q. How long were you with the police making that statement?

A. I left the American guardhouse at 5 pm and I was taken back about 3 am the following morning.

Q. 5 pm to 3 am. How much of that time was taken up with Mr De Mott taking the statement from you?

A. It was practically all of the time.

Mr JUSTICE CHARLES: All of that time?

A. Practically all the time.

Q. Did you spend the whole of that time at his office?

A. No, we were at Inspector Tarr's office.

Q. Did you spend the whole of that time at the police office?

A. Yes.

Q. From five o'clock to three o'clock?

A. Yes.

Q. And you were being questioned all of that time?

A. Yes.

Mr MAUDE: The statement that Mr De Mott says was not read to you, I am only dealing with the second statement, I am not particularly concerned with the first…

Mr JUSTICE CHARLES: That took just as long, according to Lieutenant De Mott.

Mr MAUDE: No, my lord, he said less.

Mr JUSTICE CHARLES: Just about as long, I think he said.

Mr MAUDE: I think he said two and a half hours.

Mr JUSTICE CHARLES: He said three for the second and two and a half for the first; very nearly the same.

Mr MAUDE: No, my lord, two to two and a half for the first what I took down.

Mr JUSTICE CHARLES: Yes, two to two and a half and three; there isn't much difference if there is this gruelling and exhaustion and so forth. You want to address yourself Mr Maude, to the second statement.

Mr MAUDE: I do, my lord. (To the witness) That was not read to you, we hear?

A. No, it was not.

Q. You looked through it yourself?

A. Yes, I did.

Q. Did you read it through carefully?

A. No, I did not.

Q. What did you do?

A. I glanced through it at different times and signed a paper as I did.

Q. Mr JUSTICE CHARLES: You had an opportunity of reading it as carefully as you liked?

A. I was tired, my lord.

Q. I have seen your signature, you know.

A. I was up at six o'clock that morning and up at 3 o'clock the following morning.

Q. Mr JUSTICE CHARLES: The second one is signed on every page. The signature is good, firm, bright signature on every page.

Mr Maude: My lord, I do not propose to carry that any further.

Mr JUSTICE CHARLES: That will do; you can go back.

(The prisoner returned to the dock.)

Mr MAUDE: If the police officer could be called, my lord? I think it is Mr Tarr; I think he was supposed to be present at Mr De Mott's interview, and it would satisfy my mind very much if we could have him.

Mr JUSTICE CHARLES: You shall have anyone you like. I can tell you frankly I do not believe that man.

Mr MAUDE: I dare say, but I wish your Lordship would just wait and see.

Mr JUSTICE CHARLES: He was lying to me; there is no doubt about that. I think Lieutenant De Mott was telling me the absolute truth.

A FATAL PICKUP

Mr MAUDE: I hope then, in view of what your Lordship said, I may call a police officer who has not been in court. Is there one present?

Mr MAUDE for the Defence HULTEN examined ALBERT TANSILL, sworn.

Q. What is your name?

A. Albert Tansill, Detective Inspector 'T' Division.

Q. Do you know why you have been sent for?

A. No.

Q. You were present when the written statements were taken by Mr De Mott from this man, so we understand?

A. Yes, one on the 12th October.

Q. That is Exhibit 16, the second one, the longer of two?

A. Yes.

Q. Where were they taken?

A. They were taken in the CID office at Hammersmith.

Q. That is the office available to you, the British one, you mean?

A. Yes.

Q. What time did the statement start to be taken, the questioning start?

A. Somewhere about eight pm.

Q. Have you got a note in your book?

A. Yes.

Q. Would you look at it?

A. Yes, eight pm.

Q. Who was present?

A. When the written statement was taken, myself, Lieutenant De Mott and Agent Albert J. Riddle.

Q. What happened before the written statement was taken?

A. There were preliminary questions asked.

Q. How long did they go on for before eight o'clock?

A. I would think about ten minutes to a quarter of an hour.

Q. What were they about?

A. Well, Lieutenant De Mott had memorised the facts of the case.

Q. What, from Jones's statement?

A. Yes.

Q. He had memorised Jones statement?

A. Yes.

Q. So?

A. And he put a question to the prisoner Hulten and he answered 'Yes' to nearly all of them.

Q. Were they in the nature of what we all know as cross-examination?

A. Yes.

Q. And that went on for something like ten minutes or a quarter of an hour?

A. Yes.

Q. Then the statement started to be taken?

A. Yes.

Q. And did that proceed as in cross-examination?

A. Yes.

Mr JUSTICE CHARLES: In what way did it all differ from asking questions in examination?

A. Well, it went on similar lines, my lord.

Q. Yes, but you say 'cross-examination'. What do you mean? I want to know exactly what that denotes.

A. As I have said, my lord, Lieutenant De Mott had memorised the facts from the girl's statement.

Q. And then he asked questions upon what he had memorised?

A. Yes.

Q. And answers came to him in answer to those questions?

A. Yes.

Q. That is not cross-examination; is it examination?

A. Yes, that is correct.

Q. I only want to know what you meant; I could not understand because you said, here is a man who is a lawyer who memorised a statement and who comes and asks questions upon that which he has memorised?

A. Yes.

Q. And then you said the answers came back generally 'yes.' Well, there is no room for cross-examination there; that is examination?

A. Yes, if you please.

Mr MAUDE: How long have you been a policeman?

A. Nineteen years.

Q. What is your rank?

A. Detective Inspector.

Q. You know what cross-examination is?

A. Yes.

Q. What you mean is that they were not the questions that you would have asked?

A. Not according to British jurisprudence.

Mr JUSTICE CHARLES: Oh no, of course you would not have asked any questions?

A. No.

Mr MAUDE: You would not have asked any at all?

A. Yes.

Q. Mr Tansill, we have sent for you so we could get at the truth of it, and what I am suggesting to you is that the points were being put to the man: 'Didn't you do this?' and 'Didn't you do that?' That sort of questions, suggesting matters to him?

A. Not any suggestions at all.

Q. Do you know what a leading question is?

A. Yes.

Q. It is one that suggests the answer, isn't it?

A. Yes.

Q. Were those sort of questions being put to him?

A. Yes.

Q. And that written statement, typing in other words, started at about eight o'clock?

A. Yes.

Q. What time did it stop?

A. 1.30 am.

Q. 1.30 am. The typing ceased?

A. Yes.

Q. Had he given ready answers to the questions?

A. Yes.

Q. Why did it take so long?

A. Well, it is a fairly lengthy statement.

Q. Was there any interval at all?

A. I believe there was for a meal for the prisoner.

Q. Did you have anything, you police officers, to eat or drink? Some coffee?

A. Yes something like that.

Q. How long did that last, do you remember?

A. Well, it would be no length of time.

Q. Was this interfering at all with the examination?

A. No, he seemed perfectly composed.

Mr JUSTICE CHARLES: He seemed what?

A. He was perfectly composed, my lord.

Mr MAUDE: It proceeded quite smoothly; that is to say, he was not reprimanded for drawing, or anything like that?

A. Oh no.

Q. And then it was not read to him afterwards

A. Yes.

Q. Is it fair to say he just glanced through it?

A. No, he read each page as it was typed and then signed it and initialled alterations in the statement.

Q. The only thing, is of course, that would have prevented you doing just such a thing is the Judges' Rules?

A. And being that he was an American citizen.

Q. No, but if he had been British you would not have done it because of the Judges' Rules?

A. That is correct.

Cross-examined by Mr BYRNE for the PROSECUTION.

Q. Did he at any time express any unwillingness to answer questions?

A. No, the statement was perfectly voluntary.

Q. Did he make any complaint of exhaustion or feeling tired?

A, No, he was full of energy.

Mr. JUSTICE CHARLES: Thank you, officer.

Mr Maude, do you want to add anything?

Mr MAUDE: No, My Lord

Mr JUSTICE CHARLES: Well, in this matter I have to make my decision and in case someone else had to see the decision I will say quite shortly the grounds on which I come to the conclusion to which I have arrived.

'Two statements were taken from the accused. They were taken by an officer of the CID in the American Army called Lieutenant De Mott. It is to be observed that Lieutenant De Mott is both an attorney-at-law and a barrister and has practised. He unquestionably, in accordance with their practice, asked the accused questions and those questions were not asked. I am satisfied from the evidence, in a way that put any sort of pressure on the accused. He asked questions which I have no doubt were leading in character, and received answers.

'It is not contended by Mr Maude for one moment that these statements were not absolutely voluntary. I thought I was going to hear evidence that gross pressure had been put upon this man or some gross inducement had been offered to him, so that at the end of a long and unbroken examination he was so utterly exhausted that he could not do himself justice and he was hardly in a position to know what answer he was making; indeed, it was suggested because the words 'long' and 'gruelling' were used twice by Mr Maude in his address to me. The examinations were long, but every consideration was given to the man. He was given a meal in the middle of the examination; he was not in any way exhausted; he never complained of being exhausted. Indeed the witness called on his behalf says at the end he was full of energy and every single bit of the typed statements were read, I am satisfied, right through carefully by the accused and signed by the accused. He was cautioned with the very greatest care, and I think the real question I have to consider; was there any promise of favour, was there any menace, any undue pressure such as to induce him to confess, and was he induced by such promise, menace or pressure to make that confession?

'I am quite satisfied that the answer to all those matters is negative. I have no doubt about it whatever. I have had the opportunity of seeing Lieutenant De Mott and I believe his evidence and accept it as evidence of truth.

'Cases have been quoted to me, which do no more than indicate the undesirability of questions. I quite agree according to our Rules it is undesirable, but it is quite a mistake and is bad law, and has been decided to be bad law, that answers given to questions when incorporated in a statement are not admissible in evidence.

'The first matters that are mentioned are matters of pure fact and are for me to decide, and I do decide that this was a statement voluntary in every way. The second matter is a matter of my discretion and I have come to the conclusion that I should be doing wrong and, indeed, doing violence to justice, if I exercised my discretion in these particular circumstances, having seen the accused and given him the opportunity of being sworn and giving testimony, and having seen Lieutenant De Mott, I think I should be doing wrong in exercising my discretion against the admission of such statements.

'It is perfectly true that some parts of the statements are not in my view at the present moment material to the matter we are trying. I have no doubt that Mr Byrne in consultation with Mr Maude will be able to say what parts should be eliminated, in just the same way that Mr Casswell was able to shorten the time occupied by agreeing with Mr Howard as to the matters that should be eliminated in Jones's statement. You will do that, Mr Maude?

Mr MAUDE: Of course, my lord.

Mr JUSTICE CHARLES: Mr Caswell, how long will you be?

Mr CASSWELL: My lord, not very long I think. What I intended to do was to make another application, but if your Lordship likes to hear it, I will do so now.

Mr JUSTICE CHARLES: I think I better do that tomorrow morning. It is now twenty minutes past four.

Mr CASSWELL: Might I make another application on behalf of the parents of the defendant Jones who have come up from Wales? Could they see this girl before she goes back to prison tonight?

Mr JUSTICE CHARLES: Mr Byrne, I am very much against prisoners seeing their parents and in murder cases I have never heard of it being done.

Mr BYRNE: It is a matter entirely in your Lordship's discretion.

Mr JUSTICE CHARLES: No, I cannot allow it. Then I will hear Mr

Casswell tomorrow morning. He wants to say something to me about the order in the indictment.

MR CASSWELL: If your Lordship pleases.

Mr JUSTICE CHARLES: That will not take very long?

Mr CASWELL: Not more than ten minutes.

Mr JUSTICE CHARLES: You will have to convince me that the undoubted right of the Prosecution to choose the order in which the prisoners should be set out in the indictment should be set aside.

The court then adjourned until the next morning.

Mr Maude's defence for Hulten had suffered a severe setback; the consequences of this reverse would only become clear when these statements were read to the jury and Hulten's plea for manslaughter would be crushed.

CHAPTER SEVEN

THE TRIAL - SECOND DAY

WEDNESDAY 17TH JANUARY 1945

When proceeding were resumed on Wednesday morning, Mr Casswell, defence for Jones, asked the judge if he could have the indictment altered so that Hulten's name appeared before Jones. Mr Justice Charles wanted to know why this should be granted; Mr Casswell said that the matter should not be discussed before the jury. Mr Justice Charles then asked the jury to retire from the court.

Mr CASSWELL: My Lord, I am extremely sorry to interrupt the trial in this way, I would not do so if I did not think it was in the best interests of my client. My application is that my Lordship should amend the indictment under the Indictments Act, Section 5, by ordering that the male prisoner's name be placed first in the indictment. Your Lordship has, of course, as your Lordship knows full well, power to make any amendment. I should have asked for this earlier, if I had not been assured by my learned friend that Hulten was first on the indictment. Apparently he was mistaken, although he advised the opposite. In my respectful submission, in the normal course of advents Hulten should have been put first in the indictment for these reasons; (1) There can be no doubt, that in the mind of the prosecution (or indeed I should so have submitted) it was the man who was primarily responsible; he was the owner of the revolver. He has said it in a statement, which your Lordship has admitted, that he shot the man.

Mr JUSTICE CHARLES: Apart altogether from the statement, he made that observation to a police constable.

Mr CASSWELL: Yes my lord, I had forgotten that.

Mr JUSTICE CHARLES: 'If it had not been for the girl I should not have shot Heath'.

Mr CASSWELL: He let the Prosecution know from his own lips that he shot this man; therefore he appears to be, if not in law, in fact the principle offender. (2) He is a man of full age and my client is a minor, a girl of eighteen years of age. (3) He was taken into arrest before she was. And (4) alphabetically, I am assured, 'H' comes before 'J'. So my lord, I submit on any of these grounds the normal course of events would that he should come first in the indictment. My Lord, I am told - my learned friend has made me a present of this - that the normal order of names was reversed. Your Lordship knows in the case of co-prisoners one prisoner cannot be called to give evidence against a co-prisoner except in four sets of circumstances; (1) nolle prosequi (meaning unwilling to pursue) (2) Acquittal; (3) Conviction and sentence of the first prisoner who is called to give evidence against the other, and (4) although indicted together they are not jointly tried. Only in those four instances is the Prosecution enabled to call one prisoner to give evidence against the other.

'My Lord, in this case they have decided to put both prisoners into the dock, and they therefore preclude themselves from calling one prisoner against the other, but by transposing their names they get this very remarkable fact; they force me to put my client into the box first and they not only have the witness to dot the I's and cross the T's in their case against the other prisoner, but they have the two further advantages—they examine a witness who is not their own witness, and they have this further advantage, that she is not an accomplice.

'If one prisoner gives evidence against another in the course of a trial he or she is not treated as an accomplice, as they would be if called by the Prosecution, and therefore there is no need for corroboration of their testimony. In my respectful submission it is a principle of law in a case where it is clear that one prisoner must attack the other it is a very good reason for—and in fact the case which I have here says that in such a case as the Judge should order—a separate trial.

Mr JUSTICE CHARLES: No application was made to me for a separate trial.

Mr CASSWELL: I was going on to say that. I have not made an application for a separate trial in this case, but whether I should have done so had I known the order of the names in the first place I know not. Why is it a rule of law? It is because of the embarrassment which is caused by one or both prisoners having to give evidence which incriminates the other. My Lord, that is the reason for that principle, in my respectful submission.

Mr JUSTICE CHARLES: But, Mr Casswell just let me see how that works out. You are asking that Jones should be second on the indictment because you say; in as much as I have been informed that this man is going to say that this was an accident, it does not matter to you that it prejudices him for her evidence to come first which displaced, or tender to displace, any such averment. How does it disadvantage your client that she should come first?

Mr CASSWELL: She has first to stand the ordeal of the witness box.

Mr JUSTICE CHARLES: That is not enough.

Mr CASSWELL: That may not be enough.

Mr JUSTICE CHARLES: She has to withstand the ordeal some time if she is going to be called, and some people would say the sooner it's over the better.

Mr CASSWELL: Some people may; one doesn't know about that.

Mr JUSTICE CHARLES: No, that does not affect my mind. I have not lost sight of the other points you have made.

Mr CASSWELL: I'm obliged to your Lordship for having told me that. The other point is this; that her own defence is difficult for this reason; your Lordship will have seen that certain things happened on Tuesday night and Thursday night as a result of which, my instructions are, she became thoroughly terrified, and she was threatened with what would happen to her if she said anything about it. She has got to explain why she was terrified and why he was threatening her and would not allow her out of his sight, or out of the house while he was away.

Mr JUSTICE CHARLES: Why cannot she give that evidence?

Mr CASSWELL: My lord, because it would open up other offences against her.

Mr JUSTICE CHARLES: I know, I shall be very careful to see it does not.

Mr CASSWELL: It is the last thing that one would want to happen. It is something that makes her defence difficult, and her feelings in the box difficult, and therefore I do submit she should not be first to have to go into the box and incriminate her co-prisoner, as she is bound to do.

Mr JUSTICE CHARLES: If she went into the witness box second she would be bound to incriminate her co-prisoner. She has done that already upon the statement, portions of which you have admitted to be properly produced. She has already done so, and she will do so again.

Mr CASSWELL: I should have had the advantage then of cross-examining the prisoner who, I submit, is the principle offender in this case.

Mr JUSTICE CHARLES: Well, I quite understand your points. I must hear what Mr Byrne has got to say.

Mr CASSWELL: There is one other thing I ought to say, and that is this; that so long as it remained in doubt whether Hulten's statement was admissible or not the Prosecution may have felt in some difficulty in proving the case up to the hilt, but in my respectful submission, now your Lordship has ruled that…

Mr JUSTICE CHARLES: I have got my own views about that, you know; this is a statutory discretion.

Mr CASSWELL: Oh yes, my lord.

Mr JUSTICE CHARLES: Unfortunately, you know the indictments act 1915, section 5, which is the section, applies only – only - where an indictment is defective. I doubt very much if I have any power to touch the indictment in circumstances of the sort.

Mr CASSWELL: Your Lordship will remember that at the end of that section it does not preclude your Lordship from exercising any other power:

Mr JUSTICE CHARLES: I will hear what Mr Byrne says. Mr Byrne, don't you think I ought to hear Mr Maude?

Mr BYRNE: Certainly, my lord.

Mr JUSTICE CHARLES: I think I must hear Mr Maude next, because if it is a matter of importance - whether it is or whether it is not I am not really satisfied - if it is, Mr Maude, and the application to place your client first and not second upon the indictment, I do not know whether it affects you or whether you mind one way or the other.

Mr MAUDE: My lord, I am a little at a lost what to say to your Lordship. In all my time at the Bar I have never heard of an application to alter the order of an indictment. It is something new to me.

Mr JUSTICE CHARLES: It is new to me. I have been seventeen years on the bench now and I have never heard it before.

Mr MAUDE: I have always understood it is one of the matters in which those who choose to bring charges as they will. If they choose to put them in a particular order they do. There are certain hardships involved in all criminal trials that are inevitable: for instance some may think the Prosecution having the last word in certain circumstances may tend to be a disadvantage to the prisoner; it is one of those things that happens to be a rule, but, so far as I am concerned, I don't feel I have anything really to say because I apprehend it is entirely in their discretion. As I said to your Lordship, I would not have said anything; if I had been put second and wanted to be first I should have had to be silent; but I may be wrong and Mr Casswell may be right.

Mr JUSTICE CHARLES: Yes, Mr Byrne?

Mr BYRNE: I want, if I may, before dealing actually with the submission, just to say a word about one observation of my learned friend Mr Casswell. He said he might have applied for a separate trial if he had known the order in which these two persons appeared in the indictment. My Lord, I want to say this emphatically; it is the business of my learned friend to find out what the order is in the indictment; it is not my business.

Mr CASSWELL: I did, but the indictment was not here when I came, and I asked my learned friend, thinking he would know and three times I asked him.

Mr BYRNE: It is not my business to tell him, but of course as a matter of courtesy, one would. I will tell your Lordship exactly what happened with regards to this; there is no mystery about it at all. The indictment was not drawn by counsel, it was drawn by the court; in fact I was consulted with regard to the matter and the view I took (and in my submission it is the view that anybody prosecuting is entitled to take) was that the proper order for the purpose of this trial that the woman should be first in the indictment.

I then thought no more about the matter, and when my learned friend Mr Casswell came into court yesterday morning I was looking at my notes, or doing something or other, as I sat here - my mind was upon something entirely different - and he asked me the order in the indictment. Well I looked at one spot in my papers, and if your Lordship's papers are the same as mind you will find that the depositions have been in the order 'Hulten and Jones' and the exhibits have them in the order 'Jones and Hulten'.

Mr JUSTICE CHARLES: Yes.

Mr BYRNE: With my mind upon something else at the moment I said, 'Oh yes, the man is first'. I agree I made a mistake, but really there is no duty upon me to tell my learned friend. If he had wanted to inspect the indictment he could have gone to the office of the court and inspected it. I did want to say this, that I hope there is nothing lurking in the back of his mind that he might have applied for a separate trial. I am sure your Lordship will agree with me that in such a proceeding your Lordship could order a separate trial, and if my learned friend desires to make any complaint of that, I should advise him to make an application for a separate trial and not harbour any kind of grievance that he would have done so if I had not by inadvertence misled him on the order in the indictment. As to the submission he has made, it is a most novel submission in my view. One knows perfectly well that persons are arrested, they are charged with an offence, they appear before the justices, and they appear in some order - there has to be some order - and I do not suppose for one moment - your Lordship knows these matters so well - that the police officer in the case worries his head about what order they are to appear in; they just assume some kind of position, and that position they maintain throughout the proceeding in the court below. Of course when the matter is going to be dealt with before a judge and jury the indictment has to be drawn, and in my submission the Prosecution has got an absolute right to select the order in which they propose to charge those persons in the indictment. Over and over again, I must confess, in my own experience I have changed the order in which the person had previously appeared in the proceedings. I have changed the order when I have drawn the indictment, and there has never been any exception taken to it by any learned judge. It is not an amendment of the indictment at all, because the indictment is not defective, and I would submit with great respect that your Lordship would have no power to amend it in the way my learned friend suggests. What your Lordship would have power to do, quite obviously is to say; although the indictment is in that order I think in fact the evidence by these defendants should be given in reverse order and the speeches should be in reverse order; but I apprehend your Lordship would want very good and substantial reasons to be forthcoming to exercise your discretion in that way.

Mr JUSTICE CHARLES: You see, I am looking at both of the accused. If it is to advantage one that she should be placed second, it may disadvantage the other, and I have noticed this in a case of this sort, that although the cases are considered by the judge separately and he is dealing with them in a separate compartment, I have no business whatever that I can see to give that advantage.

Mr BYRNE: With respect, I would agree with your Lordship on that discretion of duty.

THE CLERK OF THE COURT: My Lord, it does not seem to matter, but I wanted to point out that the depositions show the order as Jones first and Hulten second, as they are in the indictment.

Mr BYRNE: My copy of the depositions puts them the other way round, and my exhibits agree with that; so that one can see, so far as the order is concerned, if you go back to their first appearance it was Jones first apparently.

Mr CASSWELL: I understand the learned clerk to say in fact Jones comes first. I only want to say that in my copy Jones comes first.

Mr BYRNE: I only want to indicate how unimportant it is in an ordinary case what order the accused appear in the lower court.

THE CLERK OF THE COURT: It is so. You can look at it, Mr Casswell.

Mr CASSWELL: I don't want to look at it.

Mr JUSTICE CHARLES: The indictment is there; it could have been inspected; it was open to inspection by representatives of either of the accused, and that would have been absolute finality on the matter. I cannot accede to this application.

Mr CASWELL: If your Lordship pleases.

Mr JUSTICE CHARLES: Let the jury be brought in.

Mr Justice Charles dismissed Mr Casswell's application and the jury was recalled.

Mr JUSTICE CHARLES: Mr Byrne, I wanted to ask you – it does not matter about the jury being present – do the legal representatives of the accused want any further proof of the Home Secretary's order?

Mr BYRNE: I am obliged, my lord.

Mr JUSTICE CHARLES: Of course, it is quite easy to prove it in the regular way. At present you have stated that under a certain section – I forget which it is – the Home Secretary has made an order. Of course, strictly that order ought to be produced.

Mr BYRNE: Most certainly. It will be produced. I was not producing it at the moment, because it is produced by a police officer who gives other evidence, and it would be more convenient for him to produce it then.

Mr JUSTICE CHARLES: Oh yes, I am obliged.

Mr BYRNE: My lord the next witness is Mrs Heath, the widow of the deceased man. She was conditionally bound over, and perhaps her evidence may be read?

Mr JUSTICE CHARLES: Very well.

THE CLERK OF THE COURT: 'Winifred Ivy Heath upon her oath saith as follows: I live at 5, Hards Cottages, West Street, Ewell, Surrey. George Edward Heath was my husband. He was 34 years of age. On the 9th October 1944 I went to the mortuary at Feltham and there identified the body of my husband. (Signed) W. I. Heath.'

Mr HOWARD for the PROSECUTION examined LEONARD BEXLEY, sworn.

Q. Are you Leonard Bexley; is that your name?

A. Yes.

Q. You live at 3 Luxemburg Gardens W14?

A. Yes.

Q. Are you a coach trimmer?

A. Yes.

Q. Have you got a daughter who is a waitress in a café?

A. Yes.

Q. Whereabouts is that café?

A. In Hammersmith Broadway.

Q. Last September, were you in the habit of going into the café from time to time?

A. For some time, yes.

Q. Do you know the defendant Jones, the girl?

A. Just a slight acquaintance, yes.

Q. Where did you first meet her?

A. In this particular café.

Q. Do you remember on Saturday, 30th of September of last year, being at the café?

A. Yes.

Q. Do you know the defendant Hulten, the soldier?

A. Yes.

Q. Where did you first meet him?

A. In this café.

Q. Who introduced you to him?

A. My daughter.

Q. When was that, do you remember?

A. About the end of September.

Q. When you were introduced to him, do you remember what kind of clothes he was wearing? Was he in uniform?

A. Yes.

Q. What sort of uniform?

A. I think it was a private's.

Q. Did you know what unit he belonged to?

A. I didn't take that notice; no.

Q. Was anything said about that?

A. Nothing at all.

Mr JUSTICE CHARLES: He didn't tell you where his unit was?

A. After he was dressed as a lieutenant, yes.

Mr HOWARD: After he was dressed as a lieutenant, I think he said, my lord.

Mr JUSTICE CHARLES: I don't understand, I'm afraid.

Mr HOWARD: Did you ever see him dressed as a lieutenant?

A. Yes.

Q. Was that the first time you met him?

A. No.

Mr JUSTICE CHARLES: I see now.

Mr HOWARD: You saw him again after the end of September, did you?

A. Yes.

Q. How long after the first time you met him?

A. Almost the next day; I am not quite certain, but within a short time.

Q. Was he then dressed as a lieutenant?

A. Yes, I think so - yes.

Q. Did you know anything about his unit; were you told anything?

A. He said he could not draw pay because his unit was in Holland.

Q. He could not draw pay because his unit was in Holland?

A. Yes.

Q. Were you ever in the café at the same time as the defendants, the girl Jones and the American Hulten?

A. Yes, on one occasion.

Q. Did they know each other?

A. No, I was talking to Jones when Hulten came in and he said did I know her and I said yes, and I sort of fixed up an acquaintance there and then.

Q. Do you know when that was?

A. Roughly about the second or third of October.

Q. After you had introduced them did you hear them say anything to each other?

A. Well, I didn't take much notice.

Q. Did you know whether or not they were going to see each other again?

A. Yes, I remember now he made an appointment for that evening.

Q. That was, you say, second or third October. Did you see Hulten again after that?

A. Yes.

Q. How long after, do you remember?

A. A couple of days I should think.

Q. Do you know a bombed factory site behind the Broadway at Hammersmith?

A. Yes, it is used as a car park.

Q. Did you go there with Hulten?

A. Yes.

Q. What did you see there?

A. He showed me an automatic pistol.

Q. Just look at this. Was it like that?

A. A similar pattern, yes.

Q. Did he say anything when he showed it to you?

A. He said, 'I'd like to show you how it works.'

Q. What did you say?

A. I said, 'You'd better put that away before it goes off.'

Q. Was there any vehicle on this site that was used as a car park?

A. Yes, a huge American lorry.

Q. The day after that, after he had shown you the pistol, did you see him again?

A. Yes.

Q. Where did you go?

A. For a ride in this lorry.

Q. In the lorry that you had seen upon the car park?

A. Yes.

Q, Who drove it?

A. Hulten.

Q. Do you remember a Saturday morning, 7th October, being in the café when Hulten came in?

A. Yes.

Q. Did he say anything to you?

A. He came in quite suddenly and said 'I'm in the barber's getting cleaned up'.

Q. Did he then go out of the café having said that, or stay there?

A. He stayed for some few minutes.

Q. Did he go out then?

A. Well he produced two articles.

Q. What were the articles he produced?

A. A revolving pencil and a fountain pen.

Q. Just look at these.

A. Yes.

Q. A revolving pencil and a fountain pen?

A. Yes.

Q. He produced those, and did he say anything?

A. He said he was broke and wanted some money.

Q. What happened?

A. I gave him eight shillings for these two articles.

Q. You said he produced a gun as well, did you?

A. It was lying on the table.

Q. Did he say anything about it?

A. Nothing at all, nothing at all.

Q. That was in the morning of Saturday 7th October?

A. Yes.

Q. At about half past one or thereabouts, did you go anywhere with Hulten?

A. Yes, to a public house.

Q. After you had been to the public house, did you go anywhere else?

A. To a florist's in the station at Hammersmith, where he bought a small bunch of flowers.

Q. Then where did you go?

A. To an address in King Street Hammersmith.

Mr JUSTICE CHARLES: What number?

A. 311.

Mr HOWARD: Did you both go into 311?

A. No, I stayed outside.

Q. Did Hulten go in?

A. Yes.

Q. How long did you wait outside?

A. Until about five to two.

Q. Then what happened?

A. We got a taxi and went to the White City.

Mr JUSTICE CHARLES: 'Then we' - who is 'we'?

A. Jones, Hulten and myself.

Q. Got a taxi to where?

A. The White City Stadium.

Mr HOWARD: What time did you part from Jones and Hulten on that Saturday?

A. Roughly between four and half past.

Q. Did you notice during that afternoon what Jones called Hulten?

A. I couldn't be quite certain.

Q. Did you hear her call him anything?

Mr JUSTICE CHARLES: When she was talking to him?

A. She called him 'Ricky'.

Mr JUSTICE CHARLES: Well, that is all you were asked.

Cross-examined by Mr CASSWELL defence JONES.

Q. Mr Bexley, the first of these two accused whom you knew was Hulten, I understand?

A. No.

Q. Was he not?

A. No, the girl Jones.

Q. I got that wrong. She was a friend of your daughter's, wasn't she?

A. I don't think so, no.

Q. Who had introduced her to you?

A. Not an actual friend, just a visitor to this café.

Q. She had known your daughter?

A. Known her, yes.

Q. Your daughter introduced her to you?

A. Yes.

Mr JUSTICE CHARLES: The only thing he objects to is that she was a friend.

Mr CASSWELL: Yes, an acquaintance.

Mr JUSTICE CHARLES: Yes, she went to the café.

Mr CASSWELL: Then you got to know Hulten. Did he seem to you a well-mannered man?

A. Absolutely, yes; quite a decent chap.

Q. A decent chap?

A. Yes.

Q. And I suppose you had no hesitation in introducing him to this young girl.

A. Yes.

Q. No hesitation?

A. Yes.

Q. You didn't think that any harm would befall her because you had introduced him? That's right, is it not?

A. Yes.

Q. You had not known him long, I understand, only two or three days; is that so?

A. Possibly a fortnight.

Q. Oh, a fortnight, had you?

A. Yes.

Q. After a while he appeared in an officer's uniform?

A. Yes.

Q. Did you ask him how he got his promotion?

A. No.

Q. You didn't?

A. No.

Q. How soon after you had known him did he produce this pistol?

A. Almost immediately.

Q. Had you seen it before you went to that bombed garage or parking site?

A. Never.

Q. So that was the first time that he produced it?

A. Yes.

Q. When you say 'almost immediately' you mean on that occasion?

A. Yes.

Q. He didn't seem to mind producing the gun? Did he seem to be proud of it?

A. Absolutely, yes.

Q. I mean, you were comparative stranger and he showed you that he had got a gun?

A. Yes.

Q. Then on another occasion I understand on Saturday 7th October, he pulled the gun out of his pocket and put it on the table in the café?

A. Yes.

Q. So that it seems he had no hesitation in producing the gun?

A. Yes.

Q. With regards the accused Jones, was she known as Georgina Grayson?

A. Yes.

Q. That was her stage or dancing name, was it not?

A. Yes.

Q. You knew her fairly well, did you not? Had you been to the cinema with her?

A. Just once, yes.

A FATAL PICKUP

Q. What did you call this man? Did you call him Ricky?

A. No, I called him Karl.

Q. Had he told you his name was Karl?

A. No, my daughter told me that.

Q. Your daughter knew him before you did, did she?

A. Yes.

Q. Just one other question. During those days, from the date when you introduced the accused Jones to the other accused, did you see her at all at the café?

A. No.

Cross-examined by Mr MAUDE defence HULTEN.

Q. Mr Bexley, on the 2nd October, in the early hours of the morning, the probabilities are that Heath was killed. You know that?

A. No.

Q. You went to the racing track with these two persons, Jones And Hulten, that afternoon?

A. Yes.

Q. How long were you at the racing track, roughly?

A. Two hours.

Q. Two hours?

A. Near enough.

Q. Were you all having bets?

A. Yes.

Q. Were you all together?

A. Part of the time, yes.

Q. Most of the time?

A. Well, yes.

Q. How long does it take to get there from where you started for the track?

A. About twenty minutes.

Q. Twenty minutes there, and after the party was over at the stadium did you go away together?

A. Yes.

Q. How long were you together after you left the White City?

A. Twenty minutes, near enough, to half an hour.

Q. So that we may take it that you were something between two and three hours with these persons?

A. Yes.

Q. Did you notice anything extraordinary about either of them?

A. Just that the girl looked very ill.

Q. She looked ill?

A. Yes.

Q. Whom were the flowers for?

A. The girl Jones.

Q. He gave them to her, did he?

A. Yes.

Q. Did she wear them?

A. Yes.

Q. What was their manner together?

A. I should say…

Q. Jokes, any jokes?

A. Yes.

Q. Apart from her looking ill, did she seem distressed in any way?

A. Not absolutely, no.

Q. No, but we want to know the details of it. Not absolutely, but in any way, in some way, did she seem distressed?

A. No, I didn't notice it; just that she looked very ill.

Q. Just that she looked very ill?

A. Yes.

Q. What was her attitude towards him?

A. I should say intimate.

Mr JUSTICE CHARLES: What?

Mr MAUDE: Intimate, my lord. (To the witness) I am particularly anxious not to suggest the answer to you. I want you to give absolutely your own story about this. What does the expression 'intimate' mean; in what sort of way?

A. Very fond.

Q. Very fond of each other?

A. Yes.

Q. Or only the man for the woman?

A. Well, yes.

Q. Which is it?

A. The girl seemed very much attached.

Q. She did?

A. Yes.

Q. Was there any sign at all of fear of him?

A. None whatsoever.

Q. What was his behaviour towards her? I'm not talking now of fondness; but you put it in your own words. What was his behaviour towards her throughout the afternoon?

A. Absolutely as a gentleman, quite decent.

Q. Who suggested leaving first? Don't say if you can't remember; if you can remember tell us. Can you remember?

A. Well, we arrived in the Broadway and they went off down to the subway.

Q. I'm sorry, I didn't mean that, I meant, and should have said so; who suggested leaving the races first, or was it all over?

A. No, it was not over.

Q. Who suggested leaving, do you remember?

A. No.

Q. Had the money come to an end; perhaps that is what it was?

A. No.

Q. Still money to bet with?

A. Yes.

Q. Who was putting the money on?

A. Well, Hulten had a few bets and so did I.

Q. Did the girl have any?

A. I didn't notice that.

Q. I suppose you guessed – I say 'I suppose' from what you said – you guessed that he was absent without leave?

A. Well no, I never had any idea of that at all, not during the time I knew him.

Q. I am putting it to you, because if a man appears in a private's uniform and then appears in an officer's uniform, I am suggesting that if a man does not guess he would have commented or spoken to him about it. Why not?

A. I'm afraid I didn't go into it all that much.

Q. You didn't exercise your mind on it at all?

A. Absolutely not.

Q. Let me see if I can remind you of something else. So far as that pistol you saw is concerned, did you tell Hulten that you would be able to get thirty shillings for it?

A. Never at all.

Q. Or thirty shillings for something or other; what was it?

A. No.

Q. Perhaps it was for the pen or pencil?

A. No, I don't remember mentioning at any time that amount.

Q. It was put to you by Mr Casswell, and I want to ask you if you appreciated it, that you had seen him pull the gun out of his pocket and put it on the table. What you told the court in answer to Mr Casswell was that he put it on the table; actually he produced it from somewhere, but from where, I am suggesting you don't know?

A. Yes.

Q. Is that right?

A. Yes.

Q. Do you remember which side it was?

A. It's too far back now.

Q. When you were telling the court about the production of the pistol, on that first occasion, that was in the café was it? I don't mean, of course, in the motorcar, but he produced it, you say, in the café?

A. I think three times altogether I saw the automatic.

Q. Was one of them, you say, in the café?

A. Yes.

Q. And was it put on the table for anybody to see?

A. Yes.

Q. Quite openly?

A. Yes, with the magazine taken out.

Q. No attempt to conceal it at all?

A. No.

Q. Which occasion was that? Was that on the 7th - that was the day you went to the races?

A. No.

Q. Which day was that?

A. About the middle of the week.

Q. That is before?

A. About Wednesday.

Mr BYRNE for the Prosecution examined VIOLET FLEISIG, sworn.

Q. Is your name Violet Fleisig?

A. Yes.

Q. Are you married or single?

A. I am married.

Q. Did you know the deceased man, George Edward Heath?

A. Yes.

Q. Had you known him for some three months, was it, before he was killed?

A. That's right.

Mr JUSTICE CHARLES: About how long?

A. Three months.

Mr MAUDE: If my learned friend should so wish - it is a matter, of course, for him - I should have no objection to him putting leading questions to this witness.

Mr CASSWELL: It does not affect me, I think.

Mr BYRNE: I am much obliged (To the witness) had you lent him your fountain pen?

A. Yes.

Q. Just tell me if this is the pen you lent him.

A. Yes.

Q. Did he carry it in his outside breast jacket pocket?

A. Yes.

Q. Was he in the habit of carrying a pencil in the same pocket?

A. Yes.

Q. Is this the pencil?

A. Yes.

Q. In fact did he give that pencil to you and then had you lent it to him?

A. Yes.

Q. On Friday, 6th October, at seven o'clock in the evening, did he come to see you?

A. Yes.

Q. Do you remember whether the pen and pencil were then in their usual place in his pocket?

A. Yes.

Q. Now will you just look at this wristwatch? Do you recognise that?

A. Yes.

Q. As a watch belonging to him?

A. Yes.

Q. Used he to wear it?

A. Yes.

Q. When you saw him on that evening that you have told us about, 6th October, do you recollect whether he was wearing that wristwatch that evening?

A. Yes.

Q. He was?

A. Yes.

Q. Did he also carry with him a cigarette case?

A. Yes.

Q. Was that a cigarette case which in order to open it, one side had to be slid over the other?

A. Yes that's right.

Q. Used he also to carry on him an automatic lighter, a cigarette lighter?

A. Yes.

Q. Do you recognise this wallet?

A. Yes.

Q. Was that his property?

A. Yes.

Q. He used to carry in that wallet a photograph of you, as a matter of fact?

A. Yes.

Q. So you know the wallet pretty well?

A. Yes.

Mr CASSWELL: No questions.

Mr MAUDE: No questions.

Mr HOWARD for the Prosecution examined EDRIS MAY EVANS, sworn.

Q. Mrs Edris May Evans, is that your name?

A. Yes.

Q. Where do you live?

A. 311 King Street, Hammersmith.

Q. Were you living there last September and October?

A. Yes.

Q. You let the upper portion of those premises consisting of five rooms?

A. Yes.

Q. Do you know the female defendant, the girl?

A. Yes.

Q. Can you remember when you first saw her?

A. It was on a Friday evening when she came and asked me if I had a room to let.

Q. Do you remember when it was?

A. About eight o'clock in the evening, I think.

Q. What date, can you tell us?

A. I could not tell you exactly, no.

Q. Was it in September? A. Yes, in September.

Q. Did she come on that day that you had arranged?

A. No.

Q. About how long afterwards?

A. She was supposed to come on the Monday morning at ten o'clock, and she came on the Thursday.

Q. Did you know anything about her meeting any American?

A. Afterwards, do you mean?

Q. Yes.

A. Well, she gave me to understand that she had an extensive circle of acquaintances among American officers. I suppose she used to meet some and go out with them.

Q. Do you recollect anything being said about any particular American?

A. Well, she used to tell me different things about various ones. I do not remember anything in particular one way or the other.

A FATAL PICKUP

Q. Did you know whether or not some few days after she had been with you she had been introduced to anyone.

A. Well, she told me when she was introduced to the gentleman over there, and that was only a few days before I gave her notice to go, and she had been with me about ten days then.

Q. Let us see if we can get it in order. About ten days after she came to you, you said, something was said about being introduced?

A. Yes.

Q. What did she say?

A. She said that she had been introduced to an American in a café.

Q. Did she say anything else about it?

A. Yes, she said she thought he was a deserter.

Q. Did you know whether she was going to meet him any more? Did she say anything about that?

A. Yes, she told me various things about why she thought so, and then she told me she was going to meet him at twelve o'clock that night.

Mr JUSTICE CHARLES: She did what?

A. She told me why she thought he was a deserter and one or two other things, and then she told me she going to meet him at twelve o'clock that night.

Q. At what time?

A. At twelve o'clock.

Mr HOWARD: Did you say anything to her when she told you that?

A. Yes, I did. I said it was very foolish, and that Hammersmith Broadway was a very silly place to be at twelve o'clock at night, and quite a few other things.

Q. Do you remember the evening of Friday, which was 6th October?

A. Yes.

Q. About ten o'clock that evening were you at home at 311?

A. Yes, I was doing some sewing.

Q. Did you see the girl Jones that evening?

A. Yes, she came and sat with me.

Q. Did you know her then as Jones?

A. No.

Q. What name did you know her by?

A. She gave me her name as Georgina Grayson, and I always called her Georgie.

Q. Was she well on that particular evening?

A. No, she had a very bad cold.

Q. Did you say anything to her about her cold?

A. I said to her 'Why do you not have an early night and go to bed?'

Q. What did she say to that?

A. She said she was going out with Ricky.

Q. Later on that evening did you hear anything?

A. Well, yes, afterwards she went upstairs. I stayed in my room. I was in the front of the house and about quarter past or twenty minutes past eleven I heard some very piercing whistles, and I heard her run down the stairs.

Q. Did you hear her come back that night?

A. No.

Q. The next morning was a Saturday. What time did you go to work?

A. I had to be at work at nine.

Q. Did you see Jones on the Saturday morning before you went to work?

A. No.

Q. When was the next time you saw her?

A. On the Saturday at lunchtime.

Q. After you had seen her on Saturday, at lunchtime, did somebody come to number 311?

A. Well, I hadn't seen her - yes, I did see her - and I hadn't been in very long and the bell rang, and I went downstairs and the American was there with another fellow.

Q. Which American do you mean?

A. Hulten.

Q. Did he say anything to you, Hulten?

A. He asked if she was in.

Q. Yes?

A. And I said, yes.

Q. Did he come in?

A. He said did I mind if he went upstairs to see her, and he left the other fellow at the door. I said, no I didn't mind, and he went.

Q. Did you go upstairs to them?

A. Yes, I did.

Q. Did you at that time know Hulten; did you know who he was?

A. Oh, no I had never seen him before.

Q. Were you introduced to him?

A. Yes, she introduced me to him.

Q. How did she introduce him to you, by what name?

A. Well she said, 'This is Mrs Evans' and she said, 'This is Ricky' to me.

Q. Did they soon after that go out?

A. Oh, yes, immediately after.

Cross-examined by Mr CASSWELL Defence for JONES.

Q. Mrs Evans, you always knew her as Georgie or Georgina Grayson?

A. Yes.

Q. When she told you about this American, you told us today that she thought he was a deserter?

A. Yes.

Q. When you were giving evidence before the magistrates, did you say that she said she thought he was fishy?

A. Well, yes, I did say that, but in point of fact she did say she thought he was a deserter.

Q. She did not say 'fishy'?

A. No, not literally.

Q. I was wondering what 'fishy' meant.

A. Something queer about him.

Q. But she had no hesitation in telling you that she was going out with him that night?

A. No.

Q. She made no secret of it?

A. No.

Q. And the same on that occasion when she had a cold, you noticed she had a bad cold?

A. Yes.

Q. On that occasion too, she made no secret that she was going out with him?

A. No.

Q. Did she ever use the word 'deserter' to you? Are you sure of that?

A. Absolutely positive, because I thought she was romancing. To tell you the truth I thought if he was patently a deserter to somebody so young as her, you see, I should have thought the police would have had the sense to pick him up earlier.

Q. It was not likely he would advertise himself as a deserter?

A. That is what I thought.

Q. So at any rate you did not believe it?

A. Well, I said to her 'what makes you think that?' and she gave me all the technical reasons why she thought so, which conveyed nothing to me, to tell you the truth, and I just did not absorb any of it.

Q. When you met him, what did you think of him?

A. I thought he was a very decent chap. He seemed a bit excited, and I thought it was because he was very keen on her.

Q. You thought him a pleasant, decent chap…

My lord, I must hear what she says, and I cannot.

Mr JUSTICE CHARLES: I didn't quite catch it. You said he seemed a very pleasant fellow, rather excited, and what else did you say?

A. I put that down to the fact that he was rather keen on Georgie.

Mr CASSWELL: And that afternoon they went out, that Saturday afternoon?

A. Yes.

Q. What was the state of her cold then?

A. She seemed all right.

Q. You thought it was all right? Because we have had a witness who said she looked very ill on the Saturday afternoon. Would you agree with that?

A. No, I wouldn't say so.

Q. She had got rid of this heavy cold in the short time then, overnight. Is that what you are saying?

A. I did not take a great deal of notice about her appearance really. I mean I didn't see them very long; she just introduced me to him and I didn't stand and converse with then or anything.

Q. I suggest to you she was obviously ill that day, but you say you did not notice it. Does it come to more than that?

A. Oh, I wouldn't say that.

Q. You wouldn't say that?

A. That she was obviously ill.

Cross-examined by Mr MAUDE Defence HULTEN.

Q. Did she seem frightened of him at all?

A. No.

Q. What was her manner towards him?

A. Just an ordinary manner; I wouldn't say anything else.

Q. Nothing abnormal at all?

A. No.

Q. When you spoke to her about going out with a person who was thought to be a deserter, you gave her a very serious warning indeed, did you not?

A. Well, I did really, yes.

Q. You mentioned the possibility that she might be killed?

A. Well, I did. I said it was silly to go round Hammersmith Broadway at twelve o'clock at night to meet somebody. I said, 'Why cannot he meet you earlier?' So she said he wanted to give her something, and I said 'If a fellow wants to give you something he will give it to you at four o'clock in the afternoon, not at twelve o'clock at night'.

Q. Did you use the sensible warning that she might have her throat cut?

A. Yes, I did say that.

Q. How did she take that?

A. She just laughed. She seemed determined to go, so I didn't say anything more about it.

Q. I think my learned friend was asking you just now about the time when they must have been going off in fact to the dog races. Did you know they were going to the races?

A. Oh yes, they said they were going.

Q. They talked about it?

A. They told me they were going.

Q. May we just go to the later time when they came back. You saw them when they came back?

A. I believe I did.

Q. What were they like then?

A. Well, they didn't stay in very long.

Q. Can you give us an idea of how long, as nearly as you can?

A. They came back about teatime and I heard them go upstairs and then she came down and asked me to mind some money for her.

Q. To mind some money for her?

A. Yes.

Q. What was she like then?

A. Just as she always was.

Q. Just as usual?

A. Yes.

Q. Did you see her after that, after minding the money for her?

A No, they went out and I didn't see them any more that evening, to the best of my recollection.

Q. What money was it you minded for her?

A. I said to her – if she had any money at any time – as the buzz-bombs are about, I put anything of mine in the oven, and let me put it in the oven for her, so she asked me to mind it for her, so I said, 'Put it in the oven and you know it's there' and she did.

Q. Do you remember what she put in the oven?

A. Seven pounds she showed me.

Q. What happened to the seven pounds?

A. Well, she kept taking a little bit at a time until it had all gone, as far as I know. I let her have the run of my kitchen.

Q. Had she put any money in the oven before?

A. No, not that I am aware of.

Q. Or given it to you?

A. No.

Mr BYRNE for the Prosecution examined MORRIS LEVENE, sworn.

Q. Is your name Morris Levene?

A. Yes, sir.

Q. Are you employed as a hairdresser at a barber's shop, 18 Queen Caroline Street, Hammersmith?

A. I was until six weeks ago.

Q. In October of last year you were employed there?

A. Yes.

Q. My lord? I am told I can lead this witness. Do you know the prisoner Hulten as a customer?

A. Yes.

Q. Since when?

A. Roughly round about soon after D-Day.

Q. The early days of June?

A. Yes.

Q. About the end of September or the beginning of October, was he a fairly regular customer?

A. Practically every day.

Q. Did you ask him if he could get a watch for you through the American canteen?

A. Yes.

Q. That would mean an American watch?

A. Yes.

Q. Did he tell you it would cost you four pounds fifteen or five pounds?

A. Correct.

Q. On Saturday, 7th October last, did he come into the shop for a shave?

A. Yes.

Q. About what time was that?

A. Roughly between half past nine and ten.

Q. In the morning?

A. Yes.

Q. After he had been shaved, did he tell you that he had managed to get you a watch?

A. Yes.

Q. Did he tell you the price was five pounds?

A. Yes.

Q. Did you take the watch from him and put it in your pocket and give him the five pounds?

A. I gave him the five pounds first and then I put the watch in my pocket.

A FATAL PICKUP

Q. You put the watch in your pocket without looking at it?

A. Yes.

Q. Is this the watch?

A. Yes.

Mr CASSWELL: No questions, my lord.

Cross-examined by Mr MAUDE Defence HULTEN.

Q. Why did you put this idea into this man's head?

A. I didn't put it into his head.

Q. Did you not?

A. No.

Q. You never looked at the watch when you got it? You put it straight in your pocket, we have just heard?

A. Yes.

Q. You never looked at it?

A. No, we were very busy at the time, and, trusting the fellow - I thought he was a very decent chap the time I had known him.

Q. I know, Mr Levene, you're not in the habit, are you, of buying things for five pounds without looking at them?

A. No.

Q. Have you ever done it before?

A. No.

Q. Is it a source of supply, did you think, the American canteen?

A. Yes.

Q. For watches?

A. Yes.

Q. You thought you could get it by a quite normal, straightforward business transaction?

A. Yes.

Q. Is that what you say?

A. Yes.

Q. Do you still think so?

A. I think so.

Q. You still think so?

A. Yes.

Q. Are you going to try to get somebody else to get you one?

A. No.

Mr CASSWELL: Before the next witness is called, my lord, might I ask another question of Mrs Evans?

Mr JUSTICE CHARLES: Indeed you may.

Mr CASSWELL further cross-examined EDRIS MAY EVANS.

Q. Mrs Evans, I wanted to ask you another question I didn't know about at the time. Are you sure that these two came back on Saturday afternoon? I suggest to you it was not on the Saturday afternoon after they had been to the dog racing?

A. Oh, it definitely was.

Q. Are you sure of that?

A. Absolutely positive.

Q. And that it was on the Sunday that seven pounds was handed over to you?

A. No, on Saturday night.

Q. Well, I have to put it because I suggest you are absolutely mistaken about that?

A. No, I am absolutely positive.

Mr HOWARD for the Prosecution examined WILLIAM WATERS, sworn.

Q. Is your name William Waters?

A. Yes.

Q. Police constable 579 of the 'F' Division of the Metropolitan Police?

A. Yes.

Q. Stationed at Hammersmith?

A. Yes.

Q. On the 9th October last year, at about half past seven in the evening, where were you?

A. In Lurgen Avenue Hammersmith.

Q. On duty?

A. On duty.

Q. Were there any cars in Lurgen Avenue at that time?

A. No cars at that time.

Q. Did you go again through Lurgen Avenue at about ten minutes past eight that evening?

A. Yes.

Q. Did you see a car in Lurgen Avenue then?

A. There was a car at that time.

Q. What sort of a car was it?

A. A Ford V8, RD 8955.

Q. Was it standing stationary in the avenue?

A. Stationary, facing east.

Q. Was anybody in it?

A. Nobody in it, quite empty.

Q. Were you in fact looking out for a car bearing that number?

A. Looking out for a car bearing that number.

Q. When you saw it did you notify your police station?

A. Yes, straight from the police box on the spot.

Q. And keep observation on the car?

A. I stood at the rear of the car.

Q. About nine o'clock that evening what did you see?

A. I saw the prisoner come out of a house in Lurgen Avenue and get into the car.

Q. Which prisoner?

A. The soldier on my right there.

Q. Hulten got into the car?

A. Got into the driver's seat as though he owned the car.

Q. What did you do?

A. I stood at the rear of the car, approached him straight away, got hold of his hand and I said 'Is this your car sir?' He made no reply. I had a previous arrangement with Inspector Read and Sergeant Dowell from Hammersmith to shout them, which I did.

Q. Did they come up to the car?

A. They ran to the car and Sergeant Dowell and I got him out of the car.

Q. Was he arrested?

A. He was arrested.

Cross-examined by Mr Maude Defence HULTEN.

Q. Only one matter at this early stage. I want to ask you this; was a revolver found? A. Yes, I asked…

Q. Just listen.

A. …Hulten if he was armed. He said 'Yes, I got a gun in my back pocket'.

Q. Do listen please.

A. I beg your pardon.

Q. The answer is; yes, a revolver was found?

A. Yes, I'm sorry.

Q. Was the revolver pulled out by him from between the belt and his clothes?

A. I didn't see; it was dark.

Q. Did you know who did get it?

A. Inspector Read.

Mr BYRNE for the Prosecution examined PERCY READ, sworn.

Q. Percy Read, Detective Inspector of the 'F' Division? At about quarter past eight on the evening of 9th October last, as a result of a message from Walters, did you go to Lurgen Avenue?

A. Yes.

Q. Did you see a stationary Ford motorcar RD 8955?

A. Yes.

Q. Were you with other officers?

A. Yes.

Q. Did you decide to keep observation?

A. Yes.

Q. At about nine o'clock did the prisoner Hulten come out of a house nearby?

A. Yes.

Q. Which house was that?

A. That was the first house in Lurgen Avenue, which is actually in Fulham Palace Road, number 159.

Q. The door of number 159 Fulham Palace Road is in Lurgen Avenue, is it?

A. Yes.

Q. He came out of number 159 Fulham Palace Road into Lurgen Avenue?

A. Yes.

Q. Where did he go?

A. He went straight across and entered the car.

Q. Then did you and the other officers close in?

A. Yes, he sat in the driving seat.

Q. Were the headlights of a police car turned on so that you could see what you were doing?

A. Yes.

Q. And you saw the prisoner was sitting in the driving seat?

A. Yes.

A FATAL PICKUP

Q. Was he pulled out of the car?

A. Yes.

Q. Was he told that you were police officers?

A. Yes.

Q. What did you do with him after he had been pulled out of the car?

A. We pulled him out of the car, pinioning his arms and pushed him with his face up against the wall, and I immediately searched him.

Q. Just listen to the question and don't run on. Did you ask him first of all any questions about the car?

A. I just asked him if it was his car, and he replied 'No'.

Q. Did you then search him?

A. Yes.

Q. What did you find?

A. In a back left hand hip pocket I found a Remington automatic pistol.

Q. Having found that, what did you say to him then?

A. I told him that I should take him to Hammersmith police station, where he would be detained pending enquiries.

Q. Did he say anything to that?

A. No.

Q. Did you search him any further before you took him to the police station?

A. Yes. In his left hand trouser pocket I found a magazine containing six live rounds of ball cartridge.

Q. Then you took him to the police station?

A. Yes.

Q. How was he dressed?

A. He was dressed in khaki slacks and a brown leather jerkin bearing one gold bar of a Second Lieutenant in the American Army.

Q. At the police station did you or did some officers in your presence ask him is name?

A. I asked him is name.

Q. What name did he give?

A. He gave the name of Richard John Allen, aged 22, 501st Parachute Infantry, United States Army.

Q. Did he give his rank?

A. Yes, Second Lieutenant.

Q. At the police station, did you examine the pistol that is in front of you now?

A. Yes.

Q. What did you find?

A. I found there was six rounds of ammunition in the magazine; there was one in the breech, the hammer was back and the safety catch was unsafe.

Q. Has that pistol a safety catch and a hammer?

A. Yes.

Q. In what position were those two things when you examined it?

A. The safety catch was unsafe, and the hammer was back.

Q. What does that mean? What would happen if the trigger was pulled?

A FATAL PICKUP

A. It would immediately fire.

Cross-examined by Mr Casswell Defence JONES.

Q. Did you say unsafe?

A. Yes.

Q. May I have a look at the pistol? This is not loaded, is it?

A. No.

Q. If you pulled that hammer back - is it back now?

A. It is not right back.

Q. That is what happens when you pull it back? You hear just that noise?

A. Yes.

Mr JUSTICE CHARLES: When you pull the hammer back you hear a click?

A. Yes.

Mr CASSWELL: Am I right in saying that with this type of pistol you cannot put the safety catch on till the hammer is back?

A. Yes.

Q. Just see if you can put the safety catch to 'safe' without pulling the hammer back.

A. But there is no need to put it at safe unless the hammer is back.

Q. I am asking you; can you put it to safe without pulling the hammer back?

A. No, it is safe.

Mr JUSTICE CHARLES: Of course not. Unless the hammer is back there is no object in putting it on safe.

Mr CASSWELL: That is what I suggested: it cannot slide back.

Mr JUSTICE CHARLES: You pull the hammer back. If you leave the catch unsafe it is in the firing position; but, having got the hammer back it is open to you to make it safe by putting the safety catch forward.

Mr CASSWELL: It is dangerous although once you have pulled the hammer back, you have got to do something to make it safe – have you got to do something else?

Mr JUSTICE CHARLES: Well, I don't know about that.

Mr CASSWELL: I have had some experience of these guns.

Mr JUSTICE CHARLES: So have I, Mr Casswell, probably more than you.

Cross-examined by Mr MAUDE Defence HULTEN.

Q. My Lord, my position is very unhappy because I have not had any, but may I ask first of all, is it safe now?

A. It is safe now.

Q. There is nothing in it?

A. There is nothing in it.

Q. Then may I have it please? We don't want an accident.

Mr JUSTICE CHARLES: We do not want an accident and we do not want laughter. It disgusts me to hear laughter in court in a case of this sort.

Mr MAUDE: What have I done to it? Just take it back will you? However I move the little safety catch lever from the top I can't get the hammer to move without pulling the trigger. That is fairly strong.

A. Yes.

Mr JUSTICE CHARLES: It needs a fairly strong pull.

A. It is not too strong my lord to pull.

Mr Maude: May I just say what is happening? I pulled it halfway back. What is the effect of that? If I move one of these levers now, can I do anything with it?

A. I don't think so.

Q. Then you have got to pull it back like that?

A. Yes.

Q. If I put this safety catch in the 'up' position, do I pull it down?

A. It is down now. It should be possible to work it.

Mr MAUDE: I think your Lordship will agree it is a light trigger.

Mr JUSTICE CHARLES: Oh yes, they are not very heavy. You have got to get back the hammer and you have got to put the catch at unsafe and you have got then to pull the trigger before it goes off.

Mr MAUDE: Is it always so? For instance, supposing somebody had just fired a shot with this pistol, imagine I fired and shot that one off, there had been an explosion and the thing had worked properly...

A. Yes.

Q. Is it then automatically in a position to fire again? A. Yes.

Q. When it is in a position to fire again, does this hammer come back?

A. Yes.

Q. Or is there an internal hammer?

A. No, with that particular type the hammer comes back; it is drawn back by the breech.

Q. So that it would be in a position ready to fire?

A. Yes.

Q. You have not got to move this catch at all?

A. No.

Q. So far as the magazine is concerned, how many does it hold?

A. It will hold seven.

Q. Inspector Read tells me that what he was wearing are properly described as green slacks?

A. Yes.

Q. Is that right?

A. Yes, greenish-khaki slacks. Have you got them? Has anybody got them? Could they be got for me?

A. Yes.

Q. How many hip pockets has it got?

A. I am not certain, but I believe it has two; I wouldn't be too sure of that.

Q. It is a small matter, but when the pistol is put into the greenish slacks, how much gets down into the pocket?

A. Well, the handle of the gun sticks out.

Q. Only the handle sticks out?

A. Yes.

Q. What time was the actual arrest? I am not talking of if technically now, you know saying 'I am arresting you' or saying anything like that; but when he was pounced on, when was that?

A. It would be as near as possible nine o'clock.

Q. What time did you get to the station?

A FATAL PICKUP

A. About a quarter of an hour later.

Q. What had you been doing yourself in the quarter of an hour?

A. I had been up and searched the house.

Q. Whom did you hand the pistol to?

A. I kept it in my pocket.

Q. In your pocket?

A. Yes.

Q. What he has persisted in saying to us is - in fact it does not matter much perhaps - but he did not have it in the pocket but between a belt and himself?

A. No.

Q. You are quite sure of that?

A. Yes.

Q. Did you search him in the dark?

A. Yes, we searched him in the dark - he was up against the wall - except for the fact I had the headlight and the fog lamp on.

Q. I am not suggesting it would disturb you at all, but I suppose you had in mind the possibility that you might be tackling somebody who might use a gun?

A. Yes.

Q. Very suddenly?

A. Yes.

Q. Did you feel it quickly?

A. Yes.

Q. And pulled it out like lightning?

A. Yes.

Q. I am suggesting you are wrong, that you didn't know it was in the pocket; that you couldn't see?

A. No.

Q. Did nobody handle it until you got to the police station except yourself?

A. No one.

Q. You quite sure?

A. I am quite sure.

Q. Will you get me the trousers, the green slacks?

A. Yes.

Mr Howard for the Prosecution examined Dr. ROBERT DONALD TEARE, sworn.

Q. Dr. Robert Donald Teare, you are a registered medical practitioner?

A. Yes.

Q. And a pathologist, practising at No. 19 Harley Street?

A. Yes.

Q. On the 7th October last year, in the presence of Inspector Tarr, did you conduct a post mortem examination on the body of a man?

A. I did.

Q. A man who was later identified as George Edward Heath?

A. Yes.

Q. Did you find on the body the entrance wound of a bullet?

A. I did.

Q. Where was that?

A. That was on the back, an inch from the mid-line and at the level of the sixth rib on the right.

Mr JUSTICE CHARLES: One inch to the right of the mid-line, is that right?

A. Yes, my lord.

Q. In the middle of the back?

A. Very nearly the middle of the back.

Mr Howard: Did you find the exit wound where the bullet had come out?

A. Yes.

Q. Where was that?

A. That was an inch and three quarters to the right of the mid-line in front, over the third rib.

Q. The bullet in its passage through the body, what damage had it done? Where had it gone?

A. It had caused great haemorrhage round the spinal cord and it had pierced two lobes of the right lung, causing vast haemorrhage into the chest cavity.

Q. And a man who had received a wound of that description, would he have been paralysed quickly?

A. Very quickly, yes.

Q. About what time?

A. Within half a minute I should think.

Q. How long, in your opinion, would he have lived after being shot?

A. I think he died within fifteen minutes of being shot.

Q. Did you come to any conclusion as to when he had died?

A. Yes, I made my post mortem examination at six o'clock on the evening of the 7th and I came to the conclusion that he had died between eleven pm the previous evening, the 6th, and six o'clock on the morning of the seventh.

Q. What was the cause of death?

A. The cause of death was haemorrhage from the bullet wound of the chest.

Q. On second November last year did you go to the police station at Barnes and see a Ford motorcar?

A. I did.

Q. Did you go with Inspectors Tarr and Tansill?

A. Yes.

Q. Was the registered Number of the Ford RD 8955?

A. It was.

Q. Did you take certain measurements inside the car?

A. I did.

Q. Did you measure the height of the top of the front seat from the floor?

A. I did.

Q. What was the measurement?

A. It was thirty-three inches.

Mr JUSTICE CHARLES: Is that the front seat?

A. The top of the front seat to the floor was thirty-three inches, my lord.

Mr HOWARD: Did you notice a dent in the metalwork of the near side front door just below the window glass?

A. Yes.

Q. How far was that from the floor?

A. Twenty-eight and three quarter inches.

Q. Did you notice another dent in the lid of the cubbyhole in the dash?

A. Yes.

Q. How far from the floor?

A. That was twenty-five and a quarter inches from the floor.

Q. How far were the two marks apart?

A. Thirteen and a half inches.

Q. Was the mark on the metalwork on the near side front door consistent with a bullet having struck it?

A. Yes, it was.

Q. And the mark on the lid of the cubbyhole, was that consistent with a bullet having ricocheted on to it?

A. Yes.

Q. Did you make an experiment in that car with the aid of a human skeleton?

A. Yes.

Q. And a wooden rod?

A. Yes.

Q. Did you come to any conclusion as to where abouts in the car the bullet had been fired from?

A. Yes, I came to the conclusion that the bullet had come from a weapon held in the right side of the back of the car.

Q. Were you able to form any opinion as to the direction of the flight of the bullet?

A. The direction of the flight was downwards and to the left in relation to the long axis of the car.

Cross-examined by Mr CASSWELL Defence JONES.

Q. Have you seen the clothing of the deceased man?

A. I saw it originally. The first time I saw the body was in the ditch at Staines. I saw it then and at the post mortem.

Q. Did you examine it to see if there was any singeing?

A. Yes, I did.

Q. Was there?

A. I could see none.

Q. You would expect, would you not with that gun, if it was fired close to the body, to find singeing of the clothing?

A. Yes.

Mr JUSTICE CHARLES: How close?

A. Within six inches, my lord.

Mr CASSWELL: Could you form any opinion as to how far from the body the muzzle of the pistol when it was discharged?

A. I could only say that it was more than six inches.

Q. That is all?

A. Yes.

Q. The point of entry did not give you any sort of hint, I suppose?

A. No, It was clean cut.

Q. Besides being a doctor, if you will excuse my saying so, you acted as a detective as well. You were looking at the bullet holes and you came to the conclusion that the depression was caused first by the impact of the bullet on the car and that it was then deflected from that and hit the glove box?

A. Yes.

Q. To get over to that side of the car the body must have been leaning over? It cannot have been in the driving seat?

A. No.

Q. It must have been leaning well over?

A. It must have been leaning well over.

Cross-examined by Mr MAUDE Defence HULTEN.

Q. In fact, what you found is consistent with the driver having been leaning over to open the back door? A. Entirely.

Q. Dr Tear, would you look at the photograph that was taken by the police photographer inside the motorcar. No doubt you have seen it before?

A. I have not actually, closely.

Q. What you point out is the mark above the body of the door, and then the mark on the cubbyhole?

A. Yes.

Q. If one fired a number of shots from a weapon held in the same position, aiming the barrel slightly towards the door from the back of the car as you have been indicating, of course it would be quite impossible to say where each bullet would ricochet?

A. Yes.

Q. One might go down, and another might go up, and so on?

A. The angle of ricochet is very vague.

Q. I suppose, from what you have been telling us, that the bullet hit something hard in the body of the man, did it not?

A. Yes, it hit the vertebral column, the spine.

Q. As to the deflection that one would get from that you can't say? It's no good asking you that?

A. No. It did not appear to be great.

Mr JUSTICE CHARLES: It did not appear to be great because of the exit opening?

A. That is right.

Q. Comparing the entrance with the exit, the deflection was not very great?

A. That is so.

Mr MAUDE: You would have to do more than that, wouldn't you? You would have to take the line from the entrance to some midpoint, and then onto the exit, to see what deflection there would be?

A. Yes.

Q. If you simply see the entrance and exit holes, you cannot tell whether there has been any deflection inside at all? You have to look inside the body?

A. Naturally I did follow the track right through.

Q. There was some slight deflection?

A. Yes, there must have been.

Q. It is that fact, no doubt, that makes it impossible for you to say exactly where the pistol was held?

A. I cannot say exactly.

Q. I am asking for information here. You have talked about the singeing. Mr Casswell was asking you about the singeing of the clothing, because at six inches the flame, I suppose, burns the material?

A. Yes, that is so.

Q. If you don't know this I am sure you will tell me, but from the bullets such as have been found in this case do you know whether any powder would be deposited in the clothes?

A. I don't know precisely.

Q. You don't know at all?

A. No.

Q. Did you look for powder on the clothes?

A. Yes, I did.

Q. And you did not find any?

A. I could not find any.

Q. I think you probably may know this. If you were looking for powder in the clothes, you must have informed yourself from your textbooks on it as to the significance if you had found it?

A. I may tell you, as a generalisation, that there could not have been powder present there with that particular weapon, if it were discharged more than six inches from the coat.

Q. It comes to the same thing, the flame scorching the coat; you cannot get closer to it than that?

A. No, so far as this specific weapon is concerned.

(adjourned for a short time)

Mr BYRNE for the Prosecution examined RALPH TATE BLACKBURN, sworn.

Mr BYRNE: My Lord, I am told I can lead this witness. (To the witness) Is your name Ralph Tate Blackburn?

A. Yes.

Q. Are you the foreman of the repair garage of the Ford Motor Company of Dagenham?

A. Yes.

Q. Are you thoroughly conversant with all types of Ford vehicles?

A. Yes.

Q. On 14th October last did you examine a Ford motorcar RD 8955 in the presence of Inspector Tarr?

A. Yes.

Q. Did you measure the width of the track?

A. Yes.

Mr JUSTICE CHARLES: If you have got a note you can refer to it.

Mr BYRNE: Was it four feet, ten inches?

A. Yes.

Q. Then did you examine the underneath of the vehicle?

A. Yes.

Q. Is it fitted underneath, to put the matter quite shortly, with a spring so that the brake, when it has been put on, will be taken off again?

A. Yes.

Q. Did you find that spring was missing?

A. Yes.

Q. Just look at this spring. Does it belong to that car?

A. Yes.

Q. Is that the one that was missing?

A. Yes.

Q. Did you find when you examined that spring that it had sticking to it bits of mud and grass?

A. Yes.

Q. Did you notice that the rear window blind of the car had been torn away?

A. Yes.

Mr CASSWELL: No questions.

Mr MAUDE: No questions.

Mr HOWARD for the Prosecution examined ROBERT EARL DE MOTT, sworn.

Q. Robert Earl De Mott, is that your name?

A. It is.

Q. Are you a first lieutenant in the United States Army?

A. I am.

Q. In charge of the 8th Military Police Criminal Investigation Section?

A. I am.

Q. In civil life are you an attorney at law?

A. Yes.

Q. And a practising member of the Bar of the State of Colorado?

A. Yes.

Q. At about seven o'clock in the morning of the 10th October last year did you see the male defendant Hulten at Hammersmith police station?

A. I did.

Q. Was there also present an agent from your office, I think named Riddle?

A. Yes.

Q. And two English police inspectors, Tarr and Tansill?

A. Yes.

Q. Did you tell Hulten who you were?

A. I did.

Q. And who the others were?

A. Yes.

Q. Did you caution him?

A. I did.

Q. What did you say to him?

A. 'It is your privilege to remain silent. You need make no statement whatsoever. Any statement you do choose to make may be used either for or against you in the event that this investigation results in any trial. Do you thoroughly understand your rights?'

Q. Did he answer that?

A. Yes.

Q. What did he say?

A. 'Yes.'

Q. Is that the proper caution in accordance with American legal procedure?

A. Yes.

Mr JUSTICE CHARLES: It is very like ours, but a little more elaborate; that is all, but the effect of it is precisely the same.

Mr HOWARD: Yes, my lord. (To the witness) Did you ask him his name?

A. I did.

Q. What did he tell you?

A. He said, 'I am Second Lieutenant Richard J. Allen'.

Q. Did he tell you what unit he belonged to?

A. Yes, he said he was with the 501st Parachute Infantry Regiment.

Q. Did you ask him further questions as to who he was?

A. I did.

Q. What was his eventual answer?

A. He acknowledged that he was Private Karl Hulten of the Second Battalion Service Company, of the 501st Parachute Infantry Regiment.

Q. Did he tell you what he had been doing for the past month or so?

A. Yes, he said he had been 'over the hill'.

Q. What does that mean?

A. Absent without leave. 'Adrift' as you say.

Q. Just look at that pistol. Did you show that to him?

A. I will have to look at the number. Yes.

Q. Did you ask him anything about it?

A. I asked him where he had got it.

Q. What did he say?

A. He said that it was a pistol which he had stolen from a Staff Sergeant Irving Sherman.

Q. Did you say anything to him about a Ford motorcar?

A. Yes, I asked him where he had obtained possession of this Ford motorcar. He said that he had found it in a wood outside his camp, near Newbury, at 4.15 yesterday afternoon, which would have been the ninth.

Q. Did he say anything else about it?

A. He said it was out of gas and had a low tyre, and it was out of oil.

Q. Anything further?

A. He said that he had reported to his base in Newbury; that he had obtained two five-gallon cans of gasoline, some oil and a pump, and returned it to the car, put the gas and oil in, pumped up the tyre and returned to London.

Q. Did he say where he had gone to then?

A. Yes, he said that he went to the home of Joyce Cook at Lurgen Avenue, parked the car outside and entered the house.

Q. Did he tell you what time he left Joyce Cook's house?

A. Approximately nine o'clock.

Q. Then as we know, he was arrested by the civil police. Did he tell you that?

A. Yes he did.

Q. Did you ask him anything about his movements on the night of Friday, 6th October?

A. I did.

Q. What did he say?

A. He told me that he had slept in a truck outside of Newbury on Friday night.

Q. Did he tell you how he got back to London from there?

A. He told me that he had hitch-hiked back to London.

Q. Did he say anything about the Saturday night?

A. The Saturday night he said he had slept in the Eccleston Hotel, Victoria.

Q. The Sunday night?

A. He said he had picked up a 'commando' and stayed with her on Sunday night.

Q. What is a 'commando'?

A. A prostitute.

Q. Did you know how he had gone back to his base after that? Did he tell you?

A. He said that he had hitch-hiked back in a truck.

Q. Do you know why he had gone back? Did he tell you?

A. He said he had gone back to his base to borrow money.

Q. Then the same afternoon, about five o'clock, did you see Hulten again in your office at Piccadilly?

A. I did.

Q. What did you say to him then?

A. I again cautioned him, and questioned him further as to his movements for the preceding week.

Q. Did he say anything more with regard to Friday night 6th October?

A. He admitted to me that he had spent Friday night with Georgina Marina Jones.

Q. Georgina who?

A. Grayson.

Q. Did he say anything further about the car?

A. Yes, he said he had not obtained the car outside of Newbury but he had found it in Hammersmith.

Q. Did you ask him anything more about that?

A. I asked him where he had found it and he said he found it in a car park where they use to park their trucks, when he used to come down for the laundry.

Q. Did he say when he found it?

A. Yesterday afternoon, that would have been Monday afternoon.

Q. Did you arrange for him to be removed to the guard-house as an absentee?

A. Yes.

Q. On the 11th October, about half past ten in the morning, did you see him again at your office?

A. I did.

Q. Did he offer to do something that morning?

A. He did. He offered to show me where Georgina Marina Jones, or Georgina Grayson, as he called her, lived, and also where he had found the car.

Q. Did you take him to Hammersmith police station?

A. I did.

Q. Did you pick up Inspectors Tarr and Tansill?

A. I did.

Q. Where did Hulten take you?

A. He took us to No. 311 King Street, Hammersmith.

Q. Did he say anything to you when you got there?

A. He said, 'This is the place,' and pointed out the phone booths, as we called them, out in front.

Mr JUSTICE CHARLES: The house of Jones - Georgina Grayson, he called her then?

A. Yes.

Mr HOWARD: Did he take you to where he said he had found the car?

A. Yes.

Q, Where was that?

A. It was a car park known as the old Gaumont car park, in Sussex Place in Hammersmith.

Q. Having done that, did you take him back again to your office?

A. Yes.

Q. And did you caution him again?

A. I did.

Q. Did you ask him whether he was prepared to make a statement?

A. I did.

Q. What did he say?

A. 'Yes'.

Q. Did you then take a statement from him?

A. I did.

Q. Just look at the original Exhibit 15. My Lord, may I read this statement? I have seen my learned friend Mr Maude and he has agreed to certain pieces in both copies which it is proposed not to read.

Mr JUSTICE CHARLES: Yes, if you indicate to me as you go on.

Mr HOWARD: Would you just follow me and see that I read my copy correctly?

Mr JUSTICE CHARLES: This is the statement?

A. Yes.

Mr JUSTICE CHARLES: How does it begin?

Mr HOWARD: My Lord, it begins; 'Karl G. Hulten' then, 'Private,' and his service number 31357916. Taken by Robert E. De Mott and Walter J. Riddle, agents CID.

'Private G. Hulten, it is my duty to inform you of your rights at this time. It is your privilege to remain silent. Anything you say may be used either for or against you in the advent that this investigation results in a trial. Do you thoroughly understand your rights?' 'I do'. Then does there appear a signature; 'Karl G. Hulten'?

A. Yes.

'I make the following statement to Robert De Mott and Walter J. Riddle, who have identified themselves to me as agents CID United States Army. My name, rank, army serial number and organization are as shown above. I am twenty-two years of age, married, and my home is in Boston, Massachusetts. I have been in the Army since I was inducted, 7th May 1942.

'I have been in the European theatre of operations for approximately eleven months. My unit is now on the Continent. I have been absent without official leave from my unit for approximately six weeks. I do not remember the exact date. During this period I spent the greater part of my time in Hammersmith, SW1, until I was apprehended by the civil police at approximately 9 pm on 9th October 1944, on Lurgen Avenue, Hammersmith. I had just left the home of my girlfriend, Joyce Cook, No.159 Fulham Palace Road, and was getting in a grey Ford V8 sedan, now known to me to bear the licence RD 8955.

'On Sunday 1st October 1944, late in the afternoon, I first met Joyce Cook. I was leaving the Gaumont Theatre, Hammersmith, with a civilian known to me as Len Bexley. We looked at each other when we were inside the theatre and sort of followed each other out. It was raining and we both ducked into the same doorway. We talked for a short time, and just as she was leaving I made a date to meet her in the same doorway at 7 o'clock. She kept this date and we went to the Broadway Theatre. We came out of the theatre about ten o'clock and it was dark and cold. I told her that I had a truck and that we could pick up the truck so that we would not have to walk home in the dark and cold. The truck was a United States Army 2½ ton 6 by 6, No 'so and so' 101 Airborne Division. The truck was parked in the old Gaumont Car Park, Sussex Place, Hammersmith. This place appears to be no longer used, and I first learned of it about eight months ago when I used to come to London to pick up laundry.

'Joyce and I walked to the truck, but after we got there Joyce changed her mind and would not ride in the truck, so we walked back to her house. At her home she introduced me to her mother. At this time I was wearing Class A American Army officer's uniform, of a second lieutenant. I introduced myself as lieutenant Richard Allen.

'I had supper at Joyce's house and left at approximately eleven o'clock. I returned to the truck and slept in the back of it. I had two blankets in the truck. My personal belongings were in a B4 bag bearing the name of Werner J. Meier, which I kept checked in the check room of the Metropolitan Tube Station, Hammersmith, Broadway. On Monday, Tuesday, Wednesday, October 2nd, 3rd and 4th, I met Joyce each evening at the bakery shop where she worked, at about 5.30 pm On each of these evenings we went to a different theatre and then returned to her home. I left her house each night about nine o'clock.

'On Tuesday 3rd October 1944, I met a girl known to me as Georgina Marina Jones, who lived at No. 311 king's Road, Hammersmith. I met her in a little café at Queen Caroline Street, Hammersmith, Broadway. I do not know the name. As I was leaving I suggested that she met me there in front of the café at about 9.30 and go for a ride in the truck. She met me after I left Joyce's house at about 9.30. We went for a ride in the truck, I dropped her off at her house and returned to the car park and slept in the truck. Before I left Georgina I arranged to meet her the next night at the same place at the same time.

'On Wednesday, 4th October 1944, Joyce and I went to a movie, as I mentioned before. After the movie we went down to the car park and got the truck and I drove her home. I parked the truck in Lurgen Avenue, in front of the door to Joyce's house. When I left Joyce about nine o'clock I drove the truck over to the café, there I met Georgina. We again went for a ride and then parked the truck in the car park. I went home with Georgina and spent the night with her.

'On Thursday, 5th October 1944, I had arranged to meet Joyce at three o'clock as it was her half-day off. I called at her home about half past two and told her that I could not keep the date as I had to go to camp. I did not go to camp. I went to Georgina's house and we went down to Victoria and went to a movie. We saw 'Christmas Holiday'. After the movie we had dinner and then went up to Georgina's room.

I left Georgina's room about ten o'clock. She told me that I could not stay the night as the landlady had guests. I caught a bus in Hammersmith Broadway and took another bus to Joyce's house. I got there about 10.15. I stayed there for a few minutes and went back to the truck to sleep.

'On Friday 6th October 1944, I again met Joyce and went to the movies. We returned to her house after the movie and again remained there until eleven o'clock. I went down to Georgina's house and whistled for her. She came down and I suggested we go for a walk. She went up and got her coat and we walked down to Hammersmith Broadway. We went into a little tea-bar at No. 35 Fulham Palace Road, which is open all night. We had some tea, a sandwich and a piece of cake, and left about one o'clock in the morning. We returned to Georgina's room, where I stayed the night.

'On Saturday 7th October 1944, I got up about eleven thirty or twelve o'clock. I shaved, dressed and took the bus to the café at Hammersmith Broadway. I met Len Bexley and had lunch with him. After lunch we went across the street to a pub. I do not know the name. We had a few drinks. Len suggested we go to White City, to the dog races. I decided to go, as he said that he knew the racket there and we could pick up a few quid. We left the pub and went down and picked up Georgina. It was then about two o'clock. We took a cab to White City and Len paid the fare. When we went to the dogs I had about four pounds. I had three one-pound notes, a ten-shilling note and some change. At the races I lost about one pound ten shillings. I do not know exactly what Georgina won, but I think that she won two or three pounds. She was betting with her money and my money too.

'After the races we returned to Hammersmith. Len left and went to work. Georgina and I went down to Victoria, where we had dinner and went to a movie. I do not recall what we saw. I took her home and found that I could not stay there, so I returned to Victoria, where

I stayed the night at the Eccleston Hotel. I slept in the ballroom. I got up about nine the next day and went to Hammersmith I had lunch and looked for Len, but could not find him. I went over to Joyce's house about half past two. I took a shirt with me for her to wash. It was a pink shirt, officer's. We left about three o'clock and went to the Gaumont to a movie. After the movie, we went back to Joyce's and I stayed until about eleven o'clock.

'After I left Joyce's house I went to Georgina's house. I whistled and she came down. We did not go any place. I stayed the night in her room. I had abandoned the 21-2 ton 6 by 6 101 Airborne truck that Georgina and I had been riding in on Friday morning 6th October 1944. I abandoned this truck on a side road in Kings Road, Hammersmith as it had a flat tyre on the right outside tyre.

'On Monday 9th October 1944, I left Georgina's about 2.15 pm. I went down to Hammersmith to the Old Gaumont Car Park. In the old car park I found the grey Ford sedan, which I had when the police apprehended me. I took this car and went down to Oliver's Bakery where Joyce works. I bought a cake and told her I was going back to camp.

'I arranged to see her that night. I drove the Ford back to camp at Newbury. I stayed at camp for fifteen or twenty minutes and retuned to Hammersmith. I went directly to Joyce's house. I got there about half past four. I parked the car on Lurgen Avenue. I left Joyce's house about nine o'clock, got into the car, and the police apprehended me. When I was apprehended by the civil police I had a calibre .45 United States Army automatic revolver in my pocket. There were six cartridges in the clip and one in the chamber.

I had another clip in my pocket and it had six cartridges in it also. The only time I fired this gun since I had it was on Wednesday 4th October 1944, when I fired at a rabbit, near Reading. I missed the rabbit.

'I do not know George Heath and I have never seen him. I only

saw his picture in the newspapers. I swear I did not shoot him, and I never saw the Ford I had when I was apprehended until I found it in the car park on Monday afternoon 9th October 1944, when I was picked up by the civil police. They did not mistreat me in any way, nor did they question me. At no time was I mistreated by the CID of the United States Army, and I have made this statement voluntarily and of my own free will without threats or promises of reward being made to me and after I had been fully warned of my rights. I have read the above statement of three pages, and it is true.
(Signed) Karl G. Hulten.

A. That is correct.

Q. Then on 12th October, at about eight o'clock in the evening, did you again go with Hulten to Hammersmith police station?

A. I did.

Q. Did you again give him the caution that you have repeated to us?

A. I did.

Q. Did he make then a further statement?

A. He did.

Q. That is Exhibit 16. It is dated 12th October 1944, headed again with the name, 'Private Karl G. Hulten, taken by Robert E. De Mott', and the same caution appears at the top of the statement again signed 'Karl G. Hulten' is that right?

A. Yes

Q. 'I voluntarily make the following statement to Robert E. De Mott and Walter J. Riddle who identified themselves to me as agents, CID United States Army. My name, rank, army serial number and organization are as shown previously. I am 22 years of age, married, and my home is in Boston Massachusetts. I was inducted in to the Army 7th May 1942.

'On Tuesday 3rd October, I first met Georgina Grayson, No. 311 King Street Hammersmith. We met in a café at Queen Caroline Street, Hammersmith. I was introduced to her by a civilian known to me as Len Bexley. It was in the evening when I met her. I do not recall the exact time. When I left I arranged to meet her at half past eleven in front of the café. I was late and missed her. I was driving a two and a half ton US Army truck, 6 by 6, with ten wheels. It was No. 4544863/8 101 Airborne. When I missed Georgina I drove down Kings Street looking for her. I met her walking down Kings Street. I stopped the truck and she got in. We started to go for a ride. We drove on towards Reading.'

'Then your Lordship sees over the page, 'After we got back to Hammersmith I drove to the old Gaumont car park Sussex Place Hammersmith and parked the truck. We then back to Georgina's room where we stayed the night. Wednesday night I again saw Georgina but we did not go out in the truck. I met Georgina at her room late Thursday afternoon. I do not recall the exact time. We went to a movie. We came out of the movie before ten o'clock but I don't recall the time. We had something to eat and then went down to the car park and got the truck. We drove out to a pub near Sonning.'

'Then, my lord, missing the rest of that page and the whole of the next page, I propose to begin reading again at the bottom paragraph of page ten.

Mr JUSTICE CHARLES: At 'On Friday'?

Mr Howard: Yes, my lord. 'On Friday, 6th October 1944, I remained in bed until three o'clock. I gave Georgina a ticket for a B4 bag, which I had checked at the Metropolitan Tube Station in Hammersmith. She went down and got the bag for me.' Then I do not propose to read any more until the second paragraph at page 11, the next page: 'After I had changed clothes I left and went to visit my girlfriend Joyce Cook. We went to a movie and then returned to Joyce's house. I stayed at

Joyce's until about eleven o'clock. When I left Joyce's house I went back to Georgina's house and whistled for her. She came down and met me out in front. We walked down to Hammersmith Broadway and on towards Uxbridge. It was windy and we stopped in a doorway. We had decided to stop a cab.

'A cab went by, and Georgina called 'Taxi.' I remained in the doorway. The car stopped. It was a grey Ford sedan, which I later learnt to be driven by George Heath. I told Georgina to go and see how many people were in it. She went over and talked to the driver. She came back and said that it was a private-hire car and that only one person was in it. We both went over and got in the car. I sat behind the driver and she sat on my left.

'I told the driver to turn round and go out Kings Road past Georgina house. I told the driver that the place I wanted to go was just beyond the roundabout. It is a roundabout at this end of the Great West Road. When we got about twenty-five yards beyond the roundabout I told him that was the place. When we got to the roundabout I took my pistol from my right hip pocket. Just as the car was coming to a stop I pulled the slide back and cocked the pistol. The pistol was a calibre .45 US Army automatic. It was the same pistol which I had in my pocket when I was picked up by the civil police on Monday 9th October 1944. It is the same pistol which is now shown to me by Robert E. De Mott. It was about one o'clock when we got into the car and it must have been about 1.15 am when I told the driver to stop.

'When the car stopped I was holding my loaded and cocked pistol in front of my chest. When the car stopped I looked over towards Georgina. As I was looking back towards the front again I pulled the trigger. Just as I pulled the trigger the driver, who I later learned to be George Heath, raised up and reached over the back seat to open the rear door. He was reaching back with his left arm. When I pulled the trigger I intended to pull the trigger and fire the pistol. I intended to fire it through the car, but I did not expect George Heath to raise up to open the door just as I did it. When I fired the shot I knew that I had hit him as I heard him say, 'Oh' as I started to get out of the car, I said, 'Move over.' He did not move. When I opened the front door Heath was leaning against the left door with his head down, his chin resting sort of on his chest. His body was sort of across the car, with his right foot under the clutch. When I got into the car he moved his right leg out of the way and mumbled something to me, which I did not understand. I got in under the wheel. I told Georgina to look him over for his wallet. After a couple of minutes I drove away. As we were driving along I told Georgina to take everything out of his pockets.

'I drove on to Staines and turned left at the police station. About a mile past the police station I turned off the road to the left and followed a dirt road to the left, a short distance down this road and drove over to the left and stopped the car. I got out and walked around the rear of the car. Georgina got out the right side of the car and walked around the front of the car. I opened the left front door and put my arms through his armpits.

'I raised him up and pulled him out of the car. His feet dropped to the ground. Georgina picked up his feet and we carried him to a ditch, which was about three feet from the car. We returned to the car. I turned around and started back. I wish to state that, as we were driving to the ditch and Georgina was going through his pockets, I told her to look and see if he had a watch on. She looked and told me that she had found a wristwatch on his arm.

'As we were driving back after having disposed of the body Georgina gave me four pounds in one pound notes, a long brown United States fountain pen, a silver pencil, a small silver cigarette lighter, cigarette case and a watch. The watch as shown to me by Robert E. De Mott is the watch she gave me. As we were driving back Georgina threw all of George Heath's pictures out of the window of the car.

'When we got back to Hammersmith I parked the car in the Old Gaumont car park where I use to park the truck. We took our handkerchiefs and wiped off the fingerprints from all parts of the car, which we had touched. We stopped at the 'Black and White' and got something to eat, and then went home and went to bed.

'On Saturday 7th October 1944, I went down to the café at Queen Caroline Street, Hammersmith, Broadway, and saw Len Bexley. I left the fountain pen, the pencil, the cigarette lighter and the cigarette case with Bexley to sell for me. The watch I sold to a barber in the barbershop next to the café.

'Sunday night, 8th October 1944, I went to Georgina's house about half past nine. We went down to the car park and picked up the car. We drove it as a hire car around the West End and parked it near an air-raid shelter near her house. The next morning I picked up the car again on Monday about quarter past two and drove to the bakery where Joyce works. I took the car to my camp near Newbury and returned to Hammersmith about six o'clock. I parked the car on Lurgen Avenue across the street from the door to Joyce's house. When I came out of the house about nine o'clock and got into the car, I was apprehended by the civil police. I was carrying my pistol when I was apprehended. I was taken to Hammersmith police station.'

'Then, my lord I don't propose to read the next paragraph. The statement goes on, 'I wish to state that when I was picked up by the civil police they did not mistreat me in any way, nor did they question me. At no time was I mistreated by the CID. of the United States Army, and I have made this statement voluntarily and of my own free will, without threats or promise of reward being made to me, and after I had been fully warned of my rights. I have read my statement of ten pages and it is true.

(Signed) Karl G. Hulten.'

Mr CASSWELL: No questions my lord.

Cross-examined by Mr MAUDE Defence Hulten.

Q. Mr De Mott, the first question I want to ask you is this: am I right in saying that you appear to have seen him on at least four separate occasion? Let me give them to you; first of all on the 10th October in the early hours of the morning?

A. Yes.

Q. The second occasion is at five o'clock the same afternoon?

A. That is correct.

Q. The third occasion is next morning, 11th 10.30?

A. Yes.

Q. And the last is on 12th, that is, the next day, at eight at night or thereabouts?

A. Yes.

Q. What is the difference in paging between statements? Would you mind telling me?

A. One of them is ten pages long and one of them is three pages long.

Q. The difference, if I may tell you, between ours is three and four pages. Is it that the size of the paper is different?

A. No, the size of the paper is the same. This one happens to be double–spaced.

Q. So that in substance the difference between the length of the statements estimated by numbers of, what shall we say words – that is the only fair test – is not really very great, is it?

A. No.

Q. When I say the two statements, of course, I mean the whole statement, because only certain parts have been read. Take the first statement, will you, please? That is 10th October at three in the morning. Were you alone with him?

A. I was not alone with him at any time.

Q. Who was with you then?

A. Mr Riddle, Inspector Tarr and Inspector Tansill.

Q. We know – at least, we believe – that you have a very good memory, haven't you?

A. Well, I thank you very much.

Q. I am not flattering you. We have heard it; it is not idle flattery. It is true is it not, that you have got a very good memory?

A. I hope so.

Q. That is as far as we shall get, probably. Take the woman Jones's statement. Is it right that you managed to memorise that?

A. I think it is incorrect to say that I memorised it; I read it over sufficiently well to know the details of it that were pertinent to me. But to say I memorised the statement would be highly incorrect.

Q. Did you hear the British police officer say you had memorised it yesterday?

A. I did.

Mr JUSTICE CHARLES: This is the man, whether he memorised it or not. How can a police man say whether another officer has memorised a document?

Mr MAUDE: May we see? It may be that there is something in it after all. You see, what you did was to interview this man 12th October, that is, the last interview, the fourth interview, having seen Mrs Jones's statement, which is quite a long one.

A. Yes.

Q. You had a copy of it; is that right?

A. That is right.

Q. You had a copy of it in your office?

A. Yes.

Q. You knew that you were engaged in a murder case?

A. Yes.

Q. And you didn't take the copy down in order to question Hulten?

A. It would not have been necessary.

Q. Is the answer yes or no?

A. I did not take it down; no.

Q. And it was not necessary because you had managed to memorise what Jones had said?

A. I take exception to the memorising part. I had not memorised the statement, but I did know the facts.

Q. Are we fighting about the exact word 'memorise'?

A. I object to that word, because it is incorrect. I did not memorise that statement. I remembered the pertinent facts from it.

Q. You remembered all the details, didn't you?

A. Those pertinent ones, yes; to do with the incident, shall we put it that way?

Mr MAUDE: Is the answer yes?

Mr JUSTICE CHARLES: He said to do with the incident, yes.

Mr MAUDE: And having decided to leave her statement upstairs for some reason, what was the reason you did not take it down?

A. I attached no importance to it whatsoever. Mine was a copy that I had copied.

Q. Is the reason you did not want it, the reason you didn't take Jones's statement to see Hulten that you thought there was no need to?

A. I attached no importance to it whatsoever.

Q. And at the fourth interview, do you remember now how long it took?

A. I should think it took between two and a half and three hours to take the statement.

Mr MAUDE: I can't hear. I do not believe you answered my question.

Mr JUSTICE CHARLES: Yes he did; he said two and a half to three hours.

Mr MAUDE: I thought he said to take the statement. I did not ask that. I asked how long did the interview take?

Mr JUSTICE CHARLES: Oh well; you have got to count up all the time he was doodling on the paper, and the time he was eating sandwiches, and all the other times he was not attending.

A. I should say about four and a half hours, probably.

Mr MAUDE: You know, in fact, it started at quarter to eight and did not finish till half-past one in the morning, did it?

A. I don't know that as a fact, no.

Q. You did not take any note of the times, did you?

A. Not particularly.

Q. What?

A. No, I would not have thought it took that long.

Q. I am not asking that. What is the answer to my question: did you take a note of the time?

A. Not definitely, no.

Q. When you say 'not definitely' do not fight about it. You did not take any note of the time?

A. No.

Q. And at all those interviews, were there British officers present at all four?

A. There were.

Q. Then we shall be able to hear what they say. Tell me: The first one, the one that you say starts at about 3 am…

A. Yes.

Q. How long did that last?

A. I think I left about six o'clock; about three hours.

Q. Three hours, the first one about?

A. I think so, yes.

Q. The second one, at five o'clock that day; how long did that take?

A. That was very short.

Q. About?

A. Perhaps an hour.

Q. You're giving me the outside figures, I hope?

A. I am giving you the best I can remember, because at the time I did not attach importance to it.

Q. But you will not underestimate to me will you?

A. Not intentionally.

Mr JUSTICE CHARLES: You say you are not able to estimate it at all, really, because you took no notice of the times?

A. That is quite correct.

Mr JUSTICE CHARLES: That is a more proper way of putting it.

Mr MAUDE: On 11th October when you say – have you any idea how long that interview went on for?

A. Very short.

Q. Roughly?

A. I do not know; perhaps thirty minutes.

Q. We will ask the officers. At the first interview you told us today when asked about pistol, it is the first interview…

A. Yes.

Q. He said he had stolen it?

A. Yes.

Q. I am putting it that you made a mistake there and that he did not say that.

Mr JUSTICE CHARLES: What do you say? Did he say it? Did he say he had stolen the pistol?

A. Yes, my lord.

Q. You have no doubt about that question?

A. I am certain of it.

Mr MAUDE: Just see whether there is not an error there. Didn't he say exactly what you said in the court below when questioned about his possession of the pistol; 'He said, 'It is mine; I always carry it, but I have never used it'?

A. That is quite correct.

Q. You heard my lord talking about doodling just now?

A. Yes.

Q. The members of the jury do not know what that is about; but during the taking of the second interview he was drawing on a piece of paper? A. Yes.

Q. You have got a drawing of it?

A. No, I have not.

Mr JUSTICE CHARLES: Well, somebody has got it, pictures of tanks, bombers and cars; all sorts of things.

Mr MAUDE: Aeroplanes, motor trucks, tanks and every sort of thing?

A. Yes.

Q. He was evidently quite composed?

A. Yes.

Q. Was he quite cheerful?

A. Very.

Q. He did not appear to recognise the seriousness of it all?

A. I think he recognised the seriousness of it, yes.

Q. How did he show that?

A. Well, as anyone would show it.

Q. Some people vary, don't they, in such circumstances?

A. He did not appear to be nervous, but I would say he did appear to be solemn.

Q. He was not joking, or anything like that?

A. As time went on I think he did joke, yes.

Q. He was as happy as that, was he?

A. He was happier than I would have been in similar circumstances.

Q. Just for one moment, assuming that we are able to prove that the last statement took - I put it at its lowest - five hours at least; that is to say, I have made allowances for having tea or coffee or whatever it was; assuming that it took five hours, how does it compare with the taking of Exhibit 15, in time, that is the first of two statements?

A. The first statement took approximately two to two and half hours I would say, to take.

Q. If you really don't know nobody will want to press you; but isn't it fair to think that it probably took twice the time for the second statement as it did the first?

A. Not necessarily.

Q. No, not necessarily. But is that a fair estimate?

A. You attach more importance to the time of taking these then I did, and I have to remember the time to the best of my ability that this statement took; and in my opinion it was approximately three hours. I mentioned it before, and I mention it again.

Q. Was it done by asking him a long series of questions?

A. It was done by asking him individual questions.

Q. But in substance, if we look at the statement, the details come out one by one. Are we to imagine that they are in answer to separate questions?

A. You are, yes.

Q. Not questions like, 'Well, what happened then?' but putting questions to him?

A. Very often it would be a question, 'Well, then what did you do; what happened then?'

Mr JUSTICE CHARLES: Then what did you do?

Mr MAUDE: I heard that; but, in addition to that, questions such as this: 'What did you do there?' - putting specific things to him, specific matters to him?

A. Yes.

Q. There are certain things that I am instructed to put to you. This is on 9th October; that is probably an error in that date?

A. Yes.

Q. Is it probably the 10th, I suppose?

A. Yes.

Q. It was in Inspector Tarr's office; do you remember that?

A. Yes.

Q. That must have been the first interview?

A. The morning of the 10th.

Q. That early morning did Mr Tarr ask him any question about the car and his movements?

A. Not that I recall. I believe I asked all the questions.

Q. Did he ask what charge was being made against him?

A. I advised him, after I introduced myself to him, of the nature of the charges.

Q. What did you say to him?

A. When I found out who he was finally, then I told him he was wanted by us for certain matters not pertinent here and that, he was being detained by the civil police on suspicion of murder.

Q. I am going to ask you to help me, because it is a fact that it is extraordinarily difficult to hear; the sound is very bad. In respect of murder, did you say?

A. Yes. That he was being...

Mr JUSTICE CHARLES: That he was detained on suspicion.

Mr MAUDE: I think he said of murder. (To the witness) Did you say that?

A. Yes, I did.

Q. On suspicion of murder. Did he say, 'The murder of whom?'

A. No, he did not.

Q. He was not told 'George Heath'?

A. No.

Q. Then did one of the police officers say something to this effect, 'Seeing that you have told the truth, you won't mind making a statement,' and he said he would not mind?

A. That was after the interview was completed and we had gone downstairs, as I was getting ready to leave, yes.

Q. Then he says one of the British police officers said to him, 'Well, if it is the truth there is no harm in you making a statement about it'. I am not complaining about that, but that is quite correct?

A. That is quite correct.

Q. Then he says you said to Inspector Tarr that you would take him; that you would be claiming him for your jurisdiction. I do not suppose he has got the words right, but you then claimed him, didn't you?

A. I believe not.

Q. Was it later?

A. I think it was the next day; actually, I think it was the following afternoon.

Q. But at some time at that interview, apparently you advised him that there was no need for him to make a statement to the British Police?

A. No, I did not. How that came around was that the accused asked if he could see me alone and I went with him into a detention room. I was just getting ready to leave, as a matter of fact, and he wanted to know what was going to happen to him, whether or not he would be further questioned, and I told him that he would not be questioned further, and that if anybody did attempt to ask him any questions when I was not there, he need not answer them.

MR JUSTICE CHARLES: At that time there had been no abrogation by the American authorities to deal with their own criminals?

A. No.

Mr JUSTICE CHARLES: Or suspected criminals. The arrangement was made with them and it only comes into this court because there has been a special order at the request of the American authorities; that is all.

Mr MAUDE: What he also instructs me is that he told you at some time that he had his revolver in his right hand and had pulled the trigger whilst Heath was reaching over with his left arm to open the rear door; so far as that goes, you agree?

A. Yes; it is in his statement.

Q. What he says is that he did not say that he intended to fire through the car.

A. That is exactly what he said.

Q. Did you ask him any more details about that when he said 'I intended to fire it through the car'? Can you remember at all?

A. I remember he showed me how he held the pistol to his chest and said he intended to fire it through the car. Then he went on to say he did not expect Heath to raise up and open the door, then he showed me how he learned over opening the back door.

Q. So what he was saying to you - I am not looking at the legal aspect of it, you understand - about the facts, was that it was an accident? That he had not intended to shoot Heath, but Heath had moved across and had been in the way?

A. What he intended to say was he intended to fire through the car and that Heath raised up.

Mr MAUDE: Thank you very much.

Mr BYRNE for the Prosecution examined HENRY ALFRED KIMBERLEY, sworn.

Q. Is your name Henry Alfred Kimberley?

A. Yes.

Q. Are you a War Reserve constable, stationed at Hammersmith?

A. Yes.

Q. About two years ago were you in the habit of visiting a café called Paul's Café, in King Street, Hammersmith?

A. I was.

Q. At that time was the prisoner Jones serving in the café?

A. Yes.

Q. In that way you got to know her?

A. Yes.

Q. When did she leave the café?

A. I should imagine it must have been about two years ago.

Q. 1942, do you mean?

A. Somewhere round about there.

Q. After that did you see no more of her until quite recently?

A. Quite recently.

Q. When was it that you next saw her?

A. At 4.30 pm on Wednesday 11th October 1944.

Q. Where did you meet her on that occasion?

A. In a cleaner's shop in Hammersmith Broadway.

Q. You had gone to enquire about a suit you had left there, she happened to come into the shop?

A. Yes, that's right.

Q. Did you notice any change in her appearance?

A. She had altered considerably, yes.

Q. Did she recognise you?

A. She recognised me, yes.

Q. Did you speak to each other?

A. She said, 'Hello'

Q. Did you make any remark about her appearance?

A. I did. I told her she looked tired, and asked her where she had been for the last two years.

Q. What did she say to that?

A. 'Since I saw you last I have turned a bad girl and have been drinking heavily.'

Q. Did you say anything to that?

A. Yes, I remarked to her how old she was and tired.

Q. What did she say then?

A. 'I should think so. I have been over to the police station for some hours regarding this murder.'

Q. Did she indicate what murder she was talking about?

A. She was holding a paper in her hand, and she pointed to a column regarding the murder of George Heath.

Q. What did you say then?

A. I asked her what she had got to worry about: had she got anything to do with it?

Q. What did she say to that?

A. 'I know the man they have got inside, but it would have been impossible for him to do it as he was with me all Friday night'.

Q. Well, did the subject of the conversation change then?

A. I changed the conversation, but again remarked to her how tired she looked, and she said 'If you had seen someone do what I have seen done you wouldn't be able to sleep at night.'

Q. Then did you give her a piece of advice?

A. Yes.

Q. What did you say to her?

A. I said to her, 'You must have something on your mind. Why don't you go over to the police station and tell them the truth?'

Q. What did she say to that?

A. 'I have made a statement over there, and I have to remember what is in it I couldn't repeat it.'

Q. At that, did the two of you separate?

A. She left the shop, saying, 'Goodbye'.

Q. Then did you make a report to Inspector Tansill?

A. Yes.

Q. At about six o'clock that same evening did you and the Inspector go to her address, No 311 King Street?

A. Yes.

Q. When you and the Inspector arrived there, did you see her?

A. Yes.

Q. What was she doing?

A. Getting off a lorry.

Q. She was arriving at the same moment, getting off a lorry?

A. Yes.

Q. Did the three of you go into the house up to her room together?

A. We did.

Q. When you arrived at her room did she say something to you?

A. Yes.

Q. What was that?

A. 'I want to speak to you alone.'

Q. Did the Inspector accordingly withdraw?

A. Yes.

Q. What did she say then to you?

A. 'Why did you bring the Inspector here?'

Q. What did you say to that?

A. I said, 'Because of what you told me this afternoon in the cleaner's shop and I think you should tell him the truth.'

Q. What did she say?

A. 'All right, I will tell him.'

Q. Then did the Inspector come back into the room?

A. Yes.

Q. And did she say something to the Inspector?

A. Yes, she said, 'It was lies I told you at the station, and I'm sorry. I would like to tell you the whole truth.'

Q. Then did the Inspector say it would be better if she went to the police station for that purpose?

A. Yes.

Q. And the three of you then went to the police station?

A. To Hammersmith Police Station, yes.

Cross-examined by Mr CASSWELL, Defence for JONES.

Q. Kimberley, are you at present a reserve constable?

A. Yes.

Q. You were, of course, at the time you saw the accused Jones?

A. Yes.

Q. By that time did you know that Hulten had made a statement?

A. No.

Q. Are you sure of that?

A. I am positive of it.

Q. And it was quite by chance that you happened to meet the accused Jones, was it?

A. Quite a chance, yes,

Q. Did you go to look for her?

A. No.

Q. You had known her previously, and I understand you to say that it was in the summer of 1942?

A. Somewhere round about there.

Q. We have had pretty good evidence she did not come to London till 1943, and I suggest it was not until 1943 when she was in London serving as a waitress for a time at that café.

A. It may have been then, somewhere round about two years.

Q. You see, in 1942 she would have been under sixteen. You don't think she was that do you, in the early part of 1942?

A. She looked very young.

Q. She would be sixteen in August 1942. You said you thought it was the early summer. I suggest to you it was 1943 when she was employed as a waitress in the café?

A. No, I should say it was within two years.

Q. Would you be so sure as that if I assured you she did not come to London till 1943? Would you still be sure you saw her in 1942?

A. Well, I will give you the benefit of the doubt of four months.

Q. What name did you know her by then?

A. As 'Betty'.

Q. I do not know whether you know her well, but I suggest to you that when you saw her she had not yet begun dancing; do you know that?

A. She was dancing mad. She had got it on her brain. She was always talking about dancing.

A FATAL PICKUP

Q. But she had not yet been dancing in public?

A. Not as I know of.

Q. In fact she had an all time job at that café?

A. All I know is as a waitress.

Q. I want to get this clear. It isn't the same café of which the witness Lenny was talking about, Lenny Bexley?

A. No.

Q. Is it a café in the same street, King Street?

A. No, one is in King Street, and one is in Hammersmith Broadway.

Q. But the one you are talking about was in King Street?

A. Yes.

Q. Immediately you saw her you were struck by her looks, were you?

A. No.

Q. What was wrong?

A. When I first met her she just waited at the table and started speaking to us. She was perhaps a pretty good-looking girl.

Q. It wasn't that you were struck by her looks when you met her?

A. No.

Q. What is wrong in what I am putting to you? How am I wrong?

A. About her looks.

Q. You told us just now she was looking bad, and you asked her why and she said she had been a bad girl. Where am I wrong?

A. She was looking much different after the first time I saw her, much older.

Q. That is what I said. I suggested you were immediately struck by the difference in her looks.

A. Yes, I was.

Q. You said, no.

A. Yes I was, in that sense. The way you put the question I thought you meant when I went to the café I was struck by the looks of the girl, as though I went to see her.

Q. Did I?

A. That is what I understood you to put.

Q. What I said was, and I can be checked by the shorthand-writer, is that immediately you saw her you were struck by her looks, because as soon as you looked at her closely you saw her differently.

A. In the cleaner's in Hammersmith Broadway, or in the café?

Q. In the café, of course; I am not interested in Hammersmith Broadway.

Mr JUSTICE CHARLES: He is, you see. One moment; he says she looked much older than she did when he saw her last.

Mr CASSWELL: That is the only thing I am cross-examining about.

Mr JUSTICE CHARLES: It was a very ambiguous question. Yes you put the question, 'I must put it to you that as soon as you entered the café you were struck with her looks?' He said, 'No, I was not'.

Mr CASSWELL: No my lord, I did not say that. (To the witness) However, you understand now, don't you, that I am dealing with a certain part of your evidence?

A. Yes, I do now.

Q. I just want to find out a little more about it. That is all we are dealing with, that you said she looked different.

A. Yes.

Q. Will you tell the court how she looked different?

A. When I first met her she looked very young.

Q. She was very young, wasn't she?

A. Now I know, yes.

Q. The second time you met her, after a year or so, two years, you thought she had very much altered?

A. Very much altered.

Q. Had she simply altered because she looked as if she had grown older, or what did you notice?

A. She looked as though she was worn out.

Q. Did she look very worried?

A. Very worried, yes.

Q. We have heard that she had a very bad cold, but she looked worse than that?

A. It was not a cold that gave her that worry.

Q. That is just what I wanted to find out from you, something much worse than a cold?

A. I should imagine so.

Q. Did she tell you, as soon as she had seen you, that she had been living an artificial life, dancing at cabarets?

A. Yes.

Q. Are you sure she said she had been a bad girl?

A. I am sure of that.

Q. I notice you said after that she had been drinking a lot. A. Yes.

Q. Was that any qualification of the word 'bad' or did you understand she had been on the streets?

A. She had been on the streets. That is the way she put it to me.

Q. I presume you didn't question her about it?

A. Definitely not.

Q. Were you satisfied with that answer, or did you think there was something more behind it, something worrying her?

A. I knew she knew more about the murder then she had told; she told me she had made a statement.

Q. She had not told you about the murder at that point, but afterwards I understand you told her she was looking tired and worried?

A. Yes.

Q. She then told you she had been over at the police station for about four hours?

A. Something about four hours.

Q. Did you ask her what about?

A. She told me.

Q. Did she then have a newspaper in her hand?

A. Yes.

Q. Can you tell us at all what it had in it, the headlines of the paragraphs?

A. No, I didn't read it.

Q. I suppose you were rather interested, weren't you, when you heard she had been making a statement to the police?

A. I was not interested, no.

Q. Weren't you? You were a policeman yourself.

A. It came as a bit of a shock to me when she started talking about the murder.

Q. Four hours making a statement at the police station does not sound like a running-down accident, or anything like that.

A. No.

Q. Keeping her at the police station for four hours questioning her sounds like something serious.

A. It was serious.

Q. Did you ask her what?

A. Did I ask her what?

Q. Yes.

A. She was telling me all the answers. She told me she had been over to the station four hours regarding a murder.

Mr JUSTICE CHARLES: Wait a minute. Did you catch that answer? I know it is very difficult for you to hear. 'She had been questioned for four hours about a murder', that is what he says.

Mr CASSWELL: She said 'about.'

A. I have already told you that.

Mr JUSTICE CHARLES: He has said that already twice. It does not reach down there, I know. I have sat down there as counsel, and it is very difficult to hear. I can hear up here and you cannot hear well down there, but he said that more than once. 'She said, I have been four hours up at the police station being questioned about a murder.' And then she produced the newspaper and said something about the murder being in the paper.

Mr CASSWELL: I notice, while you were giving evidence you were referring continually to a notebook. May I see it?

A. You may.

Q. When did you write this?

A. I wrote that back at the station.

Q. I see you have written it in narrative form.

A. I always do.

Q. Saying, 'I have known the girl…' so and so?

A. Yes.

Q. In this statement you have recorded to the best of your recollection when you got back to the station the actual words that were used?

A. The notes I put down in that book before I got back to the station, as the girl left the shop. If you look at the back of that book you will find them written down there, just the statement.

Q. When did you write that?

A. I wrote that just as she went out of the shop.

Mr JUSTICE CHARLES: Almost immediately after she had said them?

A. Yes.

Mr JUSTICE CHARLES: Just as she went out of the shop, that is to say, immediately after she had made the observations. He acted with very great propriety, this gentleman.

Mr CASSWELL: I have a reason for asking these questions. As you know, I have a note of the evidence you gave before the magistrates and every now and then, there are differences and as you were reading from your notebook I wondered whether you had all the conversation down there. You see, you told me just now what she had said was, 'I have made a statement over there and if I have to remember it, I should not be able to repeat it.'

A. Yes.

Mr CASSWELL: Before the magistrates you said this: 'If I have to repeat it I could not do so.'

Mr JUSTICE CHARLES: Well that is pretty well the same.

Mr CASSWELL: Therefore it seems a little bit important to me we should know whether you were reading out of your book a statement that she had made.

A. I was reading out of my book.

Q. How comes it that it was different when you read it to the magistrates' clerk and different when you read it here?

A. In what way is it different?

Q. Let me read it to you once again. I thought you were reading it word for word.

Mr JUSTICE CHARLES: Except in terminology, there is no difference.

Mr CASSWELL: My lord, I am not on that. I am on the question of the accuracy and whether this witness, in fact, was reading from his book today or not. Were you reading from your book before the magistrates?

A. I was reading from my notebook before the magistrates.

Q. Because this is what has been taken down as your deposition and which I presume, you signed as correct. 'She said, I have made a statement over there and if I have to remember what was in it I could not repeat.' That was the evidence you gave today.

A. That's right.

Q. According to the deposition you said 'If I have to repeat it I could not do so.' You see the difference, do you?

Mr JUSTICE CHARLES: Do you?

A. It certainly means the same, my lord?

Q. I tell you frankly I don't.

A. Don't they mean the same my lord?

Mr CASSWELL: They appear to be the same. You really tell the jury that if you are reading out of a notebook you can read either 'If I have to repeat it I could not remember it,' or 'If I have to repeat it I could not do so?'

Mr JUSTICE CHARLES: No, no, Mr Casswell.

A. That is the same point.

Mr JUSTICE CHARLES: One moment. He does not say anything of the sort. He said he was reading from his book…

Mr CASSWELL: The witness my lord, is it necessary for him to go through my book, to go right the way through it?

Mr JUSTICE CHARLES: No; he must not do that. He must not look at other cases, please.

Mr CASSWELL: I am doing nothing of the sort. Are you suggesting that I am reading private parts of your book?

A. You were turning over the pages.

Mr CASSWELL: I have to turn from the back to the other part. I hope your Lordship will not allow suggestions like that to be made against me.

Mr JUSTICE CHARLES: Mr Casswell, please cease talking when I am addressing you. What he says is this. He says, 'I was reading from my notebook.' The magistrates clerk has taken down accurately the sense of it. When it was read over to him he signed it as correct. It was perfectly proper that he should do so. There is nothing whatever in it.

Mr CASSWELL: She was holding a paper in her hand in which there was a report of the murder of George Heath?

A. Yes.

Q. So you read it sufficiently to see that there was a report of the murder of George Heath?

A. I saw 'Cleft Chin' at the top in big black print.

Q. And, of course you read about that?

A. Naturally.

Q. I have now got to the part of your statement that what you said today was read apparently directly from your book.

A. Pardon?

Q. What you said today was exactly what appears in your book?

A. I read it from my book.

Q. But somehow or other it has got on your deposition differently, in different words?

A. I may have used different words reading here.

Q. What I suppose you mean to say is that you took them down, the rough notes, when she left the café, and then incorporated it into your statement after?

A. I did.

Q. I am not finding any fault. I am asked to ask you this. Do you suggest she actually used the words 'on the streets', or anything like that?

A. She used the words 'on the streets'?

Q. Yes?

A. No.

Mr JUSTICE CHARLES: He has not suggested it.

Mr CASSWELL: You said she had turned a bad girl and went on to say she had been drinking?

A. That is what she said.

Q. And she also said, did she not, that she had been - I think I have put this to you already - leading an artificial life; dancing?

A. She did not use the word 'artificial', but to that affect, yes.

Q. And you, perfectly properly, did not question her at all; you just changed the subject?

A. Yes.

Q. And then, you having advised her that she ought to go to the police again, she told you that she was worried, and said to you, 'If you had seen someone do what I had seen done, you wouldn't be able to sleep at night'?

A. She gave me the impression she could not sleep at night.

Q. And she might very well been speaking the truth?

A. She was speaking the truth.

Mr MAUDE: No questions.

Mr MAUDE: My lord I am so sorry, I have forgotten something I should have asked Mr De Mott when he was in the box. I wonder if I might be allowed to have him back? It is very short, but important.

Mr JUSTICE CHARLES: Most certainly.

ROBERT EARL DE MOTT recalled, further cross-examined by Mr MAUDE defence HULTEN.

Mr MAUDE: My lord, It is in respect of the third paragraph in Exhibit 16, but I do not want of course, to put it in, in the sense of losing the last word. Here my learned friend may help me. Perhaps I better put it in a different way.

Mr BYRNE: My lord, I can only say that I shall not take advantage of any technical situation.

Mr JUSTICE CHARLES: Oh, no; I am sure you wouldn't.

Mr MAUDE: Mr De Mott, If you wouldn't mind taking it; it is the last paragraph, the one starting 'When I missed Georgina'. May I just read it with you, as you have already given it?

A. My copy is different from yours. Yours is single space.

Q. Mine has been paragraphed and yours has not. You will see first of all 'I voluntarily make the following statement.' And then 'My name, and rank.'

A. Yes.

Q. Then you go on 'On Tuesday 3rd October' and then there is a good long bit down to the number of the truck; you can probably pick that out?

A. Yes.

Q. Then you start the next sentence 'When I missed Georgina', do you see that?

A. Yes, I do.

Mr MAUDE: My lord, may I explain it by a question? What we are now reading is Hulten's second written statement made on 12th October. It is at the beginning of his story, and he is referring to something that happened 3rd October the Tuesday; have I got it right?

A. You have.

Q. He says, 'When I missed Georgina I drove down to King Street looking for her. I met her walking down King Street. I stopped the truck and she got in. We started to go for a ride.' Now we are starting something fresh.

Mr JUSTICE CHARLES: Mr Byrne broke off at that point.

Mr MAUDE: I am much obliged. Then it is this I want.

Mr JUSTICE CHARLES: You are entitled, of course – you know that better than I do – to have the whole thing read, or any part you like can be read at any time.

Mr MAUDE: Oh, yes, my lord. What I am really apologising for is having missed it. It is a nuisance. 'During the course of the conversation she said' – that is the woman Jones – 'that she would like to do something exciting like becoming a 'gun moll', like they do back in the States. At first I thought she was kidding. I then explained to her that we had a stolen truck. We drove on towards Reading.'

A. Yes.

Q. That is all fresh, isn't it?

A. Yes.

Mr JUSTICE CHARLES: That was quite properly, by Mr Byrne for the Crown, omitted, but I quite understand you wish it to be introduced.

Mr MAUDE: Yes, my lord; I have got it paragraphed differently; it is my fault.

Mr BYRNE: My lord, the next witness is not very long on the depositions, but he is a witness who deals with Jones's statement and your Lordship may think that this statement should be read again, although I read it in opening this case, because sometimes, if statements are not read again during the course of the case, they do not get onto the shorthand note.

Mr JUSTICE CHARLES: I think that had better be done.

Mr BYRNE: If your Lordship would like me to start that witness now, so be it, but I was only pointing it out to your Lordship in case you thought you might not like to break into the witness's evidence.

Mr JUSTICE CHARLES: It will take some time?

MR BYRNE: Yes, my lord.

Mr JUSTICE CHARLES: It is after ten minutes to four now.

Mr BYRNE: We could not possibly complete it by that time.

Mr JUSTICE CHARLES: Very well; we will come back here at eleven o'clock tomorrow morning.

Mr CASSWELL: Would your Lordship allow me to apologise for interrupting your Lordship so rudely just now.

Mr JUSTICE CHARLES: Oh, no, indeed; you know I exhibit a great deal of sound and fury, but I do not feel it.

Mr CASSWELL: I wish to make an apology as publicly as I can.

Mr JUSTICE CHARLES: We know each other too well, Mr Casswell.

Adjourned till the next day at 11 o'clock.

CHAPTER EIGHT

THE TRIAL - THIRD DAY

THURSDAY 18TH JANUARY 1945

Mr HOWARD for the Prosecution examined ALBERT TANSILL, sworn.

Q. Albert Tansill, Detective Inspector of the 'T' Division, stationed at Staines. On the morning of Saturday 7th October last year, did you go to Knowle Green, where you saw the dead body of George Heath?
A. I did.
Q. Then on the 9th October did you see Lieutenant De Mott together with Inspector Tarr, at Hammersmith police station?
A. I did.
Q. On 10th October were you present when Lieutenant De Mott interviewed Hulten?
A. I was.
Q. The next day, 11th October at about twelve o'clock noon, did you go with Inspector Tarr to No. 311 King Street Hammersmith?
A. I did.
Q. Did you there see defendant Jones?
A. I did.
Q. In a room on the second floor?
A. I did.

Q. What did Inspector Tarr say to her?

A. Inspector Tarr told her who we were and asked her if she knew American officer. She said, 'You mean Ricky Allen?' Inspector Tarr said, 'Yes; will you tell me what nights he has stayed with you here?' She said, 'Let me see. I met him last Tuesday; he has been here every night except Saturday and that night he stayed at the Eccleston Hotel.'

Q. Did you notice some clothing in the room?

A. Yes, I noticed an American officer's jacket behind the door and on top of a wardrobe was a valise and blanket. The prisoner, pointing to those articles said, 'That is Ricky's.'

Q. Did you take possession of those articles?

A. Divisional Detective Inspector Tarr did.

Q. And after she was dressed did you take the defendant Jones back to Hammersmith police station?

A. I did.

Q. Did she there make a written statement? A. She did.

Q. Is that the statement?

A. Yes.

Q. Did she read that over, or was it read over to her?

A. It was read over to her and she afterwards signed it.

Q. Would you please follow while I read it. It is headed; 'Hammersmith Station, 'F' division. 11th October 1944. Statement of Elizabeth Marina Jones, No. 311 King Street Hammersmith, who saith:

'I am married but I do not live with my husband. I occupy a one-room flat at No. 311 King Street Hammersmith and I have been there about four weeks. I am a strip-tease dancer and the last engagements I had were in the Panama Club Knightsbridge and the Blue Lagoon Club in Carnaby Street W1. That was five months ago and I have not had any engagements since.

'Last Tuesday evening 3rd October 1944, I was in a café in the Broadway Hammersmith I don't know the name of it and I was introduced to a man in American officer's uniform who told me his name was Ricky Allen, although I have heard him called by the name Karl. I left him and arranged to meet him at 11.30 pm at the Broadway cinema. He met me and he had with him a big American army truck and I went with him for a ride around London. I left him at 3 am and I went home. I gave him my name and address and although I arranged to meet him at 3 pm on Wednesday 4th October I did not turn up.

'On Thursday 5th October he called at my flat at about 5 pm and I spent the evening with him and he came home with me afterwards and stayed the night. We remained in bed until 2.50 pm Friday 6th October. I got up and he asked me to go to Hammersmith Metropolitan railway to collect his valise and he handed me a cloakroom ticket. I collected his valise and that is the one the American officers took away on Wednesday 11th October. When I arrived back in the flat on Friday Ricky put on a pair of dark trouser which he took out of the valise.

'We left the flat together about 4.30 or 5 pm and we went to the Broadway cinema Hammersmith. We came out about 8.30 pm and he left me and said he would call back for me at 9.30 at the flat. He did not come until 11.30 pm.

'I heard whistling in the street and I went down and saw him there. He slept with me this night. We got up from bed at 10.50 am on Saturday 7th October and he left the flat to get a meal. He returned to the flat at 1.45 pm and a man named Lenny was with Ricky. I had seen Lenny before and I know he goes to a café in Hammersmith Broadway. The three of us went to the White City Stadium in the afternoon. In the evening I went with Ricky to Victoria and entered a cinema. He brought me home and I think he left me about 10 pm saying he was going to stay at a hotel in Victoria.

'I have seen Ricky twice since, that is on Sunday afternoon and he stayed with me Sunday night. He left on Monday morning and came back again at about 3 pm and said he would call for me at 5.30 pm but he did not come. I did not see him with a car when he called. I have not seen him since. Ricky brought the tunic that was found behind the door to my flat and on occasions I have seen him wear a leather jacket with a zip fastening.

This statement has been read to me and it is true. (Signed) E.M. Jones.'

A. That is correct.

Q. Later that same evening did Police Constable Kimberley say something to you?

A. He did.

Q. And as a result of that did you go back to No. 311 King Street?

A. I went to King Street and I saw the female defendant alight from a lorry, and we entered the house.

Q. What time was that?

A. That was about 6 pm.

Q. In the house did she say anything to Kimberley?

A. Yes, she did, 'I want to speak to you by yourself,' and I left the room.

Q. Did you go back again into the room?

A. Yes, Kimberley beckoned me into the room and I went in.

Q. Did the defendant Jones say anything?

A. Yes, she said, 'I am sorry that I told you lies at the police station; I will tell you the truth now.' I said, 'You had better tell it at the station,' and I took her back to Hammersmith police station.

Q. At Hammersmith police station at about seven o'clock that evening was she seen by Inspector Tarr in your presence?

A. Yes.

Q. Did you hear Inspector Tarr say anything to her?

A. Yes, Inspector Tarr said, 'I understand you want to tell me something.' She said 'Yes; I was in the car when Heath was shot.' Inspector Tarr cautioned her and she continued saying, 'I didn't do it.' She was going on to speak again and Inspector Tarr stopped her and asked her if she wanted to tell him about it in writing.

Q. What did she say?

A. 'Yes'

Q. And did she make another statement in writing?

A. She did.

Q. Is this the statement?

A. Yes.

Q. Was that read over to her?

A. Yes.

Q. Did she sign it?

A. Yes.

Q. It is headed: 'Hammersmith Station 11th October 1944 Statement of Elizabeth Marina Jones (YAJA/17183149) age 18, of No. 311 King Street Hammersmith, who saith: I have been cautioned by Detective Inspector Tarr that I need not say anything unless I wish, but that anything I do say will be taken down in writing and may be given in evidence,' and is that signed 'E.M. Jones'?

A. Yes.

Q. 'The statement I made to you this morning is incorrect for the most part and I wish to tell you the whole truth about my association with Ricky Allen. I first met him on Tuesday 3rd October 1944, in a café in Hammersmith Broadway, and I was introduced to him by Lenny, I don't know his last name. He asked me to meet him at 11.30 pm that night to go for a drive. T h e meeting place was outside the Broadway cinema. I turned up and he was not there. I was on my way home to King Street, Hammersmith, when I was hailed by a man driving an American lorry. I recognised the voice as being that of Ricky and I got into the truck with him. It was a big truck and it had ten wheels. We drove on into Reading. I told him in the truck that I would like to do something dangerous, meaning to go over Germany in a bomber.

'I meant that, but he got me wrong. He showed me a gun which he pulled out of an inside pocket…'

A. Just a moment: I just cannot follow you.

Mr JUSTICE CHARLES: There is something missed out, you know, if you will only follow what is read.

Mr HOWARD: It is in the same paragraph.

Mr JUSTICE CHARLES: It is only six words left out; that is all it amounts to. 'He showed me a gun which he pulled out from an inside pocket.'

Mr HOWARD: 'Or it might have been hooked to his trousers' then at the top of the next page, page 18: 'When we got to Reading he drove around the town and we started back towards London about two o'clock I think'. Then my lord, omitting some nine or ten lines, there are the last few words of that paragraph: 'It was a left hand drive and during that night he taught me to drive'. Then, my lord, missing again some ten or twelve lines until nearly the bottom of the next paragraph: 'We got back into London at five o'clock.'

Mr JUSTICE CHARLES: (To the witness): You follow that, don't you?

A. Yes, my lord.

Mr HOWARD: 'We got back into London at five o'clock in the morning and I left him and went indoors. He drove me in the truck to my door and I don't know where he went. He knew my name as Georgina Grayson, my stage name, and I gave him my address before I went. He called for me at my flat at about five in the afternoon last Thursday and we went and ate and afterwards went to the Gaumont cinema in Hammersmith. We came out of the cinema about 8.30 and entered a café in Hammersmith Broadway. Just as we got to the door the air raid sirens sounded. He took me round to the Gaumont car park where I saw the American ten-wheel truck. We got into the truck, which Ricky drove to Reading.' Then my lord, I do not propose to read any more on that page; not on the next, page 20, or on page 21, but about six lines down from the top of page 22. 'We stopped in bed' – have you found that, Inspector? – 'until ten to three on Friday afternoon.' Have you got that?

Mr JUSTICE CHARLES: 'We stopped in bed until ten to three on Friday afternoon.'

Mr HOWARD: 'We stopped in bed until ten to three on Friday afternoon and got up. He then gave me a railway cloakroom ticket and he asked me to go to Hammersmith Metropolitan station to get the valise. I did as he asked me and brought back the valise.' Then missing out the next four lines: 'He went out about 4.30 pm.' Have you got that?

A. Yes.

Q. 'He went out about 4.30 pm and promised to call for me at about six o'clock. He didn't come and I stayed in. About 11.30 pm, I heard a whistle coming from the street outside and I went down to the street door because I recognised it was Ricky's whistle. This was an arrangement we had made previously. He came indoors and then said. 'Come on, let's go and get a taxi'. I knew that meaning behind his words and that he wanted me to go with him to rob a taxi cab driver. 'We walked along Hammersmith Road and stood in a shop doorway opposite Cadby Hall. After about ten minutes a grey Ford car approached us very slowly like a taxicab; it was coming from the direction of Hammersmith Broadway. I yelled, 'taxi' and it stopped. Ricky thought it was a naval car and Ricky stopped in the shop doorway while I went over to speak to the driver. I said, 'Are you a taxi?' and he said, 'Private hire; where do you want to go?' I replied 'Wait a minute,' and I went back to Ricky. I told him it was a private car and he asked how many were in it. I told him only the driver, so we went across to the car and Ricky asked the driver to take us to the top of King Street.

'I know now that the driver was named George Heath for reasons I will tell you later. He told Ricky that the fare would be ten shillings, and Ricky said 'That's all right.' I know that Ricky had 19/- in his pockets and I had 10/3d. We got into the car and drove down King Street. After a while Heath said, 'We've passed King Street, where do you want to go?' Ricky said, 'It's farther on; I don't mind paying more.' Heath seemed cross but drove on and when we came to a roundabout Heath said, 'This is the Great West Road'.

'Ricky and I were sitting in the back seat of the saloon car and as we got into the Great West Road Ricky told Heath to drive slowly and when we travelled about three hundred yards before reaching a bridge, Ricky said to Heath, 'we'll get out here,' and Heath stopped. Just as we were passing the roundabout I heard a click and saw that Ricky had his automatic in his right hand. I realised that Ricky was going to frighten the driver with the gun and take his money because we had passed my house on the way.

'Heath learned over from his seat towards the middle of the car with the obvious intention of opening the nearside back door for me to get out. Ricky was sitting on my right and as Heath was learning over I saw a flash and heard a bang. I was surprised that there was not a loud bang because Ricky had told me it would make a big noise when it went off. I was deafened in my right ear by the bang. Heath moaned slightly and turned a little towards his front. Ricky said to him, 'Move over or I'll give you another dose of the same.' I saw that he still had the automatic in his hand. Heath seemed to understand what Ricky had said because he moved further over to the left hand side of the front seat until his shoulder was almost touching the near side door. I heard him breathing very heavily and his head slumped onto his chest. The next I realised that Ricky was in the driving seat and the car was moving.

'As we went over the bridge nearby, Ricky told me to tear down the back window blind to see if anyone was following us. I tore the right corner down, looked out and told Ricky that no one was following. Ricky then told me to go through Heath's pockets. I learned over and I heard his breath coming in short gasps. Ricky told me to look for his wallet in the breast pocket of his jacket. I felt in that pocket, but did not find the wallet. I found it instead in the left hand outside pocket of his overcoat. It was a small folding wallet with a photograph inside and four £1 notes in it. I put the wallet on the back seat. Then I removed papers and a white book from his pockets. Among these were his identity card, from which I learned his name and address, a chequebook with a blue cover, a driving licence, blue card, some petrol coupons, and some photographs and letters. I put this stuff on the seat by my side. I put in my pocket – from other pockets I took a big brown fountain pen, silver pencil, a long silver cigarette case which had a funny sliding action to open, it had '119, Regent street W1' printed on the bottom inside, an expensive-looking cigarette lighter with a snap-down action. I put all these things in my pocket.

'Ricky then asked me if Heath had a watch and I found a wristwatch on Heath's left wrist and I gave it to Ricky. I think I took everything from his pockets. All this time Ricky was driving fast along the road and I sat back examining the things I had taken from Heath's pockets. Ricky told me to put all the valuable things, which I thought he would want to keep, in my pockets and put the other stuff on the back seat. I did this and he then told me to look on the floor of the car with a torch for the bullet. I did this but did not find the bullet.

'Ricky drove on until he turned off the main road on to a sort of common. He drove on the grass and stopped two or three yards from a ditch. He got out and dragged Heath's body from the car and rolled it into the ditch. He said there was blood on his hands and I gave him Heath's handkerchief to wipe it off. He then told me to pick up the papers and get into the front seat quickly. He told me to be careful of fingerprints at the same time.

'He turned the car right round and drove over the grass and eventually on to the road again. When the car went over the grass it was very bumpy. After we got off the grass he told me to look for the bullet again with the aid of Heath's torch. I found a bronze-coloured bullet on the floor by the near side door and gave it to Ricky. After I found the bullet Ricky told me to take over the wheel and said he wanted to look at the things that I had taken from Heath's pockets. I drove along and I noticed there was no window in the offside door of the car near the driving seat. As I drove Ricky was examining the things from Heath's pockets and he threw the wallet and papers out of the window as we went on. He threw the bullet away as we were going along a wide road which had something in it to separate the traffic going in opposite directions.

'Just before we got to the roundabout near where Ricky shot Heath I asked him where we had dumped the body and he said 'Staines.' Just before we got to the roundabout Ricky took the wheel and drove the car into the old Gaumont car park behind Hammersmith Broadway. We then went to the Black and White Café in Hammersmith Broadway and had something to eat. It was then about quarter to four. There were quite a number of cab drivers in there, and I asked Ricky to asked one of them to drive us home, but none of them would. I should say that when we put the car in the car park we wiped everything inside and outside the car with our handkerchiefs.

'After leaving the car we walked home. When we got indoors I said 'He's dead, isn't he?' and he said, yes. I said, 'That's cold blooded murder then; how could you do it?' and he said, 'People in my profession haven't the time to think what they do.' Indoors we examined all of Heath's things we had taken. Then we went to bed.

'The next day, that is Saturday, we got up at ten to eleven in the morning. Ricky went out and he picked up Heath's things and took them with him. He came back at 2.45 pm and told me he had sold the wristwatch to the barber next door to the café in Hammersmith Broadway. He then told me to hurry up as he was going to the dogs. When we got downstairs we saw Lenny and the three of us went to the White City Stadium. After one or two races I offered Lenny a cigarette and whilst I was feeling for my lighter, he took one from his own pocket and I saw clearly that it was the one I found in Heath's clothes. I am sure he did not hand the lighter to Ricky.

'After the racing we left Lenny in the Broadway and we went to Victoria where we had some food and then went to a cinema where we saw 'Christmas Holiday' starring Deanna Durbin. He saw me home that night and left me about 10.30 pm saying he was going to Victoria to get a hotel room. The reason for this was because he could not stop in my room that night owing to my landlady being home all day on Sunday.

'I stayed in all day until about 8.30 pm when I went out to buy some cigarettes. I could not get any in the Black and White café. I walked over to the public house next to the Metropolitan railway station and saw an RAF man going into the public house. I asked him to get me twenty Players' cigarettes. He said he would and came out saying he couldn't get any. He suggested we went to another public house nearby and invited me to have a drink. We went into the bar and had two beers and bought some cigarettes. Then we went to another public house and had some more drinks.

'At 10 pm he asked me if he could walk me home and I said, 'Yes'. I took him up to my room. Whilst he was in my room he asked me what was worrying me and I told him about the murder. I told him that I had been with a man who had shot a fellow and that his name was George Heath of Kennington. He asked me what was the motive. I said 'Robbery,' and I asked him what I should do about it. He said 'Do as your conscience guides you,' so I asked what I should do if my conscience told me nothing. He asked me if I thought I ought to tell the police about Ricky and I said 'I don't know what to do because I am frightened.' He said, 'Would you like me to do something for you such as going to the police?' and I said, 'No.' He said, 'If there is anything you need doing, you write to me,' and he gave me his name and address. I wrote his name and address on the piece of paper, which I hand to you.

'I then heard a whistle in the street which I recognised as Ricky. I told Mac who he was and went down to the street door and let Ricky in. I told him I had a friend in my room and he became jealous, so I told him that my friend had been sent up to me by my people in Wales. He believed that. Ricky sat on the stairs, as Mac came out of the door, I introduced them. Before Mac left my room I told him that Ricky was the man who had shot Heath.

'Ricky and I went round to the car park and saw the Ford V8 there. Ricky said 'It's all right; we have no need to worry; there's nothing in the papers and the police have not found the body yet.' On seeing the car we were both reassured and went to Reading in it. I went to sleep in the car and when I woke up we were back in the car park, where we took two five gallon tins of petrol from two American trucks which were parked there. American soldiers were asleep in those trucks. We put the petrol in the car and left the two tins. He told me to tear the blind of the back of the car and wipe of all the fingerprints. We got back to Wood Lane Shepherds Bush at seven o'clock on Monday morning and went to a café and had some eats. We left the car outside the café, which was near Wormwood Scrubs.

'He then drove me home and on the way he asked me to go to Reading with him and said he would teach me to shoot. I didn't want to go and he became mad. He drove the car to the first turning past my house and parked it behind an air-raid shelter. It was then about 7.30 am and we went up to my room and slept until about twenty to two. Then he went out and promised to call for me at 5.30 and just after he left I saw him drive past the house in the car and I have not seen him since.

'Ricky never gave me any money except when we went to the dogs on Saturday. He then let me bet with his money and keep the winnings. In this way I got seven pounds.

This statement has been read to me and it is true.

(Signed) Elizabeth Marina Jones.'

That is correct.

Cross-examined by Mr CASSWELL Defence JONES.

Q. Mr Tansill, we have been told by Kimberley that she looked ill at the time. What do you say about that?

A. She looked pale.

Q. Did she look as if she had not slept?

A. Well, she looked rather pale, I should say.

Q. Rather pale, if you please. With regard to the first statement, of course, so that means that you did not at that moment, mean to charge her?

A. No.

Q. You were simply making enquiries?

A. That is correct.

Q. How long did that statement take?

A. The first statement took from about 1.30 pm to 2.30 pm on the 11th October.

Q. How long was she in the police station on that day?

A. She would have been there about one hour and a half.

Q. And you say she left about 2.30 did she?

A. Yes.

Q. When you first went to her house, was an American officer there with you?

A. Yes.

Q. I ought to have asked you; before you took that statement, when you asked her if she knew an American officer, she said at once, 'You mean Ricky Allen'?

A. That's right.

Q. And she herself pointed out the clothes which were on the back of the door; is that right? I got you as saying that she pointed them out?

A. She saw us looking at the clothing and she said, 'That is Ricky's'.

Q. So much with regard to that statement. On the second occasion you went with Police Constable Kimberley to the house No. 311 King Street and then, as I understand it, you took her to the police station. About what time did you get to the police station?

A. I should say about 6.30 pm.

Q. This was on the same day, of course?

A. Yes.

Q. I see that you said at seven she was seen by Inspector Tarr?

A. That is correct.

Q. But you did not start taking the statement until 10.30 that evening?

A. That is correct.

Q. What was happening in the meantime?

A. Well, she had told us about matters that are unconnected with this case and we were making enquiries in respect of those matters and we went back and searched her address.

Q. How long did that second statement take?

A. It took until five o'clock in the morning.

Q. From 10.30 until five?

A. That is correct.

Q. At that time did you know about this pencil and fountain pen, the cigarette case and those things?

A. Well, she mentioned them in the statement.

Q. I know she mentioned them; I was wondering whether you jogged her memory at all because she seems to have mentioned everything?

A. No, we knew, of course, the things were missing.

Q. Before that statement you did caution her?

A. Yes.

Q. It seems that throughout that statement she never said anything about her own feelings at all; that seems to have been entirely a statement of fact?

A. Yes.

Cross-examined by Mr MAUDE Defence HULTEN.

Q. Give me the times, will you, of the statements made by Hulten, the times of taking, starting on 10th October. What time did Mr De Mott start do you know?

A. There was only one statement taken from him in my presence.

Q. The interviews, let us call them interviews then. It will cover everything.

A. The first interview with Hulten, with Mr De Mott present and Divisional Detective Inspector Tarr, commenced at 3.10 am on 10th October and terminated at five am.

Q. The second one which Mr De Mott speaks of as being about five pm., give me the times of that, will you?

A. That is the written statement taking in my presence. It was commenced...

Q. No, I think not. I don't think it was taken then?

A. No, we were not present during that.

Q. It is the second interview of 10th October. There was one in the early hours of the morning?

A. We were not present.

Q. It was at Mr De Mott's office and the man was alone with him or with the Americans?

A. Yes, that is correct.

Q. What about 11th October, that was also at No. 96 Piccadilly. You would not be there then?

A. No, I was not there then.

Q. So you would only be there when the second statement of Hulten was taken?

A. Yes, the admission.

Q. Are you sure? I understood from the witnesses yesterday that you had been present before?

A. No, I was present at the first interview and I was present when the statement was taken on the 12th October.

Q. On 12th October? Then when that statement was taken, what were the times?

A. The statement was commenced at about eight pm and terminated at 1.30 am.

Q. When did the interview start?

A. The interview started, I should say, at about quarter to eight.

Q. When did the interview cease?

A. Well, at the time when the statement was commenced that would be at eight pm. I'm sorry; the interview ceased at 1.30, I should say.

Q. Then what happened to him?

A. The Americans took him back into their custody.

Q. You understand he is not complaining about that at all?

A. No.

Q. There is something I have not told you yet. He is not complaining about it, but what he instructs us is that Mr De Mott is wrong, I am not suggesting wickedly at all; I don't mean that in the least, but Mr De Mott is wrong.

Mr JUSTICE CHARLES: I say no. You can't go back to it; I have decided certain matters of fact.

Mr MAUDE: I don't know what your Lordship means by that.

Mr JUSTICE CHARLES: You are not going beyond that.

Mr MAUDE: There is no need for your Lordship to have the slightest anxiety or to mention it in any way; it has got nothing to do with the jury in any shape or form. (to the witness) If I may just pick that line up for a moment, I want you to understand it is not being suggested that Mr De Mott was saying something wickedly or wrongly, or doing any such thing; but what he says is that he was asked questions by more than Mr De Mott?

A. No.

Q. Was he never asked any question at all?

A. By me?

Q. Yes.

A. No, it was not within our province to do so.

Q. Is Mr De Mott wrong about this, Mr Tarr having said something to him about 'Well, if it is the truth there is no harm in you making a statement?'

A. When it is suggested that that was said?

Q. He remembered; I don't know what he said. Perhaps your Lordship can help; I can't remember the time he said.

Mr JUSTICE CHARLES: I have not got the actual time, but my

impression was that was antecedent to the making of the statement but when he was taken down, when the inspectors Tarr and Tansill. Inspector Tarr says, 'If you want to make a statement' – or something like that – 'there is no reason you should not.'

Mr MAUDE: I don't mind when; I am certain if it had happened you would have remembered it at some time?

A. Well, I don't remember.

Q. For instance, supposing I had said, 'Well, it is on the first occasion?'

And then you said, 'I don't remember it then' and then I said 'It is the second occasion?' and you said 'I don't remember it then,' and so on, that is quite futile. Let us just deal a little further with that day, 12th October. Do you know that he was awakened in the ordinary way in the American guard-house between five and six in the morning 12th October?

A. No, I don't know that.

Q. Had you any idea how long the man had been awake?

A. No.

Q. Assuming that it is proved for one moment, tell my lord and jury and myself this. Did he seem at all tired?

A. No.

Q. You follow that, if in fact it is proved, it means of course that he had been awake since five in the morning and had nearly five hours questioning?

A. But I don't know what happened.

Q. No, but still just assume that for one moment. Do you still say he did not seem at all tired?

A. No.

Q. Not in the least?

A. Not in the least.

Q. Can you remember anybody who did seem very tired at an interrogation?

A. I do.

Q. Very, very rarely.

A. Not really tired; because, in that case a statement would not have been taken.

Q. No, I just say, once the statement is taken, of course.

A. If a prisoner seemed to be distressed from anything at all, the statement would be discontinued and carried on at another appropriate time.

Q. And you yourself - because you were not in charge?

A. No.

Q. If it was Mr De Mott; it was not you; it was the American gentleman who was doing this, would you yourself make enquiries to find out whether the man was likely to be tired?

A. Well, it would be obvious.

Q. Would you mind saying whether it is right or wrong: do you make enquiries in the ordinary course of your practice to find out if the person whom you are proposing to interrogate is likely to be tired?

A. No, not normally; you look at the person.

Q. That is all?

A. Yes.

Q. Just look at them?

A. Yes.

Mr JUSTICE CHARLES: Have you many years' experience?

A. Nineteen years, my lord.

Q. And you say, looking at this man, he did not seem at all tired, not in the least?

A. No my lord.

Mr MAUDE: Does it matter what time one does take statements from people? Does one get better results by day or by night?

A. I couldn't say that.

Q. You don't know?

A. I can't say.

Q. You don't notice any weakening of people in the early hours of the morning?

A. It would be possible that people would get tired early in the morning, yes.

Mr JUSTICE CHARLES: But this man did not?

A. No, he was in very good order.

Q. Right up to the end?

A. Yes my lord.

Mr BYRNE for the Prosecution examined WILFRED TARR, sworn.

Q. Wilfred Tarr, Divisional Detective Inspector of the 'T' Division?

A. Yes.

Q. At half past ten on the morning of 7th October with Inspector Tansill did you see the dead body of Heath lying in a ditch at Knowle Green, Staines?

A. I did.

Q. Was the head about three feet from the tree which is marked 'A' on the plan? I think the jury have had an opportunity of looking at the plan.

A. That is so.

Q. The feet were six inches from the tree marked 'B', is that right?

A. Yes.

Q. Was that body later identified by Mrs Heath as that of her husband?

A. It was.

Q. And was that the body upon which Dr Teare made a post-mortem examination?

A. Yes.

Q. Was Heath dressed in a dark blue overcoat? Just look at the coat.

A. Yes.

Q. Just hold that up will you Inspector? You examined the coat, I suppose?

A. I did.

Q. Did you find a bullet hole in the back of the coat in the centre seam eight and a half inches below the collar?

A. I did, at that point I am indicating with my finger.

Q. Did you find another hole in the front of the right side of the coat eight inches from the point of the lapel and three inches from the centre line?

A. I did.

Q. Did you examine the area in which you found the body?

A. I did.

Q. On the grass did you observe that there were marks of tyres?

A. Yes.

Q. Did you find a spring? Just look at that, will you? That is the spring that Mr Blackburn has identified as being part of the motorcar in question?

A. Yes.

Q. Where was that?

A. That was found upon the grass verge on the south side of the roadway crossing Knowle Green and about three feet from the roadway at the end of the two grooves, which have been scored through the earth.

Q. You notice there were pieces of grass and mud sticking on the spring?

A. Yes.

Q. Later did you search the body?

A. I did.

Q. Did you find anything of any value at all upon the body?

A. Nothing whatever.

Q. I think we can deal with a great deal of your evidence shortly because there has been no cross-examination with regard to it of the other officer. Were you present at Hammersmith police station when Hulten was asked questions by Mr De Mott?

A. I was.

Q. When was that?

A. At 1.30 am on 10th October. Lieutenant De Mott asked him for particulars of his identity.

A FATAL PICKUP

Q. I don't want the details; I only want to know whether you were present. If anybody wants to ask you anything about it, there you are and you will answer the questions. At half past eight on the morning 10th October did you see a Ford motorcar in Lurgen Avenue, just off Fulham Palace Road?

A. Yes.

Q. Registered No. RD 8955?

A. Yes.

Q. Under your supervision was it removed to Hammersmith police station?

A. Yes.

Q. Did you there examine it?

A. Yes.

Q. As a matter of fact you were in court when Doctor Teare gave his evidence?

A. I was.

Q. Did you observe the marks – one mark upon the door and the other mark upon the lid of the cubbyhole – that Dr Teare told the jury about?

A. Yes.

Q. Were you present when Hulten pointed out where he said he had found the car and also where Jones lived?

A. Yes.

Q. That was on 11th October, wasn't it?

A. Yes.

Q. In fact did you and the other officer, Inspector Tansill, then interview Jones?

A. Yes.

Q. He has given evidence about that and no question has been raised about it, so I will not ask you to repeat it. The next thing is; at seven o'clock in the evening of that same day, 11th October, did you see Jones at Hammersmith police station?

A. I did.

Q. What did you say to her?

A. 'I understand you want to tell me something.'

Q. What did she say?

A. 'Yes. I was in the car when Heath was shot.'

Q. When she said that, what did you say?

A. I stopped her and cautioned her and she went on, 'I didn't do it'.

Q. What did you say to that?

A. 'Would you like to tell me about it in writing?' and she replied, 'Yes'.

Q. Then as we know, she made a statement.

A. Yes.

Q. After that did you tell her that she would be detained?

A. Yes.

Q. Did she say anything further when you told her that?

A. No, not at that stage.

Q. Upon 12th October at about eight o'clock in the evening were you present when Mr De Mott took the statement, Exhibit 16, from the prisoner Hulten?

A. Yes.

Q. At half past six on the evening of Friday 13th October, did you see Jones at Hammersmith Police station?

A. I did.

Q. What did you say to her?

A. 'I am going to take you to Staines Police station and there charge you with being concerned with Karl Gustav Hulten in murdering George Edward Heath on 7th October 1944.'

Q. Did you caution her?

A. I did; I cautioned her and she replied 'All right'.

Q. Then did you take her by motorcar to Staines police station?

A. I did.

Q. As you were going along the Great West Road and had reached a point 170 yards from the junction of Chiswick High Road, did she say anything?

A. 'That is where he shot him.'

Q. Subsequently was she formally charged at the police station and cautioned and when the charge was read over, did she say anything further?

A. She made no reply.

Q. Then did you receive a letter from her written from Holloway Prison?

A. Yes I did.

Q. When did you receive that letter, Inspector? It does not appear to be dated; that is why I asked you.

A. The letter is dated 26th October.

Q. I am much obliged.

A. I think I must have received it on the following day, the 27th.

Mr BYRNE: My lord, this is the letter I read in opening. Perhaps we might just read it again; it is quite short.

Mr JUSTICE CHARLES: I think so.

Mr BYRNE: Does she write, 'Dear sir, first of all I want to apologise to you for telling you half the truth. I should be very pleased and feel very much relieved, if you would be so kind as come along to Holloway Prison to see me and let me tell you all' – that is underlined?

A. 'All' is underlined.

Q. 'Which I have not yet told you. I am having legal aid but I want to tell you as well as the solicitor. It would be a great weight off my mind if you would come and see me before I go to court on 3rd November, which is next Thursday. You see sir, now I definitely know that Ricky is in safe hands where he cannot get out I can tell you absolutely all' – that is underlined, is it?

A. Yes.

Q. 'All the facts, one fact that is especially important to me and also to you. I am hoping with all my heart that you will not ignore this letter, sir. I am reminding you what you said to me before I came here. You said 'If ever you want to see me or tell me anything you have only to ask.' I sincerely hope to see you in a few days sir. Thank you. I am, sincerely yours Mrs E. M. Jones. PS I would appreciate a letter telling me when you are coming, if you are unable to make it for a few days. I beg of you to see me before court date. It is vitally important. Thanking you again, Betty Jones.'

A. Yes.

Q. Accordingly did you call and see her at Holloway Prison?

A. I did.

Q. What did she say to you?

A. She first of all apologised for having lied to us when we first saw her. She was referring, of course, to the very first interview and then she said, 'I merely wanted to tell you that I lied to you because Ricky had threatened me.'

Q. Is that all she told you about the matter?

A. That was all. It was an interview lasting only a few minutes.

Q. Upon 13th November did you receive this direction by the Home Secretary?

A. Yes.

Q. Made under the United States of America (Visiting Forces) Act, 1942?

A. It is.

Q. I might just as well read it through so that we know what it says. Does it read in this way: 'Whereas representations have been made to me on behalf of the Government of the United States of America with respect to the case of Private Karl Gustav Hulten, a member of the Military Forces of the United States of America, who is alleged to have been concerned with Elizabeth Marina Jones in the murder of one George Edward Heath; now I, the Right Honourable Herbert Morrison, one of His Majesty's principal Secretaries of State, in pursuance of Sub-section 1 of Section 1 of the United States of America (Visiting Forces) Act, 1942, by this Order direct that the provisions of the said sub-section shall not apply in the case of the said Private Karl Gustav Hulten with respect to the said alleged offence. Given under my hand the 10th day of November 1944,' and that is signed 'Herbert Morrison?'

A. It is.

Q. The next thing I wanted to ask you about; upon the 14th November at 3.45 pm with Inspector Tansill, did you see the prisoner Hulten at the Central District guardhouse in London?

A. I did.

Q. What did you say to him?

A. 'You know me Hulten. I am going to take you to Staines police station and there charge you with being concerned with Elizabeth Marina Jones in the murder of George Edward Heath on 7th October 1944.'

Q. Did you caution him?

A. I cautioned him and he made no reply.

Q. Then did he go with you and was Inspector Tansill with you also?

A. Yes.

Q. Did he go with you and Inspector Tansill in a motorcar to Staines police station?

A. Yes.

Q. What happened on the way?

A. He and I were sitting in the back of the car together; the car was driven by Inspector Tansill and on the way he said to me, 'I would not have been here but for the girl.' I stopped him and reminded him that I had already cautioned him and he need not say anything unless he wished, and he went on 'I wanted to go for a walk but she did not want to. We went into a shop doorway and she started yelling for a cab, the first one was a naval car it had a small anchor on it. The next one was Heath's car and he stopped. If it had not been for her I would not have shot Heath.'

Q. Then at the police station was he formally charged with the murder of George Edward Heath?

A. He was.

Q. Cautioned, and the charge read over, did he say anything further?

A. He made no reply.

Q. On the 15th November did you serve him with copies of the two statements that had been made by Jones?

A. I did.

Q. Did he make any observation?

A. No.

Q. On 16th November did you serve Jones with copies of the two statements made by Hulten?

A. I did.

Q. Did she say anything?

A. No.

Cross-examined by Mr CASSWELL Defence Jones.

Q. Mr Tarr, just to deal with what you were telling us just now first, you say that when you were taking this boy - on 14th November?

A. Yes.

Q. That was more than a month afterwards. When you were taking him with you to Staines, he said, 'I would not have been here but for the girl?'

A. Yes.

Q. He knew, of course, that at that time she had been arrested? A. Yes.

Q. Did he know that she had made a statement or not?

A. No, I don't think he did.

Q. He might have presumed that she would have said something but he did not know; you had not said anything?

A. I can't say; I don't think he knew.

Q. The reason why I am asking you is I notice that then you cautioned him or reminded him when he began to talk. Was that interruption in regard to what he was saying?

A. Yes.

Q. As I understand it, in spite of your interruption, he went straight on, 'I wanted to go for a walk, but she did not want to and called a cab?'

A. Yes.

Q. Do you think that is what he meant when he said, 'If it had not been for her I would not have shot Heath?'

A. I do.

Q. Would you mind taking the plan? I am looking at the enlarged section, which shows marks made by the car wheels. One of those marks is marked 36 feet and it is to north side of the gravel road?

A. Yes, I have it.

Q. Did you take notice of those marks? I presume you did.

A. I did, yes.

Q. It looks as if the car had been backed down there and turned in a circle and came down?

A. Yes, that is what I thought.

Q. Because very faintly on this photograph it shows the car making back to the road and apparently crossing a small bush on its way. Right down here it looks to me as if the car had come round and in getting on to the road again, it crossed over or by a small bush; that it seems to have been the route it took?

A. I am sorry; where it regained the road on the left?

Q. Yes, where it regained the gravel road.

A. Yes.

Q. Did you measure that distance between the tracks and the ditch yourself? It is shown as nine feet.

A. I did, Yes.

Q. I suppose you examined the grass for footmarks, did you?

A. Yes.

Q. Were there any visible there?

A. There were none to be seen at all.

Q. So there must have been a pretty thick carpet of grass there?

A. The grass was thick, yes.

Q. Did you notice when you saw the body whether the coat was wet?

A. No, it was not wet.

Q. It was not?

A. No.

Q. I was just wondering. You were there long after the dew would have dried off it?

A. No, The grass still bore dew even when I arrived, which was just after ten o'clock: 10.30 in fact.

Q. On 6th October?

A. Yes.

Q. That would be 9 am Greenwich time?

A. Yes.

Q. And you say the coat showed no signs of damp?

A. No.

Q. The next thing I want to ask you is this; what impression did you have of the defendant Jones? Did she seem tired to you when this long statement was taken?

A. No, I heard Inspector Tansill's answer and I do not think I can enlarge on that.

Q. She looked pale?

A. She was certainly very white indeed, very similar to her present appearance, in fact.

Q. She told Mr Kimberley in fact she had not slept for several nights. She didn't tell you that, I suppose?

A. No, in fact the statement indicates that she slept in the mornings rather than the nights.

Mr JUSTICE CHARLES: Yes, according to her statement, of course, she did generally until after midday or nearly two o'clock, with the man.

Mr CASSWELL: I understand – I may have been mistaken – that she rather gave Mr Kimberley the impression she did not look well, he said?

A. With respect, I think Kimberley meant that her appearance had changed very much. I do not think he was really...

Mr JUSTICE CHARLES: He had not seen her for two years?

A. Suggesting that she looked very ill.

Mr CASSWELL: Of course, he is not right about two years, you have made enquiries and she did not come to London until February 1943?

A. No: it obviously must have been since February 1943.

Q. It was February 1943, when she came to London?

A. Yes.

Q. Have you made enquiries about her home life at all?

A. Yes, I have

Q. She was born, I think, in July and she is now eighteen years old and however many months it is since July?

A. The 5th July 1926, she was born.

Mr JUSTICE CHARLES: That makes her eighteen years and what?

A. Eighteen years and seven months now, my lord.

Mr CASSWELL: Then at the age of three did she go with her parents to Canada, do you know?

A. Yes.

Q. And came back about four years later?

A. I think three years later.

Q. Was her mother rather delicate? Did you find that out?

A. I have seen her; she doesn't appear to be a strong woman.

Q. This girl had an elder sister, just about a year older than herself. Did you find out about that or not?

A. No, I did not.

Q. Then when she was only thirteen and a half she ran away from home three times, didn't she?

A. I have information of her running away twice; I think it quite likely she did run away again.

Q. Did you know at that time her father, of whom she was very fond, was called up?

A. Yes.

Q. Did you know that on one occasion when she ran away she got on a lorry to Usk where her father was stationed?

A. No, I have had no information about that.

Q. Then you know that she came to London in February 1943?

A. Yes.

Q. Am I right in saying that she was engaged for a short time as a barmaid?

A. Yes.

Q. A usherette at a cinema?

A. Yes.

Q. A waitress at a café?

A. Yes.

Q. And in April 1943, she did what she wanted to, she got dancing engagements?

A. Yes.

Q. I see she has been described as a strip-tease dancer. Did she in fact give that sort of entertainment?

A. I understand so, in nightclubs in the West End.

Q. I don't know whether you know; was she making quite good money dancing? Did you know that, or didn't you enquire?

A. That depends what one calls big money; I don't think it ever exceeded £4.10.0 per week, but I am not sure about that.

Q. Just one thing I have missed out. In November 1942, when she was only sixteen and four months, she was married to a man who was an old friend of the family?

A. Yes.

Q. Considerably older then herself?

A. No, I think my information is that he is not considerably older. He is twenty-six or twenty-seven, I think. Whether you consider that considerably older I don't know.

Q. Well, my information is he was considerably older than that and that they had a quarrel on the first day and never lived together; she left him on the same day?

A. Yes.

Q. And that apart from a weekend when he was on leave they have never been together?

A. That is so.

Q. One other thing I want to ask you because of certain information which has appeared in the papers; is there any evidence that she has ever lived as a prostitute?

A. No.

Q. To get back to your evidence, Mr Tarr. I notice that you say on the first occasion when you saw her she said, 'I did not do it'?

A. Yes.

Q. And I notice that perfectly correctly, if I may say so, you laid no emphasis on any of those words. Would it be correct to say she said, 'I did not do it'?

A. Yes, I think it would.

Q. I am perfectly correct that you laid no emphasis on any syllable at all?

A. Yes, I think that would be correct.

Q. This letter that you received from her, of course is written from Holloway?

A. Yes.

Q. And is it dated 26th October?

A. Yes.

Q. Can you tell us when you received it? I suppose you couldn't go straight away?

A. I am afraid I can't without referring to records, but I think the next day.

Q. I notice that you said in your deposition that you called on the 30th?

A. Yes.

Q. On the deposition is it, 'On the 30th I received a letter'. It may, of course, have taken all that time to reach you. When was it you visited her?

A. On the 30th.

Q. On the same day you received it?

A. 2.30 pm on 30th October.

Mr JUSTICE CHARLES: Was that the same day that you received the letter, do you think?

A. I think, my lord, this may have been a weekend. If I may refer to the calendar for a moment, that may have accounted for the delay.

Q. Yes.

A. I am afraid I have not a 1944 calendar here.

Mr CASSWELL: The 30th October in 1944 was a Monday.

A. Very probably I did receive that letter on that Monday morning and I went in the afternoon.

Cross-examined by Mr MAUDE Defence HULTEN.

Q. Mr Tarr, there is first of all something I want to be quite clear about. When you saw Jones in Holloway Prison you produced the letter you have got there?

A. Yes.

Q. She first of all apologises, and this is where I am not clear; she apologises for having lied to you when you first saw her. Which incident is that?

A. That was on the occasion when we went to her room and we saw her in bed.

Q. She is not referring to the interview when she makes her first statement?

A. Her first written statement?

Q. The first written statement.

A. She is referring to that also.

Q. She is referring to that as well.

A. Also.

Q. Is it one and the same interview? A . It is one and the same thing, yes.

Q. Then she says to you - we are now back in the jail - 'I merely wanted to tell you that I lied to you because Ricky had threatened me'?

A. Yes.

Q. Let us see what the position was. That first statement of hers is dated 11th October. Hulten was arrested when?

A. On 9th October.

Q. So he had been out of the way for two days?

A. Yes.

Q. And when you saw her on the 11th, when she made the first statement, did she in any way at all by words or gestures or in any shape or form indicate to you that she had been afraid of Hulten?

A. Not in the slightest way, no.

Q. Or, that she had been threatened by the man?

A. Not in the slightest. I can take it even further than that, because after she had made that written statement…

Mr JUSTICE CHARLES: Which?

A. The first written statement, my lord. I knew that it contained lies. That was before we let her go; and then I asked her, had she been advised to tell lies and she said 'No' or at least I asked her, had she been advised not to tell lies but to tell that story and she said 'No'.

Q. Now it has become not clear.

A. I knew the story she told me contained lies.

Q. Wait one moment. Can you use the words and not she?

A. Yes, I used them wrongly; I will repeat them correctly. I knew that statement she had made contained some lies and before letting her go I said 'Have you been advised by anybody to tell this story?' and she said 'No'.

Q. I am looking at my copy of that first statement.

A. Yes.

Q. You said that to her, she goes away and she is at liberty, is she then?

A. Yes.

Q. Then I have forgotten the time, but some time the next day - it was the evening, I think, wasn't it? - she starts to make the second long statement?

A. Yes.

Q. Of course, during the interval she could not possibly have seen Hulten?

A. No, she did not in fact, of course see Hulten until they appeared in the dock together at the lower court.

Mr JUSTICE CHARLES: From 11th October?

A. From 9th October, my lord.

Mr MAUDE: Go back in your mind to that moment when she is there for that second statement.

A. Yes.

Q. Which we know lasted for hours, didn't it?

A. Yes.

Q. What was it – about seven hours?

A. Six and a half hours, I think eight till 5.30, rather more in fact. I am so sorry. The statement of the girl – excuse me you are talking, are you not, of the second statement? That was 10.30 pm to five am.

Q. I am interested in the one you say was eight to 5.30.

A. No, that is my mistake entirely.

Q. What did you mean?

A. I did not mean anything like that.

Q. Where did you get the time 5.30 from any of these statements?

A. That was a mistake. I did not get the time from anywhere; it was just a mistake.

Q. The time 5.30 just came into your mind by mistake?

A. Yes.

Q. I accept it, if you say so. You are sure it is?

A. I am positive, the time was 10.30 pm to 5 am.

Q. Till 5 am?

A. Yes.

Q. Ah, I agree. I quite see. I didn't think we had got a five anywhere. I agree, Mr Tarr; I quite understand. I thought five was quite a new figure. From 10.30 to five in the morning is seven hours?

A. Six and a half.

Q. A good long time?

A. Yes, a very long time.

Q. During that time did she then give any indication that she had been frightened, by the man?

A. Not the slightest.

Q. Of no sort or kind?

A. Not the slightest.

Q. The court was relying, I think on your experience not long ago, which is many years. You have reached this distinguished position after many years as a police officer?

A. Yes.

Q. It would be fair to say that for a girl aged eighteen you would expect her at such an interview to be nervous?

A. Yes.

Q. Was she?

A. No.

Q. When you finished with her on the 11th – we know that she is arrested and I want to get these dates clear – on the 13th she is formally charged?

A. She was charged on the 13th.

Q. On 13th October. As you know, the defence of both these persons, the British and the American, is being done by the British Government; it is not a private defence. Do you know when she first saw a lawyer; I am not talking about barristers, but do you know when she first saw a lawyer?

A. If I may refer to my notes. It would be within a day or two, I think, of her first appearance before the court. I should say within a few days of 14th October I think.

Q. Can you get it closer? Have you got there a note that you can refresh your memory from?

A. No, I have not.

Q. Because of course, she was granted a certificate and I don't know when her solicitor first saw her. You see, I have not even got the dates of the police court hearings?

A. The first hearing in her case would be 14th October.

Q. Was she represented then?

A. No.

Q. What is the next hearing?

A. I think 3rd November.

Q. The 14th October. She was granted legal aid then?

A. Yes, I am reasonably sure she was granted legal aid at the first hearing.

Q. Have you any doubt, before the letter of the 26th arrived, she had been granted legal aid?

A. In this letter, if you will see, she refers here to her solicitor in the last paragraph, I think, of this letter, she says, 'I want to tell you as well as the solicitor.'

Q. But it is ambiguous. What she is saying there is, 'I am having legal aid, but I want to tell you as well as the solicitor' - which might well mean that the girl had not seen the solicitor?

A. In fact, she had legal aid and had seen her solicitor by that date; I do know.

Q. I am now looking at the second paragraph of the letter to you: 'You see, sir, now I definitely know that Ricky is in safe hands where he cannot get out, I can tell you absolutely all the facts.'

Is 'all' underlined?

A. Yes.

Q. 'One fact that is especially important to me and also to you'?

A. Yes.

Q. There is no doubt it is right, is it not, what she puts in the last paragraph; 'I am reminding you what you said to me before I came here. You said, 'If ever you want to see me or tell me anything you have only to ask"?

A. Yes, that is right.

Q. You told her that?

A. Yes.

Q. So on 26th October she sends for you and the only thing you are told is that she lied to you, that is to say, on the first occasion?

A. Yes.

Q. Because Ricky had threatened her?

A. Yes.

Q. There was other conversation apparently, but nothing of importance?

A. No, I don't think there was other conversation. This interview lasted a few minutes; I should think less than five minutes, certainly less than five minutes.

Q. When I said 'other conversation', don't think I mean anything to do with her or her activities or anything like that; but I notice you said in the court below, it may not be clear, 'She told me nothing else of importance.' I imagine that you had some conversation, I dare say of a kindly nature, did you?

A. Yes, in fact, very briefly, yes.

Q. That is what I understood. When she said that she had been threatened did anybody say when or how? She was not asked any questions about it?

A. No.

Q. And did not volunteer any particulars?

A. No.

Q. She did not mention that pistol?

A. No.

Q. Or any implement?

A. No.

Mr CASSWELL: I wonder if your Lordship would allow me to ask a question on that?

Mr JUSTICE CHARLES: I will indeed.

Further cross-examined by Mr CASSWELL Defence JONES

Q. I notice you told us Mr Tarr, that on the first occasion you say she did not indicate to you in any way that she was frightened. May I take it even further than that: after she made the first statement you knew it had contained lies?

A. Yes.

Q. And so then you said to her, 'Have you been advised by anyone to tell lies?'

A. No, I corrected that. 'Have you been advised by anyone to tell this story?'

Q. Yes, to tell this story and she said, 'No'?

A. Yes.

Q. At that time did she not know that Hulten was not still at large, did she?

A. I think she knew quite well at that time where he was.

Q. How could she know?

A. I don't know how she knew; I think she must have guessed it. You will remember that that very day she told Kimberley she knew a man inside.

Q. That was after she got a newspaper: which she showed to Kimberley.

A. Yes, that is true enough, that may be the explanation; I don't know.

Q. Only one thing I wanted to ask you on the depositions. Of course you do not know when her solicitor first saw her?

A. No, I don't.

Q. I am hoping they will check that up. One thing and that is: her husband was reported missing at the end of September, wasn't he?

A. The letter announcing the fact that he was missing arrived upon the day she was charged, 13th October.

Q. But all the time he has been making her a separation allowance of thirty-five shillings a week?

A. He has been making her an allowance, but I don't know the amount.

Re-examined by Mr BYRNE for the Prosecution

Q. I only want one matter cleared up if I may. So far as you yourself are concerned can you tell me, when was the first time that Jones alleged that she had been threatened by Hulten?

A. When I visited her in Holloway Prison on 30th October.

Mr JUSTICE CHARLES: Holloway Prison on the what?

A. 30th October, my lord.

Mr BYRNE: As far as you are concerned, up till then had she ever suggested either by words or demeanour that she had been threatened by him?

A. Not in anyway.

Mr BYRNE: My Lord, my learned friend Mr Casswell would like me just to clear this up for him. I sent for the legal aid certificate and it appears it was granted on 14th October.

Mr JUSTICE CHARLES: That, I think, that is what he said, wasn't it?

Mr BYRNE: Was that the date?

Mr CASSWELL: I didn't know the certificate was granted at the first hearing.

Mr JUSTICE CHARLES: That is what he said. She saw her lawyer within a few days of 14th October, when she was granted legal aid.

Mr CASSWELL: My lord, I do not think this officer knew when she saw him.

The witness: I did say I was reasonably sure that was the date, but I was not positive.

Mr BYRNE: That is the document.

Mr CASSWELL: That document simply says she was granted legal aid on that date, but not when the solicitor saw her.

Mr JUSTICE CHARLES: No, of course it doesn't. He says she was granted legal aid 14th October. Then you were right, officer.

Mr BYRNE: My lord that is the case for the prosecution. May I just say this? I am wondering whether your Lordship at some appropriate time might think it was convenient to indicate the question of fact that your Lordship was leaving it to the jury to determine in order to arrive at their verdict, because obviously that would be of great assistance to us at the Bar.

Mr JUSTICE CHARLES: Well, there are a very great many questions of fact, a very great many, which I shall have to refer to at the proper and at the appropriate time.

Mr CASSWELL: Which, I may suggest, your Lordship will not know until you have heard the defence?

Mr JUSTICE CHARLES: I cannot now, that is quite obvious; and whether I can do it at all I do not know. There are one or two given questions of fact that you all know I must ask in order that the jury may come to a determination, but there are a very great many questions of fact, which have a bearing on their decision as to the given facts to which, of course, I shall have to refer.

Mr BYRNE: I had in mind…

Mr JUSTICE CHARLES: I was misunderstanding you, perhaps.

Mr BYRNE: Perhaps I did not put it clearly. Your Lordship will recollect, when I opened this case, I ventured to say for your Lordship's ear what I conceived the law to be. At some time or other when you sum this case up I have no doubt your Lordship will arrive at a point when if the jury find certain circumstances as facts, as your Lordship will direct them that, that in law amounts to murder or whatever the verdict may be. Your Lordship follows? You see, it is quite obvious from the cross-examination that has taken place, for example, that there is a possibility – of course, we don't know until we have heard the evidence – that some kind of defence of accident may be put forward so far as Hulten is concerned; and one of the matters that one would like to determine, in order to save time, undoubtedly would be whether the defence of accident in those circumstances is open to him, your Lordship follows? It has been adumbrated quite clearly by Mr Maude.

Mr JUSTICE CHARLES: The defence quite clearly in terms, as I took it down, is he is going to say that this shooting was an accident.

Mr BYRNE: Your Lordship will recollect the way in which we put the case for the Prosecution is that Hulten was engaged in the commission…

Mr MAUDE: One moment. I am all in favour of simplification, but, if it involves my learned friend making a second speech for the Crown in front of the jury, I really must object. I don't wish to hear from my friend's point of view the way he puts the case for the Crown. He has had an opportunity to do that.

Mr JUSTICE CHARLES: He will have an opportunity of summing this case up and he ought to in cases of this sort.

Mr MAUDE: Although I would very much like to hear he puts his case for the Crown in different surroundings, I don't want to at the present moment.

Mr JUSTICE CHARLES: I quite understand both of you, but you see the force of the observation made by Mr Maude. I think on the whole – in fact I have no doubt and I so decide – that on the whole I had better hear the evidence and you will be able to put the case in your summing-up of the case, your final address; you will be able to put the case as the Crown envisages it. I don't want and I don't think I ought to say how you ought to put it, because all you have to say is, 'I cannot agree with the Judge'. I want to know how the Crown put it.

Mr BYRNE: I have indicated it and I was only wondering whether it agreed with your Lordship's view.

Mr JUSTICE CHARLES: I know. After you have heard all the evidence, and all the evidence has been taken, and you are making your final address to the jury, I think, would be the time for you, if I may say so, to say upon what facts as revealed by the evidence the Crown rely in order to obtain a conviction.

Mr BYRNE: Of course, if your Lordship says that, it is quite sufficient; but it did seem to me that there was a question of law arising which would make a material difference. But at any rate, so far as that is concerned, I could deal with that in cross-examination.

Mr JUSTICE CHARLES: That would be more appropriately discussed when you are making your final observation. Of course, I don't know quite what directions of law it will be necessary for me to make when I have heard all the evidence. I might be jumping before I come to the stile, if there be a stile.

Mr BYRNE: I was only suggesting perhaps one or two broad principles might have fallen from your Lordship's lips.

Mr JUSTICE CHARLES: No, I think the proper time for me will be after you have addressed the jury; then I shall tell the jury what in my view the legal position is having regard to the facts as disclosed by admissible evidence. I think that is the proper way.

DEFENCE

Mr CASSWELL: My Lord, the time has come for me to make my defence.

I have no witnesses to call except the prisoner herself.

Mr JUSTICE CHARLES: It is now seven minutes to one, and I think it would be most inconvenient to take five or six minutes of her evidence and break off.

Mr CASSWELL: If I may say so, my lord, I agree.

Mr JUSTICE CHARLES: I don't think it is fair to me or to the jury. Members of the jury, at two o'clock we will meet again and Jones will then, I am told by Mr Casswell, go into the box and give her evidence.

(Adjourned for a short time)

Mr CASSWELL: Mrs Jones, will you go into the witness box, please?

Mr CASSWELL examined ELIZABETH MARINA JONES, sworn.

Q. Mrs Jones, is your name Elizabeth Marina Jones, or is it Maud Jones?

A. Maud Jones.

Q. Elizabeth Maud Jones is your proper name. I think your last address was no. 311 King Street, Hammersmith?

A. Yes.

Q. How old are you?

A. Eighteen.

Mr JUSTICE CHARLES: Eighteen years and seven months, isn't it?

Mr CASSWELL: Yes, my lord. (To the witness) I think you were born in Wales, were you, on the 5th July 1926?

A. Yes.

Q. And after some two or three years did you go to Canada with your parents?

A. Yes.

Q. Have you an elder sister?

A. Yes.

Q. How much older than you is she?

A. A year and two months.

Q. Has she always been delicate?

A. Yes.

Q. Then you went to Canada when your mother and father and sister went there, and remained there for how long?

A. Nearly five years.

Q. And came back to Wales again?

A. Yes.

Q. Did you get on very well with your mother?

A. Yes.

Q. Did she seem as fond of you as she was of your invalid sister?

A. I didn't think so.

Q. I think you and your father were fond of one another, were you not?

A. Yes.

Q. So you lived there until you were thirteen and a half - I think that is the next time I need come to - and when you were thirteen and a half, was your father called up to serve?

A. Yes.

Q. Were you happy after he left home?

A. No.

A FATAL PICKUP

Q. I think three times, for short periods, you left home, did you not?

A. Yes.

Q. And on the third occasion did you get on a lorry hoping to be taken to Usk, where your father was stationed?

A. Yes.

Q. When you got there, you didn't see him, did you?

A. Yes.

Q. Did you see him?

A. Yes.

Q. Were you ultimately taken on to the police station?

A. Yes.

Q. And sent home by the police?

A. Yes

Q. I think you came to London, did you not, in February 1943?

A. 25th January.

Q. January, was it?

A. Yes.

Q. You were then sixteen and six months old?

A. Yes.

Q. What did you do when you first came to London?

A. I had several jobs.

Mr JUSTICE CHARLES: What?

A. I had several jobs here, my lord.

Mr CASSWELL: Mr Tarr told us that you had been a barmaid for a short time.

A. Yes.

Q. Did you earn your own living and keep yourself?

A. Yes.

Q. I think all the time from when you were a little girl, you wanted to go in for dancing; is that so?

A. Yes.

Q. And in April 1943 did you get your opportunity?

A. Yes.

Q. I think you were trained somewhere, were you not?

A. Yes.

Q. Where was that?

A. At the school.

Mr JUSTICE CHARLES: Where?

A. In Manchester.

Q. What?

A. In Manchester.

Q. What school?

A. The approved school.

Mr CASSWELL: At Sale wasn't it?

A. Yes.

Q. And you took up dancing in April 1943?

A. Yes.

Q. Did you then obtain engagements at various nightclubs?

A. Yes.

Q. What sort of money did you get?

A. When I first started I earned about four pounds ten.

Q. I should have said that, before you came to London, in November 1942 you married, did you not, when you were only sixteen and a few months?

A. Yes.

Q. Did you marry a man who had been well known to you and your family for many years?

A. Yes.

Q. Did you marry with the approval of your parents?

A. Yes.

Q. Your husband afterwards, I think, joined the Army, did he not?

A. He was already in the Army.

Q. In September of last year he was reported missing, was he not?

A. Yes.

Q. You have heard no more of him since?

A. No.

Q. But the whole time has he been making you a separation allowance?

A. Yes.

Mr JUSTICE CHARLES: You have not told us they were separated.

Mr CASSWELL: I ought to have done that. Did you live with your husband for any length of time?

A. I never lived with my husband.

Q. How did that come about?

A. Because my husband struck me on the first night we were married.

Mr CASSWELL: I don't know whether your Lordship could hear that?

Mr JUSTICE CHARLES: No.

A. Because my husband struck me the first night we were married.

Mr CASSWELL: Because he struck you the first night you were married and you left him, did you?

A. Yes.

Q. After that, did you only see him for about a weekend's leave, once?

A. I saw him several times but never lived with him.

Q. You saw him quite often but did not live with him?

A. Yes.

Q. But for a weekend you were together, were you not?

A. No, we did not live with each other.

Q. Let me come to the time we have already had, when you were dancing.

Mr JUSTICE CHARLES: Mrs Jones, you are likely to be here some time. Would you like to sit down? You can if you like.

A. Yes.

Mr CASSWELL: My lord, I made a mistake. I thought it was a separation allowance. (To the witness) It was an Army allowance, was it not?

A. Yes.

Mr JUSTICE CHARLES: As I understand, rightly or wrongly I know not, there was no formal separation.

Mr CASSWELL: No, my lord.

Mr JUSTICE CHARLES: They disagreed the very day they were married and they did not live together and shortly after he went into the Army and he transmitted the regular allowance to his wife, who is this woman?

Mr CASSWELL: That is so my lord.

Mr JUSTICE CHARLES: Is that right?

A. Yes.

Mr CASSWELL: Unfortunately I used an inaccurate term. It should have been the Army allowance.

Mr JUSTICE CHARLES: They had a row the very day they were married and they never lived together and then he, being in the service, transmitted the ordinary allowance to his wife?

Mr CASSWELL: Therefore it was two months after this marriage of yours that you came to London?

A. Yes.

Q. Did you have engagements through 1943 and the beginning of 1944?

A. Yes.

Q. After you had ceased to have engagements, on what did you live?

A. My husband's Army allowance.

Mr JUSTICE CHARLES: How much was the allowance?

A. £1-15-6p.

Q. Mr JUSTICE CHARLES: Thirty-five and six a week.

Mr CASSWELL: We have heard you went to live at Hammersmith, no. 311 King Street, in September last. Did you go to a café, which was in Hammersmith Broadway, for some of your meals?

A. Yes.

Q. Is there any truth in the suggestion, which has appeared, unfortunately in the press, that you were a prostitute and lived in that way at any time?

A. No, sir.

Mr JUSTICE CHARLES: You did live with other people?

A. There was only one man.

Mr CASSWELL: I was talking about the café. In that café did you meet a man we have seen, who you knew as Lenny?

A. Yes.

Q. How did you come to meet him?

A. Through his daughter.

Q. You knew his daughter, did you?

A. Yes.

Q. Was she a waitress at that café?

A. Yes.

Q. How did you come to meet Hulten?

A. Lenny introduced me to him.

Q. We have been told that was on the 3rd October. Is that right, a Tuesday?

A. Yes.

Q. How was he introduced to you, in what name?

A. As 'Ricky'.

Q. Did he give his surname?

A. No.

Q. How was he dressed when he was introduced to you?

A. An officer's uniform.

Q. What impression did you get of him? Did you think he was a decent fellow?

A. I thought he was a gentleman.

Q. Did he tell you anything about his unit, or what he was engaged on?

A. No.

Q. Did he say where he was stationed?

A. He told me he had just come back from Holland.

Q. Had you any reason to believe that he was a deserter?

A. No, sir.

Q. When did you first know that?

A. When the police told me.

Mr JUSTICE CHARLES: When?

A. When the police told me.

Mr CASSWELL: In the course of the conversation, did he ask you to go out with him?

A. Yes.

Q. Did you have any hesitation in agreeing to do that?

A. No, Sir.

Q. Did he tell you whether he was on duty during the day or not?

A. No, sir.

Q. Did he give any explanation of why he should want to start driving at eleven o'clock at night, or something like that?

A. No.

Mr JUSTICE CHARLES: Did he not say why he wanted to start what?

Mr CASSWELL: Driving, my lord.

Mr JUSTICE CHARLES: She has not said that.

Mr CASSWELL: I am sorry. Did he give an invitation the first day he met you to go out with him?

A. Yes.

Q. At what time?

A. Eleven-thirty at night.

Q. Did he tell you where to meet him?

A. Yes.

Q. Did you go; I think that was somewhere in the Broadway, wasn't it Hammersmith Broadway?

A. Outside the Broadway Cinema.

Q. Did you go to meet him?

A. Yes.

Q. Did you find him there or not?

A. No.

Q. What happened?

A. I waited a few minutes and he did not come, so I started on my

A FATAL PICKUP

way home and then a big Army truck was coming along the street and stopped and he shouted my name.

Q. My lord, I could just hear it, perhaps knowing what it was. (To the witness) Just try and speak a little louder, Mrs Jones. I thought you said, didn't you, that you went to meet him and you waited for some minutes; I didn't hear anything after that.

A. I was on my way home, up King Street, and an Army truck drew up and Ricky shouted my name.

Q. You heard somebody call your name?

A. Yes.

Q. That was he, was it?

A. Yes.

Q. What sort of vehicle was he driving?

A. A ten-wheeled lorry.

Q. Did he tell you where he was going for the drive?

A. As we were going along the street, he told me that he was going to drive me to Reading.

Q. As you were driving along, did he say anything to you which struck you that you can remember?

A. I don't understand you sir.

Q. Did you say anything to him about what you wanted to do?

A. I said I should like to do something dangerous.

Q. Did you explain what you meant by that?

A. Yes.

Q. What was it?

A. I said I would like to go over to Germany in an aeroplane.

Mr JUSTICE CHARLES: Did you tell him that?

A. Yes.

Mr CASSWELL: Did you say anything more that you remember?

A. I don't think so.

Q. Did he then tell you anything about himself?

A. Yes.

Q. What did he say?

A. He told me he was a gunman.

Q. 'He told me he was a gunman,' yes. Did he tell you where he came from or where he had been a gunman, or anything like that?

A. He told me he had been a gunman in Chicago.

Q. Did he say anything about a gang, or anything like that?

A. He told me he was the leader of a gang operating in London.

Mr JUSTICE CHARLES: I am afraid I did not quite hear.

A. He told me he was the leader of a gang operating in London.

Mr CASSWELL: Did he show you anything?

A. He showed me a gun.

Q. Where did it come from, this gun, do you know?

A. I think he took it out of a belt.

Q. Mrs Jones, did he say this in a boasting sort of way or in a way that made you believe him?

A. He said it in a way that I believed him.

Q. Did he say anything to you about what would happen if you told other people about this?

A. Yes, he said he would use the gun on me.

Mr JUSTICE CHARLES: 'He would use the gun on me if I told anyone about this' – about what he had told you?

A. Yes.

Q. That was on 3rd October?

A. Yes.

Mr CASSWELL: The first time you were out with him?

A. Yes.

Mr JUSTICE CHARLES: The very first time you were out with him?

A. Yes.

Mr CASSWELL: What effect did that have on you?

A. I was very frightened.

Q. Did you ask him at all about his work in the Army?

A. No.

Q. How long were you driving with him that night?

Mr JUSTICE CHARLES: What time did you get back?

A. I can't remember.

Mr CASSWELL: In the early hours of the morning, was it, the next morning?

A. Yes.

Mr JUSTICE CHARLES: It must have been, they went down to Reading.

Mr CASSWELL: What did he do the next morning, which would be the morning of Wednesday 4th October? You say you can't remember what time you got home. Can you remember the circumstances in which you got home; did he drive you home?

A. Yes.

Q. Did he come in with you, or not?

A. No.

Q. Did he say anything to you before he left you?

A. Yes.

Q. What was it?

A. He told me that I would always have somebody watching me.

Q. What were you to do? Did he tell you what you were to do?

A. He said I was to stay in.

Q. That was on Wednesday 4th October, did you stay in that day?

A. I only went to have my meals, at the café next door.

Q. Did you meet him at all that day?

A. No.

Q. When did you see him next?

A. I saw him and Leonard Bexley when they called for me on Thursday.

Mr JUSTICE CHARLES: October what?

Mr CASSWELL: Thursday would be the 5th.

Mr JUSTICE CHARLES: You did not see him till Thursday?

A. No.

Q. Is that so?

A. Yes, my lord.

Q. That was with Leonard Bexley?

A. Yes, my lord.

Mr CASSWELL: At what time did you see him on 5th October?

A. I think it was getting on for about five o'clock.

Q. Where did you see him?

A. At my house.

Q. He came for you, did he?

A. Yes.

Q. Was anybody with him at the time?

A. Leonard Bexley.

Q. Did he seem very friendly with Lenny Bexley or not?

A. Yes.

Q. He came and fetched you. Where did he take you on the Thursday afternoon? A. We went and had a meal and then we went to a cinema.

Mr JUSTICE CHARLES: 'We went and had a meal,' and what?

A. And he took me to a cinema.

Mr CASSWELL: What time did you come out from the cinema, about?

A. About eight-thirty, I think; I am not sure.

Q. What did you do after that?

Mr JUSTICE CHARLES: What then?

A. Then we went and had a meal.

Mr CASSWELL: Had he still got this Army truck with him then?

A. I had not seen it at all that day.

Q. You had not seen it, I know by that time; but you had been to a cinema and had a meal?

A. Yes.

Q. Did he propose to do something after you had that meal?

A. Yes.

Q. What did he propose to do?

A. He took me over to the garage in Sussex Place and told me to get into the lorry.

Q. He took you over to the garage and told you to get into the lorry. What garage was that?

A. In Sussex Place.

Q. Did you want to go out with him again?

A. No, sir.

Q. Why did you?

A. Because I was frightened of him. He told me I had to do everything he told me.

Q. Did you in fact drive with him to Reading that night?

A. Yes.

Q. Did he say anything more to frighten you, which frightened you that night?

A. I don't think so.

Q. Then when did you get back from that drive, the Thursday - Friday – drive, do you remember?

A. In the early hours of the morning; I don't know what time.

Mr JUSTICE CHARLES: That would be October what?

Mr CASSWELL: That would be the 6th, the early hours of Friday morning. What were your feelings towards this man by that time, Mrs Jones?

A. I was terrified of him.

Q. Having brought you back in the early hours of Friday morning, what did he do? Did he come in with you or not?

A. Yes.

Q. And spent the night in your room, or the early hours of the morning?

A. He took the truck some place first.

Mr JUSICE CHARLES: What?

A. He took the truck some place first, and then he took me home.

Mr CASSWELL: I am very sorry; I can't hear that. I know it is difficult for you, but try and make it a little louder, would you?

A. He took the truck some place and then he took me home. He hid the truck round by Ravenscourt Park.

Mr JUSTICE CHARLES: He took the truck away and then he came back to your house?

A. Yes.

Q. Did he sleep with you? A. He did not sleep in bed with me.

Mr CASSWELL: Were you prepared to allow him to be intimate with you?

A. There was nothing of that.

Q. How long did he remain in your room?

A. Until the afternoon, about three o'clock.

Mr JUSTICE CHARLES: Wait a minute. 'He stayed in my room till three pm the next day'?

Mr CASSWELL: That would be Friday, my lord; it would be the same day that he brought her back. He brought her back in the early hours of the morning, your Lordship will remember. (To the witness) Then did he send you on some errand?

A. He gave me a cloakroom ticket and told me to go down to the Metropolitan station and get a B4 bag for him.

Q. Did he show you anything else besides this revolver - not revolver, pistol?

A. After I got the bag for him he brought out two daggers.

Q. As you got out of bed, do you say?

A. After I got the bag from the station for him.

Mr JUSTICE CHARLES: What did he show you?

A. Two daggers.

Q. How long were you away getting the bag?

A. About half an hour.

Q. You saw hundreds of people?

A. Yes.

Q. To any of whom you could have complained of your terrified state?

A. He told me before I went out that he had got two people watching me.

Mr CASSWELL: Did you believe him when he said you were being watched?

A. Yes.

Q. Where did these daggers come from?

A. From the bag I brought from the station.

Q. Did he say anything about them?

A. He had hold of the blade and he showed me how he used them.

Q. When he was in the house with you, did he let you leave the room without him?

A. No.

Q. What did he do?

A. He always followed me about.

Mr JUSTICE CHARLES: He what?

A. He always followed me about.

Q. He did not follow you about when you went away to get the bag, when you were away half an hour?

A. No.

Mr CASSWELL: You told my lord and the jury that you went and fetched his bag from Hammersmith station?

A. Yes.

Q. What happened after that? I mean, did he stay with you or did he go out?

A. He went out.

Q. At what time did he return? Before I come to that, did he tell you what you were to do while he was out?

A. He warned me not to go out. He told me I was to stay in. He said people were watching the house.

Q. At what time did you see him next; that was on Friday, you know, 6th October?

A. I think he said he would call back for me at nine-thirty.

Q. At nine-thirty, you think. Do you remember how he let you know that he was there?

A. Yes.

Q. How?

A. About half past eleven I heard some whistling.

Q. Do you still say it was nine-thirty?

A. No, it was about half past eleven.

Q. He let you know he was there by whistling. Did you go downstairs to him?

A. Yes.

Q. Did he tell you what he wanted to do then? In the first place, had he got a truck or any sort of vehicle with him then?

A. No.

Q. Did he tell you anything about what he wanted to do, or tell you to do it?

A. He said, 'We will get a cab.'

Q. He said you would take a cab?

A. Yes.

Q. Did you take a cab at first, or did you walk?

A. We walked.

Q. How far?

A. Until we got to Hammersmith Road, about the middle of Hammersmith Road.

Q. What sort of a night was it, do you remember?

A. It was light, I believe. I think it was a light night.

Q. Having got as far as the middle of Hammersmith Road, somewhere down Hammersmith Road, what happened? Did you go on walking or what?

A. We stopped in a shop doorway.

Q. Did you want to go on walking with him?

A.   We just stopped and I didn't question him.

Q.   I beg your pardon. I could not hear that.

A.   We just stopped and I didn't question him.

Mr JUSTICE CHARLES: You stopped in a doorway. What time of night was it then?

A.   About twelve o'clock.

Q.   About twelve o'clock midnight and you stopped in a doorway? What counsel asked you was what did you do?

A.   Ricky said to me, 'Call a taxi.'

Mr CASSWELL: He told you to call a taxi, did he?

A.   Yes.

Q.   What did you do?

A.   I called several taxis but they did not stop.

Q.   Did you stop any cars?

A.   There was a car coming along the road from Hammersmith Broadway and I called 'Taxi,' and it stopped and Ricky told me to go over and see if it was a private car - I beg your pardon, see if it was a taxi.

Mr JUSTICE CHARLES: What?

A.   Ricky told me to go over and see if it was a taxi.

Q.   A car stopped. Do you say you went over to see if it was a taxi?

A.   Yes, my lord.

Q.   What did you want a taxi for?

A.   I don't know.

Mr CASSWELL: He did not tell you why he wanted a taxi?

A. No, sir.

Q. Did you ask him?

A. No, sir.

Mr JUSTICE CHARLES: Did you know where you were going?

A. No, sir.

Mr CASSWELL: Was that a taxi, the one you stopped or not?

A. It was a private car.

Q. The one we have been hearing about, or some other car?

A. The one you have been hearing about.

Q. The one that was driven by the man we now know was Heath?

A. Yes.

Q. That was not a taxi car, was it?

A. It was a private hire car.

Q. Did Heath tell you it was a private hire?

A. Yes.

Q. Did he say anything more? What did you do then?

A. He said, 'Where do you want to go to?' so I went back and…

Q. You didn't know where you wanted to go?

A. No.

Q. You went back to Hulten, did you?

A. Yes.

Q. Did he then go with you and speak to Heath?

A. I told him it was a private hire car and he said to me, 'How many people in it?' and I said, ' One.'

Q. Then did he go with you to speak to the driver of that car? A. Yes.

Q. What did Hulten say to him?

A. He said, 'Are you a taxi?' and the driver said, 'I am private hire,' and he said, 'Where did you want to go to?' so Ricky said, 'To the top of King Street.'

Q. That was where you lived, wasn't it, in King Street?

A. Yes.

Q. Did he tell you then what he intended to do with the taxi?

A. Pardon?

Q. Did Hulten tell you then where he intended to drive with the taxi? He told the taxi driver the top of King Street, I understand?

A. Yes.

Q. Did he tell you anything different?

A. No.

Q. Was anything said about what the fare would be?

A. Yes.

Q. What was that?

A. The driver said, 'It will cost you ten shillings.'

Q. Had you money on you enough to pay for that, if necessary, or not?

A. Yes.

Mr JUSTICE CHARLES: How much had you got?

A. Ten and three pence.

Q. Do you know what he had got?

A. About nineteen shillings.

Mr CASSWELL: And so you two got into the car and drove off, did you?

A. Yes.

Q. Did you then know what Hulten intended to do?

A. I thought we were going home.

Q. Did the drive take you along King Street or across the end of it, or what?

A. We went up King Street.

Q. You had to go along King Street?

A. Yes.

Q. Did it go past your lodging?

A. Yes.

Q. But it did not stop there?

A. No.

Q. Did you then ask Hulten what he was doing?

A. No.

Q. What happened?

Mr JUSTICE CHARLES: Did you say you thought you were going home?

A. Yes.

Q. When he passed your door, didn't you say to him, 'Here is my door; you know it; you have been there; why don't we stop?'

A. I was afraid to question him, my lord.

Mr CASSWELL: What about the driver? The driver has been told to go to the end of King Street, I understand and here you were going past King Street. Did he say anything about it?

A. He said, 'We have passed King Street,' and Ricky said we had not come to the place where he wanted to go. The driver got very cross and said it would cost him more and Ricky said, 'I don't mind.'

Q. Just go on. What happened as you went along there? The driver drove on, I suppose?

A. Yes.

Q. What is the next thing that happened?

A. The driver said, 'This is the Great West Road,' so Ricky told him to drive slowly.

Q. Yes.

A. As we passed the roundabout we drove on for about fifty yards and then Ricky said he wanted to get out there, so the driver stopped. Before the car stopped…

Q. One moment; before you get there, I want to ask you this: During that drive in the taxi from where you started to that point, had Hulten told you what he intended to do?

A. No.

Q. Had he told you why you were driving past your home?

A. No.

Q. During that evening, had he produced that revolver at all?

A. As we were driving along, just as we got past the roundabout, I heard a click and when I looked over to Ricky…

Q. Yes, that is just where you had got to the roundabout, or past the roundabout, but up to that time had he been flashing his revolver about at all?

A. No, only in the afternoon before he left.

Q. Now let us continue the journey. You had got to the place where Hulten had told the driver to slow down. That was where he wanted to get out. What happened then?

Mr JUSTICE CHARLES: She says the driver stopped.

Mr CASSWELL: If your Lordship pleases. (To the witness) What happened then?

A. Before the driver stopped I heard a click and when I looked towards Ricky, I saw he had the gun in his right hand. Then the car stopped and the driver put his hand over the back of the seat to open the door for me to get out.

Q. I have not asked you which side where you were sitting, the near side or the off?

A. I was sitting on the left hand side.

Q. The near side of the car?

Mr JUSTICE CHARLES: Well, go on.

A. Just as I was about to get out of the car I heard a shot and saw a flash and the shot deafened my ear for a few minutes and then I saw Ricky standing. Ricky had opened the door of the driver's seat and he was standing there with the gun in his hand.

Mr CASSWELL: It is very necessary that we should get what she said after that.

Mr JUSTICE CHARLES: It is very difficult. Will you speak up? You say that you heard a shot and saw a flash?

A. Yes.

Q. Then what after that? It is my fault, I dare say, but I could not catch what you said.

A. It deafened my right ear for a few minutes. Yes, I got that.

A. And then I saw Ricky standing at the front door of the car, with the gun in his hand.

Q. Yes.

A. He said to the driver, 'Move over or I will give you another dose of the same.'

Mr CASSWELL: Did the driver move over?

A. Yes.

Mr JUSTICE CHARLES: He was alive then?

A. Yes, sir.

Q. Then what happened?

A. Ricky got in the driving seat and he said to me, 'Go through his pockets.'

Mr CASSWELL: Were you willing to do that?

A. I did not do it.

Q. What happened then?

A. So Ricky picked up the revolver that was lying on the seat and said, 'You heard what I said. I can easy do the same to you.'

Mr CASSWELL: I didn't catch that.

Mr JUSTICE CHARLES: 'Ricky took up the revolver and said, 'You heard what I said; I will do the same to you.' I think that is right, isn't it?

A. He said if I did not he would do the same to me. He said if I did not search his pockets he would do the same to me.

Mr CASSWELL: What was Ricky's condition, as far as you could see then - was he calm and collected, or what?

A. He was very touchy.

Q. He seemed to be on edge, did he?

A. Yes.

Q. Did you go through Heath's pockets?

A. Yes.

Q. And take out the things which you mentioned in your statement?

A. Yes.

Q. Did you notice anything about the driver Heath then?

A. He was breathing very heavily.

Mr JUSTICE CHARLES: While you were searching him?

A. Yes.

Mr CASSWELL: Did you say anything to Hulten about it?

A. No, sir, I don't think so.

Q. After a time did Heath stop breathing altogether, as far as you could see?

A. Yes.

Q. Did you say anything to Ricky then about it?

A. I don't think so.

Q. Meanwhile what was happening? Was the car being driven on?

A. Yes.

A FATAL PICKUP

Q. What happened next?

A. We were driving along the road and then Ricky drove off the road and he drove for a few minutes on to a sort of common and then he stopped the car and got out.

Q. When he got out what happened then?

A. He opened the left-hand front door and dragged the body out of the car.

Q. What were you doing all this time?

A. I was sitting in the back of the car.

Q. Did you help him at all to carry the body from the car?

A. No.

Q. You are sure of that?

A. Yes.

Q. What happened after he had taken the body out of the car?

A. He rolled it into a ditch.

Q. Did he drive away at once, or wait for any time?

A. He asked me for a handkerchief and I gave him the one which was in the man's pocket.

Q. Yes, and what then?

A. He said he had blood on his hands. Then he told me to get into the front of the car.

Q. He told you to get into the front?

A. Yes.

Q. In which seat, the driver's seat or the other?

A. No, the other seat and he got in the driving seat and back on to the road.

Q. Did you then come back towards London?

A. Yes.

Q. Did he continue to drive all the way, or did he get you to drive part of the way?

A. I drove part of the way.

Q. What was the behaviour of Ricky coming back? What was his manner? Did he seem to have regained his calm, or not?

A. No.

Q. What was his manner?

A. He was still very touchy.

Q. How far did you get? How far did you drive back?

A. Just before we got to the roundabout.

Q. You pulled up at the roundabout - did anyone throw anything out of the window on the way?

A. Yes, Ricky threw all the man's papers out of the window on the way.

Q. Was that while you were driving or while he was driving?

A. While I was - I am not sure.

Q. I don't want to go into this at length, but you got back. Where did you come to the end of this journey? Where was the car put, for instance?

A. I didn't get what you said then.

Q. All I wanted to know was what place did you reach at the end of this journey when you came back to London. Did you come back to Hammersmith?

A. Yes.

Q. Where did you stop?

Mr JUSTICE CHARLES: Where did you stop when you came back after this occurrence?

A. We drove the car into Sussex Place, the old garage.

Mr CASSWELL: Where did you go from there?

A. We went into a milk bar.

Q. Did you then go back to your home, to your room?

A. Yes.

Q. Did Hulten come with you?

A. Yes.

Q. What was your state of mind then?

A. I was terrified and I was dazed: I just couldn't believe it had happened.

Q. Did you sleep that night?

A. No.

Mr JUSTICE CHARLES: Where did Hulten go?

A. He came back with me.

Q. But where did he sleep?

A. He did not sleep either.

Q. What?

A. We sat up.

Q. You sat up together, did you?

A. Yes.

Mr CASSWELL: Did you say anything to him about what had happened to Heath, when you got back there?

A. Yes.

Q. I want you to tell the jury, and tell them so that they can hear, what was said then.

A. I said, 'The man is dead, isn't he?'

Mr JUSTICE CHARLES: You knew, didn't you? He had been pulled out and dumped into the ditch?

A. Yes.

Q. You knew he was dead quite well, didn't you?

A. Yes.

Mr CASSWELL: And at any rate the question I was asking you was, what you said to Ricky.

Mr JUSTICE CHARLES: She said, 'The man is dead, isn't he?'

A. Yes.

Mr CASSWELL: This is what I wanted to know. What did he say as a result of that?

A. He said, 'Yes'.

Q. You said what?

A. I said 'That is cold-blooded murder. How could you do it?' and he said, 'People in my profession are used to things like that.'

Q. You have told us how he let off this revolver in a closed car. Had you heard him let off this revolver before? Had you ever heard it fired?

A. No.

Q. What happened on that morning - this was, I suppose early in the morning of Saturday 7th October, wasn't it?

A. Yes.

A FATAL PICKUP

Q. What happened during that day? How long did he stay with you?

A. Till about ten to eleven.

Q. Did you talk to him at all during that time and mention this murder again? Did he say anything to you about it?

A. I don't think so.

Q. Was it worrying you?

A. Yes.

Q. Did you say anything to him?

A. He wouldn't let me smoke. He said that would make me nervous.

Q. Did you tell him you were worried?

A. Yes.

Q. What did he say to you?

A. He told me to forget it.

Q. Did he say anything about people who informed against him?

A. Yes.

Q. What did he say?

A. He said he always got them first and asked questions after.

Q. You say he went out during the morning. Did you say at ten-thirty or eleven? I didn't quite catch.

A. About ten to eleven.

Q. Did he tell you where he was going?

A. He said he was going to the barber's shop.

Q. Did he tell you what you were to do while he was out?

A. He told me I was to stay in.

Q. When did he come back again?

A. He came back at a quarter to two.

Q. Did he tell you where he had been?

A. No.

Q. Was anyone with him when he came back?

A. Yes.

Q. Who?

A. Leonard Bexley.

Q. When he went out on that morning - I ought to have asked you this - did he take anything with him?

A. Yes, he took all George Heath's belongings.

Q. Lenny, as you call him, told us the three of you went to the dog races. Is that right?

A. Yes.

Q. Did you have any bets on the dogs?

A. Yes.

Q. Did you make any money?

A. Yes.

Q. How much?

A. About seven pounds.

Q. What time did you leave?

A. After it was finished.

Q. Can you tell us at all what time it was it did finish?

A. About four to half past.

Q. Where did you go from there? Did you go back to your lodgings or not?

A. No.

Q. Where did you go?

A. We went down to Hammersmith Broadway and we left Lenny; then we got on the Underground and went up to Victoria.

Mr JUSTICE CHARLES: Underground to where?

A. Victoria.

Mr CASSWELL: Was Lenny with you all the time, or when did he go?

A. He left us at Hammersmith Broadway.

Q. After the dogs, was it?

A. Yes.

Mr JUSTICE CHARLES: You went on then with Hulten alone?

A. Yes.

Q. Walking?

A. We got on the Underground.

Q. Then you got out at the Underground and you went where?

A. Went and had something to eat.

Q. What?

A. We went and had a meal.

Mr CASSWELL: After that, did you go anywhere?

A. We went to a cinema.

Q. Do you remember what you saw?

Mr JUSTICE CHARLES: This is all with a man you knew had murdered somebody?

A. Yes.

Mr CASSWELL: Did you go to your lodgings at all that day, that afternoon? Mrs Evans has told us that you deposited seven pounds with her and she says it was on Saturday afternoon.

A. No.

Mr JUSTICE CHARLES: Did you deposit anything with her?

A. On the Sunday morning.

Mr CASSWELL: We will come to that. That night, what happened after you had been to the pictures? Did Ricky see you home or not?

A. Yes.

Q. Did he stay with you that night?

A. No.

Q. Did he give you any instructions when he left you that night?

A. He had told me he had put men to watch me.

Q. He told you not to leave?

A. Yes.

Mr JUSTICE CHARLES: 'He told me he had put men to watch me.'

Mr CASSWELL: So you stayed at home that night did you? What did you do during Sunday? Did you see him at all?

A. I didn't see him until the night; I don't think I saw him till the night.

Q. Let us go through Sunday. You told us just now that on Sunday you gave seven pounds to your landlady?

A. Yes.

Q. At what time was that, do you remember?

A. Just before lunch.

Q. Did you have lunch with her in the house?

A. Yes.

Q. She told us that on weekdays she was out all day. Did you ever have lunch with her on weekdays?

A. No.

Q. When you gave her the seven pounds, was it in her own room that you gave her that?

A. Yes.

Q. To look after?

A. Yes.

Q. Does that help you at all to remember how soon that day, on Sunday, you saw Ricky again? Does that remind you at all?

A. I think I saw him that night.

Q. Did you go out with him again that night?

A. Yes.

Q. Why did you do that?

A. Because he asked me to.

Q. Did he come back with you and stay with you that night, or not?

A. Yes.

Q. Did you see somebody else and tell them about this?

A. Yes.

Q. When was that? Which night was that?

A. Sunday night.

Q. How did you come to see him?

A. I had no cigarettes, so I took a chance and went down to Hammersmith Broadway.

Q. What do you mean by 'took a chance'?

A. I knew somebody would be following me.

Q. Took a chance of who was watching you?

A. Yes.

Q. You went down to Hammersmith Broadway. Where did you go?

A. I went to a milk bar, but they did not have any cigarettes.

Q. Since you could not get any cigarettes in the milk bar, did you go somewhere else?

A. I crossed the street and I saw an Air Force man going into a public house. I gave him some money and asked him if he would get me twenty Players.

Q. Was he an officer?

A. No.

Q. An airman?

A. Yes.

Q. You asked him to go in and get some for you. Did he manage to do that?

A. No.

Q. Did you go anywhere else with him?

A. Yes, he said he would take me across the road to another public house and see if he could get some for me there. Then he asked me to go in and have a drink.

Q. I think you had a drink with him at another public house and then did you have a conversation with him?

A. Yes.

Q. What did you tell him?

A. I told him I knew the man who had done the murder.

Q. Did you give him a description of what happened? Did you tell him in any detail of what had happened on the Friday night?

A. I told him I was in a car when Ricky shot him.

Q. Why did you tell him that?

A. I felt I had to tell somebody.

Q. Did you hope that he would tell somebody else, or not?

A. Yes.

Q. Did you ask his advice as to what to do?

A. He ask me if I wanted to go to the police and I told him I didn't know what I wanted him to do.

Q. Did he give you his address?

A. Yes.

Q. Did he write it down, or did you - do you remember?

A. I don't remember.

Q. I think you handed that to the police?

A. Yes.

Q. As he was going out, did you meet anybody else? I had forgotten this. Did you meet anybody else when the airman was leaving your room or when he was there?

A. Well, I heard a whistle and I went downstairs and It was Ricky.

Q. Now we get to the time when you saw Ricky on Sunday. About what time was it?

A. About eleven o'clock, I think.

Q. Late at night?

A. Yes.

Q. And Ricky was coming in, and this Air Force man was there at the time, was he?

A. Yes.

Q. What happened, quite briefly?

A. He asked me who I had got in my room and I told him that he was a friend of my people. I said my people had sent him up from Wales, but I don't think he believed me. Then I took him upstairs and I said to the Air Force man - Ricky waited outside - I said to him, 'I will introduce you to Ricky.' I told him that he was the man who had shot George Heath.

Q. You told the Air Force man but not in front of Ricky, I suppose, not whilst Ricky could hear?

A. Yes.

Q. You told the Air Force man that Ricky was the man who had shot Heath?

A. Yes.

Q. Did the Air Force man then leave?

A. I introduced them to each other.

Q. Ricky stayed, did he?

A. Yes.

Q. I am sorry, it is my mistake. I got that in the wrong place. Then Ricky and you went out and you have told us what happened after that. When did you last see Ricky?

A FATAL PICKUP

A. On the Monday.

Q. Had he made any further arrangement to meet you?

A. Yes. He said he would come back at five o'clock, or five thirty.

Q. And you did not see him from that time onwards, I think?

A. No.

Q. Now, you have heard Mr Kimberley give his evidence. That was the police officer, you know. Had you met Mr Kimberley before?

A. Yes.

Q. When you were in the café?

A. Yes.

Q. I don't think we have got much to complain of, but Mr Kimberley says that you told him you had been a bad girl, when he remarked that you were looking ill and very changed. Did you tell him you had been a bad girl?

A. Yes.

Q. Had you in fact been a bad girl in the way he took it?

A. No.

Q. What had you been doing?

A. I had been drinking more than a girl of my age should have.

Q. Mr Kimberley agreed with me that you had been living an artificial life and dancing in cabarets. You told him that, did you?

A. Yes.

Q. Was anything else said to Mr Kimberley that you remember?

A. I told him that I had been over at the police station.

Q. At the time, had you been talking to anybody about this case that afternoon?

A. No, only the police.

Q. You had been to the police that morning and made a statement?

A. Yes.

Q. We heard about the newspaper. When did you get the newspaper?

A. I got the newspaper after I had been in the café.

Q. From the police - they told us you left them about half past two - you went to a café, did you?

A. Yes.

Q. And in the café did you see somebody you knew?

A. I saw Leonard Bexley and his daughter.

Q. Did she tell you something about this case?

A. Yes. She told me that they had got Ricky inside.

Q. She knew Ricky of course?

A. Yes.

Q. Was that the first time you knew that Ricky had been arrested?

A. Yes.

Q. Then after that you told me you got the newspaper?

A. Yes.

Q. Had that newspaper got something about it?

A. Yes.

Q. Do you remember what it said - not the actual words but what it told you?

A. It said an American soldier had been arrested on suspicion.

Q. And that was the newspaper, was it, that you showed to Mr Kimberley?

A. Yes.

Mr JUSTICE CHARLES: When was it you went to this café?

A. After I had been to the police station.

Mr CASSWELL: Mr Kimberley came into that same café, did he?

A. No.

Q. Was it another café he told us of?

A. It was a cleaner's shop.

Q. Did you say anything to him before? He told us you said, 'If you had seen someone do what I have seen done, you wouldn't be able to sleep at night'. Was there something you said to him before that which led to that?

A. He said I looked very worried and I told him I had been over to the police station in regard to the murder.

Q. I really can't hear. It is making it very difficult. Would you speak a little louder?

A. He said I was looking very worried and I told him that I had been over to the police station regarding the murder.

Q. Wasn't there something more that you said that led to this - about if you had seen someone do what I had seen done you wouldn't be able to sleep at night?

A. I told him I knew the man they had got inside.

Q. Then Mr Kimberley has told us how he came round with Inspector Tansill afterwards and you went to the police station. Did you realise that in the whole of that statement you had not said anything about your own feelings and had not said you were frightened and so on?

A. I just gave the police the facts; that was all.

Mr JUSTICE CHARLES: Now the greater part of your evidence is that step by step you were terrified, dazed, frightened, ordered to do this, ordered to do that. Why didn't you say a word of that to the police?

A. Because I didn't think it concerned me, that I would be drawn into it.

Q. You didn't think it concerned you? Why do you think it concerns you today?

A. Because it has all been explained to me now.

Mr CASSWELL: At that time you did not think they were enquiring about your being guilty in any way, I understand?

A. No.

Q. Later on, we know that you wrote that letter and although we were told in the first place it was written on the 30th October, it appears it was written on the 26th. Do you remember writing that letter from Holloway Prison?

A. Yes.

Q. I want you to throw your mind back. Had you been speaking to your solicitor before you wrote that letter or not?

A. No.

Q. You are perfectly sure about that?

A. Positive.

Q. Did you know, until a solicitor came to see you, who had been allotted to you as a solicitor?

A. No.

Q. I see in this letter you say, 'I should be very pleased and feel very much relieved if you would be so kind as come along to Holloway Prison to see me and let me tell you all which I have not yet told you. I am having legal aid but I want to tell you as well as the solicitor.' Did you mean by that you had not seen the solicitor yet, when you said, 'I am having legal aid'?

A. Yes.

Q. You had not yet got a solicitor. You had not yet seen him?

A. No.

Q. Mrs Jones, when you went on that journey that evening in Heath's car, did you know that Hulten intended to rob the driver?

A. After we drove past my house I thought I knew he was going to do something.

Mr JUSTICE CHARLES: The question is a simple one, which your counsel asks you and you don't answer. When you went on that journey did you know that Hulten meant to rob the driver?

A. No, sir.

Q. You say you knew he meant to do something. What did you think he was going to do?

A. I thought he was going to rob the man after we passed our house.

Q. What?

A. When we got past our house I thought then he was going to do something.

Q. What?

A. Perhaps rob the cabman.

Mr CASSWELL: Were you prepared to help him do that?

A. No, sir.

Q. Did he ask you to help him or give you any instructions as to what you were to do?

A. No.

Mr JUSTICE CHARLES: I think tomorrow morning Mr Maude, don't you? I think tomorrow morning would be more convenient than now.

Mr MAUDE: Yes, My Lord.

Adjourned till tomorrow morning at eleven o'clock.

CHAPTER NINE

THE TRIAL - FOURTH DAY

FRIDAY 19TH JANUARY 1945

Mr MAUDE Defence HULTEN cross-examined ELIZABETH MARINA JONES.

Mr JUSTICE CHARLES: You may sit down if you wish. I know you will speak up if you can, won't you, it is very difficult for those gentlemen to hear down there, more difficult than it is for me to hear; and of course, the members of the jury are the people who want to hear you most.

Mr MAUDE: Mrs Jones, I am going to ask you a lot of questions. Will you take your time in answering, all the time you want and if you don't understand anything, tell me? The whole of your acquaintance with Hulten up to the time of Heath's death was something like four whole days and some of them nights, that is to say, Tuesday 3rd, Wednesday and Thursday - that's right isn't it? - Tuesday, Wednesday, Thursday the 5th and Friday the 6th?

A. I didn't see him on the Wednesday.

Q. You didn't see him at all on the Wednesday?

A. No.

Q. You remember telling my lord yesterday that there had been nothing of a sexual nature between you?

A. Yes.

Q. I am not going to suggest that it is untrue; that is true isn't it?

A. Yes.

Q. The reason is this, isn't it; that, when you first met him, you told him that you had a rash on your body?

A. No.

Q. Had you got a rash on your body?

A. Yes.

Q. How could he know, if you hadn't told him?

A. I didn't tell him.

Q. Can you think of any way in which he could get to know that?

A. He was there one night when I undressed.

Q. May I suggest how he knew? You told him, did you not, that the reason why you had given up striptease dancing was because of the rash?

A. No.

Q. Did you give up striptease dancing because of the rash?

A. I had a very bad cold.

Q. Did the rash have something to do with it?

A. No.

Q. When did you develop the rash?

A. On the Saturday night, I believe.

Q. What Saturday are you speaking of? How long before you met him?

A. It was after I met him.

Q. After you met him?

A. Yes.

Q. The rash didn't develop until after you met him?

A. No.

Q. On a Saturday night?

A. I don't think so.

Q. That won't do, will it; it wouldn't be till Saturday the 7th?

A. Yes.

Q. Will you just think again? Am I not right in suggesting to you that you have had it for some time and told him about it when you first met him?

A. No.

Q. You told my lord there had only been one man. Do you remember that, yesterday?

A. Yes.

Q. Whom were you speaking of? Not Hulten?

A. No.

Q. Not your husband?

A. No.

Q. Tell me, as your imagination is concerned, are you a girl who likes to imagine stories about yourself?

A. No.

Q. Have you had an idea at any time that somebody had had connection with you and then said afterwards it was wrong?

A. I don't understand you, sir.

Q. Don't you understand that?

A. No.

Q. Let me put it a little plainer. You haven't at any time told somebody that a man had had sexual intercourse with you and then later said you made a mistake?

A. No.

Q. Never something like that?

A. Not that I know of.

Q. Not some years ago?

A. Yes.

Q. That had been pure imagination, hadn't it?

A. No.

Q. What I put to you was correct, that you had said that somebody had; and then you had withdrawn it completely afterwards, hadn't you?

A. When I was thirteen and a half, a man had tried.

Q. You are saying he tried?

A. That was all.

Q. I suppose you told the police?

A. Yes.

Q. And later you told the police that that was quite wrong?

A. No.

Q. Have I got the form of words wrong? You withdrew the whole story, didn't you?

A. No.

Q. Did you persist in it? Are you swearing that?

A. Yes.

Q. Having given up the striptease dancing, there you were for something like five months living on this Army allowance

A. Yes, and money I had saved.

Q. Let us go to your landlady, Mrs Evans, do you remember the lady with the black conical hat?

A. Yes.

Q. She seemed a nice, kind woman. Was she? Did she treat you well or not?

A. I didn't have very much to do with her.

Q. I was thinking of one particular instance. Do you remember she was telling my lord and the jury about how you had told her that you had met an American, in a café, do you remember telling her that?

A. Yes.

Q. And you said you thought he was a deserter?

A. I did not say that.

Q. What did you say to her, because we have heard, what did you say?

A. I told her I had got introduced to an American officer by a friend of mine and that I was going out with him that night. I told her he appeared to me to be a gentleman.

Q. He appeared to you to be what?

A. A gentleman.

Q. What else did you tell her?

A. I told her I was going out with him that night at 11.30.

Q. Then she is quite mistaken - let us put it that way - in saying that you said you thought he was a deserter?

A. Yes.

Q. Or thought there was something fishy about him?

A. Yes.

Q. Did you say that?

A. No.

Q. Nothing like that?

A. No.

Q. Did Mrs Evans say she thought it was foolish to go to Hammersmith Broadway at night?

A. Yes.

Q. What did you say to that?

A. I said if he didn't seem to me to be a gentleman, I would not go out with him.

Q. How did she take that? I suggest you know that is quite untrue what happened between you and Mrs Evans?

A. No, it is quite true.

Q. Didn't she say something to you about you might have your throat cut?

A. Yes.

Q. There would not be any reason, would there for her to think that, if you had said you were going out with an American officer who was a gentleman?

A. I don't think she likes Americans.

Q. You don't think she likes them?

A. No.

Q. But didn't you hear what she said about Hulten when she saw him? She said, 'I thought him a very decent fellow'?

A. Yes.

Q. She didn't seem to mind him?

A. That was after I introduced him.

Q. Certainly. She was not rude to him, was she?

A. No.

Q. Half past eleven was the time that you were to meet him on the 3rd, that was the first night?

A. Yes.

Q What were you to do?

A. Go for a ride with him.

Q. If you start at half past eleven at night, how long were you to go riding with him?

A. I didn't ask him.

Q. You didn't ask him?

A. No.

Q. It wasn't a motorcar in the ordinary sense was it?

A. No.

Q. It was a truck?

A. Yes.

Q. Weren't you surprised when you found that an officer was going to take you round in a truck?

A. Yes.

Q. A great big truck?

A. Yes.

Q. Did you think there was anything odd then about it? What do you think? Can you just try and recall what you were thinking when you found you had been picked up by an officer at half past eleven at night with a ten-wheeled truck?

A. American officers, if they want a Jeep or truck, they usually managed to get it.

Mr JUSTICE CHARLES: What? I am afraid I didn't catch that.

A. American officers, if they want a Jeep or a truck, they usually manage to get it.

Mr MAUDE: You have not had experience, have you, of them turning up to take a girl out with a ten-wheeled truck?

A. No.

Mr JUSTICE CHARLES: At 11.30 at night?

A. No.

Mr MAUDE: Was he nice to you?

A. Yes.

Q. Right up to the very end, I am suggesting he was very nice to you?

A. No.

Q. But you went to the cinema with him; that was on the 7th; the very afternoon after Heath had met his death, you went to the cinema together, didn't you? You remember the name of the film?

A. Yes.

A FATAL PICKUP

Q. What was it?

A. 'Christmas Holiday.'

Q. Who was in it?

A. Deanna Durbin.

Q. Do you remember what it was about?

A. Yes.

Q. What else was there on the programme, do you remember?

A. I believe we only saw the one big picture.

Q. How were you sitting in the cinema; just you two alone, or was Lenny or somebody else there?

A. No.

Q. Did you sit with your head on his shoulder?

A. No.

Q. Did you hold hands at all?

A. Ricky had his arm in mine.

Q. And you had a bunch of flowers, hadn't you?

A. A spray of flowers.

Q. Were you wearing them?

A. Ricky pinned them on my coat.

Q. Is the court to understand that, sitting there in the cinema in that way, you were terrified of the man?

A. Ricky reminded before we went into the cinema that he still had his gun on him and it was loaded.

Q. I dare say; that may well be true. But what I am asking is: are you telling my lord and the jury that you were terrified of him?

A. Yes.

Q. It must then have been a very great relief to see Mr Tarr and the other police officers?

A. The first time I saw Mr Tarr and the other police officers I didn't know they had got Ricky.

Q. Let me just persist in what I was asking you: was it a great relief to see Mr Tarr privately?

A. Yes.

Q. Why?

A. I was glad that they had found out.

Q. And as you sat there with them - we are talking now of the morning, because they saw you twice on the 11th October - they saw you in the morning, then you went away and you came back - when you sat there in the morning, you sat with them for quite a long time, half an hour, something like that?

A. It was about two hours, I believe.

Q. Two hours the first time?

A. I think so.

Q. And Mr Tarr, was he kind to you?

A. Yes.

Q. No bullying?

A. No.

Q. No shouting?

A. No.

Q. How about the other gentleman who were there, the other police officers; how did they behave?

A. They were also very kind.

Q. Quite kind to you?

A. Very kind.

Q. And you knew, of course, what they were?

A. Yes.

Q. You knew they were policemen?

A. Yes.

Q. You knew they were detectives; did you think they were from Scotland Yard?

A. I think they told me so.

Q. You could hardly have been anywhere safer, could you?

A. No.

Q. Then why didn't you tell them that you thought you were being watched?

A. I was afraid, if they let me go – because I didn't know they had got Ricky – that Ricky may do something to me.

Mr JUSTICE CHARLES: What?

A. I was afraid that, if they let me go, if I saw Ricky after, that he would do something to me.

Mr MAUDE: You mean, as I understand it, if you were allowed to walk away, at any rate just temporarily, to get out from where they were, that something might happen to you?

A. Yes.

Q. Why did you not tell them?

A. That was the reason.

Q. But why not say, 'Do you realise I am in danger of my life?' or words something like that?

A. At the time I didn't think.

Q. Didn't think?

A. No.

Q. I am suggesting to you that, if your story was true, it would be the only thing you would be thinking about practically, that you might be killed when you got outside. What do you say?

A. I didn't know they had got Ricky.

Q. You didn't know, but you were anxious as to where he was, weren't you?

A. Yes.

Q. Then why didn't you ask the police?

A. I was afraid to ask them.

Q. Afraid to ask them if they had got him?

A. Yes.

Mr JUSTICE CHARLES: But why? Here you were in the midst of Scotland Yard detectives, you knew they were Scotland Yard detectives and if you thought you were in danger of your life from Hulten, why didn't you say, 'Have you got Hulten yet?' And, if you didn't say that, why didn't you say, 'He has threatened me; he says he is having me watched and I am afraid that he is going to do me some harm'? They were there to give you protection. Why didn't you tell them, if it is true?

(The witness did not reply.)

Mr MAUDE: Well, I did not want to hurry you about that, but if there is an answer to that, let me have it. Now let us think what happened. You were released - when I say 'released', of course you went away - and what time was it that you were again with the policemen that day on the 11th?

A. About six o'clock.

Q. Then following on that, they started to take that very long statement from you?

A. Yes.

Q. You knew, of course, then that you had not told them the whole truth?

A. Yes.

Q. Something had made you change your mind, hadn't it? Something had made you change your mind and decide to tell the whole truth?

A. Yes.

Q. What was that?

A. After I left the police station I went into the same café where I was introduced to Ricky and the waitress told me that they had got Ricky in custody.

Q. A waitress told you that they had got Ricky: is that right?

A. Yes.

Q. And you believed it, did you?

A. Yes.

Q. Just take that letter in your hand, will you? Is that the letter that you wrote to the police, do you remember, asking them to come and see you?

A. Yes.

Q. I just want to read it with you; it is quite short. It is written apparently on the 26th October; at any rate that is the date?

A. Yes.

Q. I don't know if that is the date the prison people put on when they handed you the piece of paper, or whether it was the date you wrote it?

A. The day I wrote it.

Q. The day you wrote it, the 26th. Just look at the second paragraph first, the one starting, 'You see sir'. Do you see that?

A. Yes.

Q. 'You see sir, now I definitely know that Ricky is in safe hands, where he cannot get out, I can tell you absolutely all the facts. One fact that is especially important, to me and also to you.' In fact you had seen them twice on the 11th and before you saw them for the second time, you knew that he was arrested?

A. Yes.

Q. I am suggesting that is humbug, that second paragraph?

A. I don't understand you sir.

Q. Let me see if we can explain it. What do you mean by 'You see, sir, now I definitely know that Ricky is in safe hands'? That is on the 26th. You knew it on the 11th?

A. Yes.

Q. I will try and put it in very simple language. What had happened was that by the 26th you had decided to try and put all the blame, the whole of the blame, for this on to the man?

A. No.

Q. Well, that is surely true, that by the 26th you had decided to put all the blame on the man?

A. No.

Q. We must explore that. The whole point of sending for a policeman was to tell him, wasn't it, that you had been terrorised?

A. Yes.

Q. And in telling the policeman that you had been terrorised, that the whole blame should be put upon him, that you had been a frightened child?

A. I was terrified of him.

Q. I dare say, but what was the object of sending for the policeman?

A. To tell them.

Q. That it was fear; you had been a frightened child?

A. I was frightened.

Q. That was the idea, was it not, to explain to the policeman at last how you had been terrorised?

A. Yes.

Q. What I want to ask you again is: why did you say on the 26th, 'You see, sir, now that I definitely know that Ricky is in safe hands'?

Mr JUSTICE CHARLES: You knew on the 11th?

A. Yes.

Mr MAUDE: The reason why, if I may anticipate, the court suggests that to you, is that, having heard it from the waitress or through the waitress between the two police interviews, if you had not believed it, the very first thing you would have asked the policeman, 'Is it true that Ricky has been arrested?'

A. I didn't ask them.

Q. No, because you believed that he had been, didn't you?

A. Yes.

Q. Therefore, when you saw Mr Tarr the second time, there was a great load off your mind of fear, wasn't there?

A. Yes.

Q. Did you try your hardest to tell them everything that had happened?

A. I told them the facts, sir.

Q. I know you told them certain facts; I am not putting it against you as hard as that. For the moment this is what I am asking: you tried your hardest to tell them all that you could remember?

A. Yes.

Q. If you would just look at your second statement. We need only look at the beginning: 'The statement I made to you' - if I read it wrongly, will you correct me, because I have only got a copy?

A. Yes.

Q. 'The statement I made to you this morning is incorrect for the most part and I wish to tell you the whole truth about my association with Ricky Allen. I first met him on Tuesday, 3rd October 1944, in a café in Hammersmith Broadway and I was introduced to him by Lenny, I don't know his last name. He asked me to meet him at 11.30 pm that night to go for a drive. The meeting place was outside the Broadway Cinema'. Just pause there for one moment; it was not to make money out of him, was it? I am not suggesting it, but it wasn't to make money out of him that you went for the drive?

A. No.

Q. What was it for - the thrill?

A. Put it that way.

Q. What did you say?

A. If you like to put it that way.

Q. But do you agree with me? Was it for the thrill?

A. I thought there was no harm in going out with him, because as I said before, he appeared to be a gentleman.

Q. I will just read on. 'I turned up and he was not there. I was on my way home to King Street Hammersmith when I was hailed by a man driving an American lorry. I recognised the voice as being that of Ricky and I got into the truck with him. It was a big truck and had ten wheels. We drove on into Reading.' I am suggesting the very next thing in your statement is the thing that had been worrying you all along. 'I told him in the truck that I would like to do something dangerous.' There is a comma there, and something else comes after it. Pausing there for a moment, how long had you been driving before you told him that? Was it almost at once, or had you gone miles, or what had happened?

A. Just a couple of miles.

Q. Gone a very little distance? Can you remember how you said it to him?

A. I think he asked me what my work was and I told him.

Q. What did you say your work was?

A. I told him I was a striptease dancer.

Q. So then what happened?

A. He said I must have a lot of pluck to go and do that.

Q. He said you must have a lot of pluck, so what did you say to that?

A. Then I told him I should like to do something dangerous.

Q. So did you propose something to that effect: 'Oh, no' - laughing it off, the suggestion that you were a plucky girl - 'What I should like to do is something really dangerous'?

A. Yes.

Q. Is that what happened?

A. Yes.

Q. The statement reads like this, reading the whole statement: 'I told him in the truck I would like to do something dangerous, meaning to go over to Germany in a bomber'?

A. Yes.

Q. It isn't the same thing as saying, 'I told him I should like to do something dangerous.'

Mr JUSTICE CHARLES: Really dangerous. Today she said 'really dangerous'.

Mr MAUDE: Oh, 'really'. It is not the same thing as saying, for instance, 'Go to Germany in a bomber.'

A. You told me you were still on the first page.

Q. Yes, I am on the first page.

A. I was waiting for you.

Q. What is it we have got wrong? Are you still looking at the same sentence? 'I told him in the truck that I would like to do something dangerous'?

A. Yes.

Q. 'Meaning to go over Germany in a bomber'?

A. Yes.

Q. You never said to him, did you, 'I would like to go over Germany in a bomber'?

A. Yes.

Q. That I am suggesting to you, is the reverse of the truth, unless you can tell me what he said. What did he say?

A. I don't follow you sir.

Q. Let me see if you can't understand this. For a girl to say, 'I should like to go over Germany in a bomber' would surely lead to the answer, wouldn't it, 'Well you can't do that'?

A. He didn't say so.

Q. What did he say?

A. I don't recall what he said.

Q. I am suggesting the statement is correct, you see. You did tell him you would like to do something dangerous, but 'meaning to go over Germany in a bomber' is something you had thought of afterwards?

A. I told him that.

Q. Did you say anything else about the dangerous thing you would like to do? A. No, I don't think so.

Q. You must have been trying to think, to remember; you have tried to remember this back, haven't you? A. Yes.

Q. You see, the very next thing you say is: 'I meant that, but he got me wrong'?

A. Yes.

Q. How could that have happened? What could be simpler than saying 'I would like to go over Germany in a bomber'? I heard a comment from my learned friend and I think it is a fair one; I think that is a very difficult question, very involved. Let me make it much more clear. 'I meant that, but he got me wrong.' What was it that he seemed to muddle?

A. I still don't follow.

Q. What you are trying to say, aren't you, in your statement, that from that moment he thought you were some sort of woman criminal?

A. No, I shouldn't say that.

Q. What did you mean by 'He got me wrong'? you meant, clearly, wasn't it, that at that point this apparent gentleman officer took the view that you were a person at least likely to fall in with some dishonesty. Isn't that what you meant?

A. Yes.

Mr JUSTICE CHARLES: 'He thought I was the sort of girl who would fall in with some dishonesty'?

A. Yes.

Mr MAUDE: Did you encourage him in that idea?

A. No.

Q. Did you discourage him? Perhaps you didn't discourage him?

A. The reason why I knew he had got the wrong idea was because he pulled a gun out of his pocket.

Q. That would have been an appalling thing, very frightening?

A. Yes.

Q. What did you do about it? What did you say?

A. I didn't say anything about it.

Q. The mere pulling of a gun out of his pocket, without anything else, after he told you he was a gunman. He told you he was a gunman?

A. Yes.

Q. Have you heard the expression 'gun moll'?

A. No, not before.

Q. Never?

A. Not from him.

Q. No, not from him, but from someone else; had you heard it from someone else?

A. In the books I have read.

Q. And indeed you didn't hear it from him, because it was you who said it to him?

A. I didn't say anything of the sort to him.

Q. What does it mean?

A. Someone who went round...

Q. Who what? Someone who goes armed?

A. Someone who goes round with a man like Ricky and helps him of his own free will.

Q. Did you say 'and helps' something? I am told you added something we didn't hear here. Did you say something more?

A. Someone who goes round with a man like Ricky and who helps him of their own free will.

Q. In his statement, you know, to the police? You remember he said this? We have heard it read, but let me read it again: 'During the course of the conversation she said she would like to do something exciting like becoming a 'gun moll', like they do back in the States. At first I thought she was kidding, but she told me she was serious.' Is that true or not?

A. No.

Q. Very well. When he told you he was a gunman, how did you treat that; what did you say?

A. When he told me he was a gunman, he told me he had been a gunman back in Chicago and was operating a gang in London. He told me he was the leader of a gang.

Q. We are on the way to Reading in the truck?

A. Yes.

Q. On the first ride to Reading. What did you say?

A. I don't think I said anything.

Q. Nothing at all?

A. No.

Mr JUSTICE CHARLES: How far had you gone when that happened?

A. I don't know.

Q. Of course you know; you went all the way down to Reading. You must have spoken to him. After that, what was the next thing that you said after he had told you he was a gunman from Chicago and operating a gang in London and that he was the leader? What was the next thing you said after that? You were going all the way down to Reading, you know?

A. Ricky asked me if I would like to drive.

Mr MAUDE: You see, we are trying to get a picture of a man suddenly disclosing to a woman who has only met him an hour or so that he is a gunman. Didn't you indicate in any way whether you would be likely to give him away, or disapprove, or help?

A. No, he told me without me saying anything to him that if he was suspicious of anybody, he always got that person first and asked questions afterwards.

Q. Was it then that he said that, on the first drive?

A. I think so.

Q. Well, I won't press you about it if you don't remember. Looking back on it, do think you did anything at all to show that it was not quite your line of business?

A. I was too frightened to say anything.

Q. You know what I mean, that it was not the sort of thing that you would help him in. Did you say anything at all, looking back on it, to indicate that?

A. I don't think so.

Q. In addition to that, let us follow up. You see if you did not tell him you would like to be a gun moll and so on, did he ask you whether you had got any experience of crime?

A. No.

Q. Not a word?

A. No.

Q. So the 3rd finishes and I think that was the night wasn't it that you got back in the early hours, it must have been of the 4th? Is that the night - when I say 'night' I mean the hours of darkness - that first night that you were together in the room?

A. No.

Q. You were not, that first night, together?

A. No.

Q. Did he kiss you when he went off?

A. No.

Q. Did he try to?

A. No.

Q. Any appointment made?

A. He told me I was to stay in and not go out until he came for me.

Q. The one thing you did not want was ever to see that man again, wasn't it?

A. Yes.

Q. He had driven you in the truck to your door: is that right?

A. Yes.

Q. And he did not know your address, did he?

A. No.

Q. You gave it to him?

A. He asked for it.

Q. I dare say, but you gave him it and gave him it correctly?

A. Yes.

Q. And he called for you, did he not, according to your statement, on the 5th that same afternoon, because you got in at five in the morning? Hadn't you got into London at five in the morning?

A. About that.

Mr JUSTICE CHARLES: That was the 4th. The first meeting was on the 3rd and they got back in the early hours of the 4th.

Mr MAUDE: That is right, yes. I am much obliged, my lord; the early hours of the 4th. Then on the Thursday – that is what I think your Lordship is correcting me about – Thursday is the 5th. Then on the Thursday he called for you at your flat?

A. Yes.

Q. Were you expecting him?

A. No.

Q. What did you say when he arrived?

A. He told me to get ready; he said he was going to take me out.

Q. What did you say?

A. I didn't say anything; I just put my coat on.

Q. You are young, you are only eighteen, but you had two years alone in London?

A. Yes.

Q. And you have been able to look after yourself, haven't you?

A. Yes.

Q. We heard from Mrs Evans you had men friends, like a lot of other perfectly ordinary girls, and had been able to look after yourself?

A. Yes.

Q. Did you protest, or think of some excuse not to go with him?

A. Somebody had already called for me on that Thursday afternoon and I told Ricky that I had some friend there and he told me I was tell him to go, so I told my friend to go and I told him I would meet him at six o'clock.

Q. I think I may be wrong, but I am suggesting you are talking of some quite different time. What I am talking about now is the Thursday. Do you see the statement 'He called for me at my flat'?

A. Yes.

Q. 'At about five in the afternoon last Thursday we went and ate and afterwards we went to the Gaumont Cinema in Hammersmith'?

A. Yes.

Q. 'We came out of the cinema at about 8.30 and entered a café in Hammersmith Broadway. Just as we got to the door the air raid siren sounded.' What you have been telling us about the friend is quite a different day, isn't it?

A. No, I don't think so.

Q. He has never raised a finger to you from first to last, has he raised his hand?

A. Yes.

Q. When was that?

A. On the Thursday after we had been to Reading.

Mr JUSTICE CHARLES: After what?

A. After we had been to Reading on the Thursday.

Q. That is the second journey to Reading?

A. Yes.

Mr MAUDE: You tell my lord, will you, what happened after you had been to Reading? I don't want to suggest it to you. What did you say?

A. Ricky stayed with me that night after we came back from Reading and I went downstairs to have a wash and Ricky came down afterwards and he told me I should have asked his permission and he struck me.

Q. Asked his permission to go down and have a wash?

A. Yes.

Mr JUSTICE CHARLES: You went downstairs to wash and he followed you and struck you?

A. Yes.

Q. What for?

A. Because I did not ask his permission.

Mr MAUDE: Would I be right in guessing that you never told a soul that until this minute? Whom have you told, do you remember?

A. My counsel.

Q. When was that?

A. I thought they would come down last night.

Q. Last night?

A. I thought they would come down and see me last night and as they didn't come I wrote a note.

Q. So you have told that story to me.

A. Yes.

Q. And you wrote a note about it, putting it down for the first time when - during the night?

A. Last night after I left the box.

Q. How many times have your solicitors seen you in all?

A. I don't know.

Q. Very often I mean, what, three times or four times?

A. About three times.

Q. This guess would certainly be right, wouldn't it, that you as a result of those interviews and during them, have been trying to remember any single incident where the man struck you?

A. No.

Q. When you were sensible enough to realise the importance of saying that you had been terrorised by Hulten, when was that? It was explained to you; you told my lord it had all been explained to you. When was that?

A. I don't understand you, sir.

Q. Yesterday, do you remember when your attention was drawn to this defence of yours, you told my lord that it had been explained to you?

Mr CASSWELL: I may be wrong but I do not think she said it had been explained to her before she wrote that letter.

Mr MAUDE: Which letter is this?

Mr CASSWELL: The letter we have been talking about.

Mr MAUDE: No, I am not talking about that letter at all.

Mr JUSTICE CHARLES: No, it came out in another way.

Mr MAUDE: This is what you said, wasn't it, words to this effect: 'I did not say in my statement to the police that I had been frightened. It has all been explained to me since'?

Mr JUSTICE CHARLES: Yes that is what she said.

Mr MAUDE: That is right, isn't it? I don't want there to be any mistake about it. 'I did not tell the police I was frightened; I did not think it concerned them. Now I know, because it has all been explained'. That is what you were saying yesterday, wasn't it?

Mr JUSTICE CHARLES: Yes, that is what she said; that is right.

Mr MAUDE: Mrs Jones, you are not telling me you don't remember that? I am suggesting you have probably been worrying about it ever since you left the court yesterday, having said that to my lord?

A. I don't recall it.

Q. About it being explained to you, have you not been worrying about that answer?

A. No.

Q. What did the answer mean? Explained by whom?

(The witness did not reply.)

Q. I do not want to prolong it, just let me turn to one other part of your story. Let us go to that night when you hailed the taxi. Let us deal with your story yesterday. It is this, is it not? You stood in a shop doorway; he told you to call a taxi; you called, 'Stop,' but they did not stop. 'I called a taxi and Ricky told me to see if it was a taxi.' That is part of the story and that is correct, is it?

A. Yes.

Q. 'I don't know why he wanted a taxi and I did not ask him,' is that right?

A. I didn't question him.

Mr JUSTICE CHARLES: That is not quite the point.

Mr MAUDE: The point, I think, is explained isn't it a little further on. You said, 'I did not know where I was going and I did not know where he wanted to go.' Is that true?

A. Yes.

Q. There you were calling a taxi, just thinking you were going for a ride, I suppose?

A. I didn't think anything.

Q. You must have thought something, surely; you must have thought something Mrs Jones. What did you think you were stopping the taxi for? Was it for him to drive home in? Was he going back?

A. When Ricky told the driver he wanted to go to the top of King Street I thought we were going home.

Q. Thought you were going home?

A. Yes.

Q. Then I was correct in my guess about that; you thought it was simply the end of the evening?

A. Yes.

Q. And indeed no thought of robbery, if that is so, no thought of crime had been in your mind at all?

A. No.

Q. As innocent as you sit there? Is that right, quite innocent?

A. I told you before, when Ricky said he wanted to go to the top of King Street, the top of King Street I lived and I thought he was taking me home.

Q. I am now putting it strongly; you were as innocent in your mind and heart as you are now?

A. Yes.

Q. Then you look back at your statement, I will see if I can find a passage for you. It is on page 7 of the original and the hand writing, although extremely good, is very faint; it would be more convenient if she could have a copy if there is one. This is a copy of mine; it is a copy of the two exhibits and it is the same as mine. Have you got that?

A. Yes.

Q. 'He went out about 4.30 pm and promised to call for me about six o'clock. He didn't come and I stayed in. About 11.30 pm. I heard a whistle coming from the street outside and I went down to the street door because I recognised it was Ricky's whistle. This was an arrangement we had made previously. He came indoors and then said, 'Come on, let's go and get a taxi'. Was that just meaning to fetch a taxi; is that what it meant; just 'let's go and fetch a taxi'?

A. No.

Q. The last five minutes, all this about you being innocent has simply been untrue hasn't it?

A. No.

Q. Let us read then. 'He came indoors and then said, 'Come on, let's go and get a taxi.' I knew the meaning behind his words and that he wanted me to go with him to rob a taxi cab driver.' What has it all meant, what you have been telling the jury in the last ten minutes about you being as innocent as you are now, thinking that you were going to drive home?

A. When we got outside the house, we walked down the Hammersmith Road and stopped in a doorway and when he said, 'Call a taxi,' I called a taxi and when I asked if it was a taxi the driver said it was a private hire car and when I told Ricky, Ricky came across and said to the driver would he drive us to the top of King Street. Then I thought he was driving me home. When he first told me 'Let's go out and get a taxi,' I was suspicious.

Q. You were what?

A. Suspicious.

Q. Suspicious when he said, 'Come on, let's go and get a taxi.' Do you notice the way you phrased it to Mr Tarr? I must draw you attention to this; just look at it. 'He came indoors and then said, 'come on, let's go and get a taxi.' I knew the meaning behind his words and that he wanted me to go with him to rob a taxi cab driver'?

A. Yes.

Q. Is that true?

A. Yes.

Mr JUSTICE CHARLES: Then you did not know when he said, 'Let's go and get a taxi,' that he meant 'Let's go and rob a taxi cab driver'?

A. Yes, sir.

Q. Why did you say that no thought of robbery entered your mind at all?

A. Because when he told the driver he wanted to get to the top of King Street…

Q. No, that it not what you said, you know. 'When he said, 'Let's go and get a taxi,' I knew, I gathered that he meant 'Let's go and rob a taxi cab driver'?

A. Yes.

Q. And you say that is true?

A. Yes.

Q. There is no question about getting to King Street and passing King Street, or anything of that sort?

A. Not then, sir.

Mr MAUDE: And so at the moment when you are standing in the doorway with the suspicion, at any rate in your mind, at no time had you indicated to this man that you were not willing to take part in some crime?

A. No.

Q. Nothing like: No Ricky, don't; I can't,' or 'What are you going to do?', nothing like that at all?

A. No.

Q. Not a word?

A. No.

Q. All the time there was Mrs Evans, who was rather a strict landlady, wasn't she? I notice he did not sleep there when Mrs Evans was back. She was strict, wasn't she Mrs Evans?

A. No, I would not say that.

Q. Not?

A. No.

Q. I do not mean horrid to you, but a woman who was careful about the honour of her house?

A. Yes.

Q. There she was; she had warned you, hadn't she, that it would be dangerous to go out that first night?

A. Yes.

Q. And you found that you had gone with a bad fellow and you never went near her and never said a word to her about it, did you?

A. No.

Mr JUSTICE CHARLES: Mr Maude, I just want to put this together. (To the witness) You said, 'I was suspicious when he said, 'Let's go and get ta taxi.' I thought he meant that we should rob a taxi driver.' And when you knew and you told me yesterday, you believed that he was a Chicago gunman, he was a leader of a gang?

A. Yes.

Q. Yet you hailed a taxi and got into it with him?

A. I hailed the taxi under his orders.

Mr MAUDE: Let us follow that out. You see your story in the box is that you thought he had changed his mind, or that he had made a mistake when he mentioned King Street?

A. Yes.

Q. Did you whisper something to him like 'So you are not going to do it after all'? A. No.

Q. Or 'I am so glad'?

A. No.

Q. Not a word?

A. No, because Ricky had told me before that I was to obey his orders and ask no questions.

Q. Obey his orders? It would not be right for the jury to think you were sort of going round with him like a silly dog, wouldn't it?

A. No.

Q. You were joking, we have heard, even after the death of Heath?

A. No.

Q. He was giving you flowers – did he often give you flowers?

A. That was the only flowers he gave me.

Q. Let us just go on with it, if you will just follow it: 'We walked along Hammersmith Road and stood in a shop doorway opposite Cadby Hall. After about ten minutes a grey Ford car approached us very slowly like a taxicab; it was coming from the direction of Hammersmith Broadway. I yelled, "Taxi," and it stopped.' Am I right, just look when I point out to you that you have not said in your statement that it was he who told you to get the taxi at all? It is what you say now, isn't it that you were working under the orders of Hulten, and your friend Ricky, that he told you to stop the taxi?

A. Yes.

Q. You did not tell the police that, did you?

A. I just told the police the plain facts, that's all.

Mr JUSTICE CHARLES: You didn't tell them that he told you to call a taxi?

A. No.

Q. You thought when he said, 'Come on let's get a taxi,' that he meant he wanted you to go with him to rob a taxi driver and then you called a taxi?

A. He told me to call a taxi.

Q. Why did not you tell the police that he told you to call a taxi?

A. I told the police nothing about myself.

Mr MAUDE: 'I yelled, "Taxi," and it stopped. Ricky thought it was a naval car and Ricky stopped in the shop doorway while I went over to speak to the driver. I said, "Are you a taxi?" and he said, "Private hire, where do you want to go?" I replied, "Wait a minute," and when back to Ricky. I told him it was a private car and he asked how many people were in it. I told him only the driver, so we went across to the car and Ricky asked the driver to take us to the top of King Street.' What you ought to have put in there at least once is that he had ordered you to stop the car: 'He had ordered me to go and see how many people were in it'?

A. No.

Q. In that respect how come, if you were quite blameless and only a terror-stricken girl, that you used that expression 'Where we have dumped the body'? Do you remember that?

A. Yes.

Q. Let us find that. If you turn onto page 6 of the copy you have got there, you will find it at the top. Mrs Jones, have you got that?

A. Yes.

Q. ' Just before we got to the roundabout where Ricky shot Heath I asked him where we had dumped the body.' I want to find it in the original in case it is a typewriting error; 'we' might be 'he'. Which did you say to them, do you remember?

A. I think it was 'we'.

Q. You said 'we', did you?

A. I think so.

Q. Why did you use that expression?

A. Because I was with Ricky when he did it.

Q. If you were not a cold-blooded girl I am suggesting you could not possibly have said that, if you were a terror-stricken frightened girl; and the truth of it is that 'We had dumped the body' describes it very well, for you helped him carry that corpse, didn't you?

A. I didn't help him.

Q. He may not have been dead, but you helped him to carry that body, didn't you?

A. No.

Q. It was your hands or fingers that took the wristwatch off his body?

A. Yes.

Q. And took the other things off his body?

A. Yes.

Q. And that afternoon you sat in the cinema and you remember it very well, don't you? One other matter, when you get back you say, 'That's cold blooded murder then; how could you do it?' You remember that. That you were telling us yesterday, and it is following that that I am interested in. You told us yesterday, 'I was terrified and dazed and I just could not believe it had happened.' Then I have in my note, 'I did not sleep that night. We sat up together.'

A. Yes.

Q. There are armchairs in the room, aren't there?

A. We sat on the bed.

Mr JUSTICE CHARLES: For how many hours?

A. I don't know.

Q. Till what time the next day?

A. Till about ten to eleven.

Mr MAUDE: About ten to eleven?

A. Yes.

Q. Alter it now if what I am saying is not correct, that you never just sat on a bed. That you went to bed and got up?

A. No.

Q. You had never done that in your life before, had you sat up without going to bed like that? Had you ever done that before?

A. Yes.

Q. Not very often?

A. Yes.

Q. Not in circumstances like that, at any rate?

A. No.

Q. In fact when you look at your statement on page 6 it says this, doesn't it: 'Indoors we examined all of Heath's things we had taken' not that 'He had made me take,' but 'that we had taken'. 'Then we went to bed'?

A. I made a mistake there.

Q. 'The next day that is Saturday we got up at ten to eleven in the morning' - that is the truth isn't it? Look at the bottom of page two. You are describing how you were being asked by the man what was worrying you and so on. 'I told him that I had been with a man who shot a fellow and that his name was George Heath of Kennington. He asked me what was the motive, I said 'robbery'.' Had you ever said to Hulten, 'You know I thought you had changed your mind. I never realised that you were going to do this thing'?

A. No.

Q. Not a word like that?

A. I never questioned Ricky at all.

Q. Not a word like 'My God I thought you had changed your mind'?

A. No.

Q. Then, if we read on: I said, 'Robbery' and asked him what I should do about it. He said, 'Do as your conscience guides you', so I asked what I should do if my conscience told me nothing.' I put it to you that that is utterly cold blooded. What did you mean?

A. I could not do what I wanted to do. All the time I was with Ricky I could not call my life my own.

Mr JUSTICE CHARLES: But when you weren't with Ricky you never told the police. When you had got Scotland Yard detectives all round you, you never told them that you were terrified or frightened in any way. 'I asked him where he had dumped the body.'

Mr MAUDE: If you turn over to the next page you will see, 'I then heard a whistle in the street which I recognised as Ricky. I told Mac who he was.' Is that the man whose name and address you gave to the police?

A. Yes.

Q. 'I told Mac who he was and went down to the street door and let Ricky in'. I am assuming Mac was a real person; was he?

A. Yes.

Q. 'I told him I had a friend in my room and he became jealous. So I told him that my friend had been sent up to me by my people in Wales, he believed that. Ricky sat on the stairs as Mac came out of the door I introduced them. Before Mac left my room I told him Ricky was the man who shot Heath.' That is the incident, isn't it, that you were telling us about earlier when I was cross-examining you, you had muddled the dates?

A. No, sir that is not the same one.

Q. After Mac had been on the scene, you and Ricky according to your statement go round to the car park and see the Ford there, and he says 'It's all right; we have no need to worry; there's nothing in the papers and the police have not found the body yet.' 'On seeing the car we were both reassured'...

Mr JUSTICE CHARLES: 'We were both reassured.'

Mr MAUDE: 'And went to Reading in it. I went to sleep in the car and when I woke up we were back in the car park.' Is that right?

A. Yes.

Q. You still say you were terrified of the man?

A. Yes.

Q. The only sign in the whole of your statements of anything even approaching violence is this, isn't it, in the paragraph at the bottom of the page: 'He then drove me home and on the way he asked me to go to Reading with him and said he would teach me to shoot. I didn't want to go and he became mad.' How did he show it on that occasion? That was very courageous of you. How did he show it? 'He became mad'?

A. I hadn't been to sleep the night before, and when he told me he wanted to take me out to teach me to shoot, I told him I didn't want to go.

Q. Yes, and he became mad. 'Mad' is a common expression; it is not insane; it means he became cross, angry?

A. Yes.

Q. Well, the interesting part about it is that, as a result of your saying you did not want to go you did not?

A. No.

Q. And is this the first time you had ever put your foot down, isn't it?

A. Yes.

Mr JUSTICE CHARLES: When you said you did not want to go, you did not go?

A. No.

Mr MAUDE: If you turn back to the part where the actual shooting of Heath takes place, which you will find on page 4: 'Ricky and I were sitting in the back seat of the saloon car and as we got into the Great West Road Ricky told Heath to drive slowly and when we have travelled about 300 yards before reaching a bridge Ricky said to Heath, 'We'll get out here' and Heath stopped. Just as we were passing the roundabout I heard a click.' What did you do?

A. I looked towards Ricky.

Q. It was night?

A. Yes.

Q. Not a busy road?

A. No.

Q. What could you see?

A. I saw Ricky had his revolver in his hand.

Q. How could you possibly see that? Where did the light come from?

A. It was not a dark night.

Q. It has been pointed out to me there was a moon, but that does not shine inside a car. Was it a closed car?

A. Yes.

Q. What did you do? Did you put your hand out?

A. I went to get out.

Q. It all happened so suddenly as that?

A. Pardon?

Q. You see, I am suggesting you are quite inaccurate about when you heard the click, that you heard any click at all and so on. If this version is right, that while you were passing the roundabout you heard a click and saw a pistol in his hand which he was probably going to let off and you had never heard one go off, you would have done something, touched him, done something to prevent it. You did not?

A. No.

Q. The reason for that is that you neither saw it nor heard it?

A. I did.

Q. Can you explain why you did not do anything at all?

A. Because one look from Ricky was enough.

Q. One what?

A. One look from Ricky was enough.

Q. You could see his eyes as well could you?

A. I saw his face.

Mr JUSTICE CHARLES: But were you surprised? You knew he was a gunman, you knew he had got his gun and you knew he was going to commit a robbery: were you surprised when he used his gun?

A. When I heard the shot I was.

Q. Mr MAUDE: What I am suggesting is that both you and he undoubtedly had in your minds and you knew it quite well a robbery.

A. I didn't know it…

Q. But I suggest…

Mr CASSWELL: Let her answer.

Mr MAUDE: Certainly.

A. I did not know it until after we had passed our house.

Mr JUSTICE CHARLES: You know, you told me quite different. You told me that when he said, 'Let's go and get a taxi,' you understood that he meant, 'Let's go and rob a taxi cab driver.'

A. Yes.

Q. Very well. That is long before you got into the cab. You say it was not until you passed your house?

A. When he told the driver he wanted to go to the top of King Street I thought he was taking me home.

Q. Well, it is no good putting it to you again. You told me twice quite clearly and in your statement to the police that when he said, 'Let's go and get a taxi,' you understood that he meant, 'Let's go and rob a taxi driver'; that is long before you were passing the house.

Mr MAUDE: My lord, I don't want to go into more details; I want to be allowed to suggest to her that her account of the actual incident, the click and so on, is quite unreliable. (To the witness) It is all quite unreliable? I am suggesting it is quite unreliable?

A. It is all true.

Q. Let me put one thing to you then. Although he made you rob the body, according to you, although he made you take the watch off the wrist, he never asked you to help to move it?

A. No.

Q. I am putting to you that it is quite untrue and that you and he had either end and carried that man?

A. I did not touch that man except when I searched his pockets.

Q. Did you have to move his arm in order to get the watch off?

A. Yes.

Q. Did he seem to be alive?

A. Yes.

Q. What did you do? See if he had a wound anywhere?

A. No.

Q. Why not? That was the moment when you could have helped, wasn't it? You could have helped him?

Mr JUSTICE CHARLES: You say that his breath was coming in short gasps when you robbed his body?

Mr MAUDE: Was it you who put the collar up to hide his face?

A. No.

Q. Did somebody do that?

A. I don't know.

Mr MAUDE: My lord, I hope it will not be taken against me if I have not put everything to her.

Mr JUSTICE CHARLES: I want to ask you one question. How do you say he got the body into the ditch? How do you say the body became dumped in the ditch?

A. Ricky got hold of the man under his armpits and dragged the body from the car.

Q. Dragged the body across the grass?

A. The car was near the ditch.

Q. We know where the car was. Did you hear the policeman say there was no sort of dragging on the grass at all?

A. Yes.

Cross-examined by Mr BYRNE for the Prosecution.

Q. How many nights did this young man spend in your room?

A. Three.

Q. Did he sleep in your room?

A. On two nights, yes.

Q. What?

A. Two nights he slept there, yes.

Q. The third night he did not sleep in the room but spent the night in the room, is that what you mean?

A. Yes.

Q. Did he sleep in the bed with you?

A. He slept on the bed.

Q. On the bed?

A. Yes.

Q. On the bed you were sleeping in?

A. Yes.

Q. Do you tell the jury that that young man never had connection with you?

A. Yes.

Q. The night that he spent in your room when he did not sleep, was that the night after Heath had met his death?

A. Yes.

Q. Was that the night, or the few remaining hours of daylight of the twenty-four when most people are asleep that you and Hulten spent examining the dead man's property that you had brought back with you?

A. Yes.

Q. Your association with this young man lasted, did it not, from 3rd October until just about midday on Monday 9th October?

A. Yes.

Q. During those days of your association with him, were you earning your living?

A. No.

Q. Had you had any money put aside?

A. Yes.

Q. How much?

A. I had a few pounds in the Post Office.

Q. During those days of association with him, did you withdraw any money from the Post Office?

A. Saving stamps, yes.

Q. What?

A. They were saving stamps.

Q. Did you cash any of the saving stamps during the time that you were associating with Hulten?

A. I cashed them all.

Q. How much did that come to?

A. About three pounds.

Q. Three pounds?

A. Yes.

Q. How did you cash the stamps?

A. I just handed my book in and they tore the stamps out.

Q. And handed you the cash for them?

A. Yes.

Q. Are you sure of that?

A. Yes.

Q. Is it true that on that Sunday morning – I won't be sure about the morning but on that Sunday, 8th October, you handed to your landlady seven pounds for her to take care of?

A. Yes.

Q. Was some of that money that had been taken from Heath's clothing?

A. No.

Q. Where had you got it from?

A. I won it at the races.

Q. The races on the Saturday afternoon?

A. Yes.

Mr JUSTICE CHARLES: Where did you get the money to bet with at the races?

A. I used some of my own and some of Ricky's.

Q. Ricky, you tell us, had only nineteen shillings when he started out for Reading. Wasn't he, through you, betting with the dead man's money? Weren't you putting the dead man's money on? Weren't you?

A. I didn't think so at the time.

Mr BYRNE: When you hailed Heath's car you had 10s 3d in your possession, hadn't you?

A. Yes.

Q. Had you any other money anywhere else?

A. I believe I had some at home.

Q. And he had, that is to say Hulten had, nineteen shillings in his possession, hadn't he?

A. Yes.

Q. Had he got any more?

A. I don't know.

Q. How did you know that he had got nineteen shillings in his possession?

A. Because he told me.

Q. You were both rather short of money, weren't you? A. I was not.

Q. Was that the reason why the decision was made to rob a taxi cab driver?

A. There was no decision made.

Mr JUSTICE CHARLES: You knew he was probably going to; you told me so?

A.   Yes.

Mr CASSWELL: My Lord? In my respectful submission that was a very fair answer of hers. Decision might mean a decision of two people or of one.

Mr JUSTICE CHARLES: Very well.

Mr CASSWELL: If your Lordship pleases.

Mr BYRNE: Now tell me this, will you? I understand you to say a short time ago after you had been to the police station on 11th October the waitress at the café told you that the police had arrested Hulten; is that right?

A. Yes.

Mr JUSTICE CHARLES: After her first visit?

Mr BYRNE: Yes. I was just going to get that clear, my lord. (To the witness) When you heard that from the waitress in the café, was that before you saw Kimberley, the Special Constable?

A. Yes.

Q. When you saw Kimberley, the Special Constable, you knew, did you, that Hulten was safely under lock and key?

A. Yes.

Q. Were you glad?

A. Yes.

Q. Your troubles were at an end then, I suppose, weren't they? No more of these threats that you told the jury about?

A. Not from Ricky.

Q. Not from anybody else?

A. I was afraid of the gang which he was supposed to have been the leader of.

Q. Have you ever seen the gang?

A. No.

Q. There was no such a thing, was there?

A. I didn't know that until I was later told.

Q. I suggest that you knew perfectly well there was no kind of gang at all.

A. I didn't know.

Q. Would it be true to say that, although you knew that Hulten had been arrested by the police, you were still trying to protect him when you had a conversation with Kimberley? Do you follow?

A. No, sir.

Q. Let me remind you of Kimberley's evidence and tell me whether you agree with it. You met Kimberley, did you at about half past four that afternoon, 11th October, is that about right? In a cleaner's shop?

A. Yes.

Q. Is it true, is it, that he had not seen you for some time, though you had known each other previously?

A. Yes.

Q. Did he make a remark about you looking rather old and tired?

A. Yes.

Q. Did you tell him you been a bad girl and had been drinking heavily?

A. Yes.

Q. Did he say that you looked worried?

A. Yes.

Q. And did you use the words 'I have been over at the police station for about four hours regarding the murder'? Did you say that?

A. Yes.

Mr CASSWELL: 'This murder' it should be.

Mr BYRNE: Quite right, 'regarding this murder.' When you said 'this murder', you referred to an account in a newspaper that you had with you; is that right?

A. Yes.

Q. Did Kimberley ask you what you were worrying about and say to you, 'You had nothing to do with it, did you?' Do you remember that?

A. Yes.

Q. Did you reply, 'I know the fellow they have got inside, but he could have had nothing to do with the murder as he was with me all Friday night'?

A. Yes.

Q. That was a lie wasn't it?

A. Yes.

Q. Why did you tell Mr Kimberley, the Special Constable, a lie?

A. Well, I knew the police had got Ricky and I left Ricky to tell them himself that he had done it.

Q. Would you be kind enough just to apply your mind to my question? Why did you tell Mr Kimberley a lie?

A. Because I wanted him to think I had nothing to do with it.

Q. Why did you want him to think that in fact the police had got hold of the wrong man because he had spent the night with you? That was what you were trying to tell him, wasn't it?

A. Yes.

Q. Why did you want to tell him that?

A. Because I didn't want him to know that I knew such a bad man.

Q. But you were making it quite plain that you knew the man against whom the allegation was being made, because you were saying that he had spent all Friday night with you. That answer won't do, will it?

A. I don't follow you there, sir.

Q. You told me a minute ago that you did not want Mr Kimberley to know that you knew such a bad man?

A. Yes.

Q. Did you really mean that answer? Did you really mean that?

A. Yes.

Mr JUSTICE CHARLES: But just think. It can't be so, because you had just told him that Ricky could not have done the murder because he had spent the night with you, and yet you say you said that because you wanted him to understand that you did not associate with such a bad man?

A. Yes.

Q. Well, I think I see what she means; when she had associated with Ricky, Ricky was such a good man that they must have got the wrong one. I think that is a logical explanation of her answer.

Mr BYRNE: You knew in your own mind that they had not got the wrong man, didn't you? You knew perfectly well, didn't you, because you had been there when he had shot Heath?

Mr JUSTICE CHARLES: Sitting next to him when the shot was fired.

A. Yes.

Mr BYRNE: There was no doubt about it; the police had got the right man?

A. Yes.

Q. They had not only got the right man, but they had got a man who, according to you, had put you in fear of your life?

A. Yes.

Q. The result of telling that policeman that in fact the man they had got could not have done it because he was with you all Friday night, might be that he would become free again, mightn't it?

A. I didn't think so.

A FATAL PICKUP

Q. You see, weren't you in fact, as it were, making an alibi for the very man of whom you were in fear of your life?

A. I didn't think that.

Q. It is quite plain that is the effect of what you said, isn't it?

A. I didn't think that, though.

Q. No, but it is quite plain, looking at it now, that is the effect of what you said?

A. Looking at it now, yes.

Q. You see, I am suggesting in the plainest possible terms to you - and it is only right you should understand it - that this story about being in fear of your life is a lot of lies?

A. No.

Q. You follow the suggestion? Then did you go on talking to Kimberley a little later, saying, 'If you had seen someone do what I had seen done you would not be able to sleep at night'? Did you say that to him?

A. Yes.

Q. What did you mean by that, having just told Kimberley that the police had got the wrong man, in effect? What did you mean by saying that, if he had seen someone do what you had seen done, he would not be able to sleep at night?

A. I was referring to the murder, sir.

Q. Did you go on to tell him - well, first of all, did he suggest to you that the best thing for you to do would be to go back to the police station and tell the truth?

A. Yes.

Q. And did you say that you had made a statement over there and if you had to repeat it you could not do so?

A. Yes.

Q. What did you mean by that?

Mr CASSWELL: That is not what he said here. You are reading the depositions.

Mr BYRNE: Well, you correct me, Mr Casswell.

Mr CASSWELL: What he said here was 'If I have to remember what is in the statement I could not repeat it.' It is the very point I made the other day. She makes it quite clear: 'I could not remember it.'

Mr BYRNE: Let us take it in that way then, that you were in effect saying that you could not remember the statement that you made to the police?

A. Yes.

Q. The statement you had made to the police, in fact was not a true statement was it?

A. No.

Q. Why did you tell them lies?

A. Because I did not know they had got Ricky.

Q. Let me understand where we are getting to, you first of all tell the police lies, because you did not know that they had arrested Ricky.

A. Yes.

Q. Then when you hear that Ricky has been arrested, you tell Kimberley lies by saying he could not have done it because he had spent the night with you. That is the position, isn't it?

A. Yes.

Q. So no matter what the true state of affairs happened to be, you told a lie about it?

A. Yes.

Q. After that, later that evening at six o'clock, you were seen by Inspector Tansill and Mr Kimberley; do you remember?

A. Yes.

Q. And having been seen by them, you made that statement which is the longer of the two statements; is that right?

A. Yes.

Q. I don't want to repeat what has already been dealt with in cross-examination if I can help it, but just let me see if I understand the position. When you made that second statement you knew that Ricky was safely locked up?

A. Yes.

Q. When you made the statement you were in the security of a police station?

A. Yes.

Q. You were in the hands of Scotland Yard Officers?

A. Yes.

Q. According to the story that you have told, you at the time were still frightened of the Hulten gang, shall we call it?

A. Yes.

Q. Did it occur to you to tell the police of your fear?

A. No.

Q. Did it occur to you to tell the police that you were afraid of Hulten?

A. No.

Q. When did you first decide to tell this story of being in fear of your life from Hulten?

A. I decided in Holloway Prison that I better tell everything.

Q. You decided in Holloway Prison what?

A. That I better tell them everything.

Q. I am sorry I couldn't catch that?

A. I decided in Holloway Prison that I better tell them everything.

Q. When did you make that decision? Do you recollect?

A. Do you mean when did I write?

Q. If it helps you, let me assist you, do you mean that, having made the decision, you wrote the letter to the Inspector?

A. I decided to tell the police when I wrote the letter.

Q. And you wrote the letter as soon as you had decided to tell the police, did you?

A. Yes.

Q. Did you date the letter yourself, put the date on it?

A. No, one of the sisters of Holloway Prison put the date on.

Q. Well, she put on the date upon which you wrote it, did she?

A. Yes.

Q. We know the letter is dated 26th October, so may I take it that it was upon 26th October you decided to tell the police that you had been frightened of Hulten; is that right?

A. Yes.

Q. Can you tell me this; what time of day was it that you wrote that letter?

A. About a quarter to ten in the morning.

Q. Had you seen your solicitor before you wrote that letter?

A. No.

Q. When did you first see him?

A. After I had written the letter.

Q. Was it the same day?

A. No.

Q. Just think about it. Did you see your solicitor at Holloway Prison on 26th October?

A. I believe it was a few days after I wrote the letter.

Q. Well, I suggest to you in perfectly plain terms that you saw your solicitor on the 26th October at Holloway Prison. What do you say to that?

A. I don't think so.

Q. Just look at the letter. Do you see you begin by saying 'First of all I want to apologise to you by only telling you half the truth,' do you see that?

A. Yes.

Q. What did you mean by that?

A. I did not tell them anything of my feelings.

Q. You did not tell them anything of what?

A. Of my feelings.

Q. Is that what you meant by 'half the truth'?

A. Yes.

Q 'I should be very pleased and feel very much relieved, if you would be so kind as to come along to Holloway Prison to see me and let me tell you all, which I have not yet told you.' What did you mean by 'all', which is underlined; 'Let me tell you all'?

A. I wanted to tell the police that Ricky had threatened me.

Q. You wanted to tell the police Ricky had done what?

A. Threatened me.

Q. 'I am having legal aid, but I want to tell you, as well as the solicitor. It would be a great weight off my mind if you would come and see me before I go to court on 3rd November, which is next Thursday. You see sir now that I definitely know that Ricky is in safe hands, where he cannot get out, I can tell you absolutely all the facts.' Pausing there for one moment, you knew on the 11th October that Ricky was in safe hands when you made your statement to the police in the evening, didn't you?

A. Yes.

Q. Why had it taken you from 11th October until 26th October to come to this decision? Do you follow?

A. No, sir.

Q. Because you see, you are saying in your letter, 'Now that Ricky is in safe hands and cannot get out I can tell you absolutely all the facts.' Well, you had known on 11th October that he was in safe hands, hadn't you?

A. Yes.

Q. You had not told all the facts on the 11th October, had you?

A. I told you everything, I tried to remember everything and I told the police.

Q. But you had not told all the facts, had you?

A. No.

Q. What I am asking you is: Why did you wait till 26th October before you decided to do that which you could have done just as easily on 11th October? What is the answer?

A. My mind was very confused when the police questioned me.

Q. You see, what I am suggesting to you is that by 26th October you had an opportunity of considering what kind of defence you were going to make to this charge, and that was why you were then going to put forward this story about being in fear of your life?

A. No.

Q. And when you saw the Inspector in response to that letter, is this what you said to him: 'I merely wanted to tell you that I wrote to you because Ricky was threatening me'?

A. Yes.

Q. Did you give him any kind of particulars at all?

A. He never asked me.

Q. What? A. He didn't ask me.

Q. Did you offer him any particulars?

A. No, he didn't ask me.

Mr JUSTICE CHARLES: Did you offer him any?

A. No.

Mr BYRNE: You had written a letter to him asking him to call so that you could give him all the facts, as you say?

A. Yes.

Q. When you got him there, when he answered your letter by calling there, what I am asking you is: Did you offer to tell him all the facts?

A. No, sir.

Mr JUSTICE CHARLES: What was the good of getting him there?

A. I told him that Ricky had threatened me.

Q. What was the good of getting him there on 26th October? You knew Ricky was under lock and key on the 11th, and you say you had told them the truth then, but you did not mention that you were terrified. Was there anything other than the fact that you had been threatened that you wanted to tell Mr Tarr?

A. No.

Mr CASSWELL: My learned friend put questions that made it look as if he has some information which I have not got about this visit to Holloway Prison. If he has, perhaps he would put it to the witness.

Mr JUSTICE CHARLES: He will do just as he thinks proper.

Mr CASSWELL: Yes, I dare say he will, but I was just inviting him to do so. If your Lordship thinks it is an improper invitation, I will not pursue it.

Mr JUSTICE CHARLES: If Mr Byrne thinks it is his duty to, but he has prosecuted with such infinite fairness that I shall not say he should.

Mr CASSWELL: If your Lordship pleases.

(Adjourned for a short time)

Re-examined by MR CASSWELL defence for JONES.

Q. Mrs Jones, just one or two question I want to ask you. You remember at the beginning of my learned friend's cross-examination he asked you whether you had a rash?

A. Yes.

Q. Do you know what kind of rash it was?

A. I didn't know until after my landlady took me to the doctor.

Q. Your landlady took you to the doctor?

A. Yes.

Q. It was not a venereal disease, was it?

A. No.

Q. You have never had venereal disease, have you?

A. No.

Q. Your landlady took you to a doctor and then he prescribed for it?

A. Pardon?

Q. The doctor prescribed for it?

A. Yes.

Q. The next thing was, it was put to you that some years ago a man tried to assault you.

A. Yes.

Q. Was it as a result of that that you ran away from home?

A. Yes.

Q. Did he go with you?

A. No.

Q. You were found alone, were you not, in a room in Swansea?

A. Yes.

Q. Was he ever with you, that man?

A. No.

Q. That was when you were only thirteen and a half years old?

A. Yes.

Q. The next thing I want to ask you is this: did it occur to you that the police were just the sort of people who could protect you from Ricky? Did that occur to you when you were at the police station, that they were the people who could protect you?

A. It did not occur to me then.

Q. I think your previous experience with the police was when they had sent you home again when you had run away from home, was it not?

A. Yes.

Q. With regard to the stolen property, it was pointed out to you by my lord that if you put Ricky's money on the dogs that some of it, if he had only nineteen shillings the day before, must have been money which he got by the robbery of Heath. Did that occur to you at the time?

A. No.

Q. Did you have any of that property which was taken from Heath?

A. None.

Q. As far as you know, did you have any of the proceeds of it?

A. No.

Q. Did Ricky give you any money? Apart from this money I understand you put on the dogs that afternoon, did Ricky give you any money at all?

A. No.

Q. Then you were asked about this passage in your second statement in which you said this: 'I told him in the truck I would like to do something really dangerous, meaning to go over Germany in a bomber. I meant that,' and your statement goes straight on: 'He showed me a gun which he pulled out from an inside pocket, or it might have been hooked to his trousers.' Do you mean that he showed you the gun immediately after you said that?

A. Yes, I think so.

Q. Do you think that he was suggesting to you that you should join him in using the gun?

A. After he showed me the gun he told me about himself.

Q. You were also cross-examined - I am not suggesting at all improperly - about your further statement: 'Come on let's go and get a taxi. I knew the meaning behind his words and that he wanted me to go with him to rob a taxi driver.' You quite agree that is what he thought he meant when he came to the door?

A. Yes.

Q. After you had called the taxi, why did you tell the police about how much money you had in your pocket and how much you thought he had? The taxi driver had asked for 10 shillings?

A. Yes.

Q. Did you think then that you would have to pay him 10 shillings?

A. No.

Q. Why were you telling the police about the amount of money you had in your pocket?

A. I believe the police asked me.

Q. The police asked you, I suppose, whether you had money to pay the ten shillings fare?

Mr JUSTICE CHARLES: No, you must not put it that way. It might be asked in view of the questions asked by Mr Byrne as to whether they were not both of them precious hard up.

Mr CASSWELL: It comes directly after that, my lord.

Mr JUSTICE CHARLES: I quite agree, Mr Casswell.

Mr CASSWELL: 'I know now that the driver was named George Heath for reasons I will tell you later. He told Ricky that the fare would be 10 shillings and Ricky said, 'That's all right.' I know that Ricky had 19 shillings in his pockets and I had 10s 3d.' That followed because of some questions the police asked you?

A. I think so.

Q. When the driver passed your house, did you think that his decision had changed, that Ricky still meant to rob the taxi driver, or when you heard him give the address of King Street Hammersmith, did he think he meant to take you home?

A. Yes.

Q. I think you have told us that when you passed the house you then realised that he did not mean to take you home?

A. Yes.

Q. Were you prepared to help him to rob that taxi driver?

A. No.

Q. Do you think if you had interfered it would have stopped it?

A. No.

Q. Now with regard to you being frightened. In your statement you speak in one place of being frightened when you were talking to the RAF man: 'He asked me if I thought I ought to tell the police about Ricky. I said, 'I do not know what to do because I am frightened'.' Is that what you told him?

A. Yes.

Q. In fact, that of course, is a statement you made to the police; you told the police that you had told the RAF man that you were frightened?

A. Yes.

Mr JUSTICE CHARLES: She does not say she was frightened of Ricky. She had been in the midst of what she said was a horrible affair and that had frightened her.

(The prisoner returned to the dock)

Mr CASSWELL: My lord, there was one other question I should have asked Mrs Jones.

Mr JUSTICE CHARLES: Ask her where she is.

Mr CASSWELL: Mrs Jones, you are still on your oath. When your solicitors did see you in prison, was anything said about the letter which you had written

A. I told them I had written a letter to the police.

Q. What did they say, do you remember? However it does not matter. You had told them that you had already written a letter, did you?

A. Yes.

Mr CASSWELL: My Lord, that is my case.

Mr MAUDE: My Lord, I am calling Hulten and no other evidence.

Mr MAUDE examined KARL GUSTAV HULTEN, sworn.

Q. Is your full name Karl Gustav Hulten?

A. Yes.

Q. Were you born on the 3rd March 1923?

A. 1922.

Q. In Stockholm?

A. Yes.

Q. Your parents were Swedish?

A. Yes.

Q. And your mother went to America and became a personal maid to a lady in Boston?

A. That's true.

Q. Were you taken to the United States as a child aged nine months?

A. One year and eight months.

Q. I know you will help all these gentlemen; do not bother about me so much, but they have to hear. My Lord has got to hear and Mr Byrne, so you must keep your voice up.

A. Yes.

Mr JUSTICE CHARLES: He says not nine months, one year and eight months.

Mr MAUDE: Well, we might still call you a baby. Is there any truth whatever in the story about you having been a Chicago gunman, if I may put it shortly?

A. No, there is not.

Q. Have you ever been to Chicago in your life?

A. I have been there, yes.

Q. But so far as America is concerned, were you in the United States until the war?

A. Yes.

Q. Coming over here in the American Forces?

A. Yes.

Q. Up to that time had you been to a farm and trade school at Boston?

A. Yes.

Q. And you had been employed as a clerk, a mechanic and assistant manager and things, I think, to do with taxis and the Firestone Tyre Company?

A. Yes.

Q. Then you were inducted into the United States Army at Boston, Massachusetts, in May 1943?★

A. Yes.

★*At the Court Martial Criminal Investigation Division it was stated that Hulten was inducted into the Army on the 7th May 1942. However, on the charge sheet they are saying 24th May 1943. The sheet of Evidence Of Previous Convictions states date of current enlistment as being the 24th May 1943.*

Q. When did you arrive in England?

A. I am not sure of the date.

Q. Can you give it me roughly?

A. Sometime a little after January 1944.

Q. About a year ago?

A. Yes.

Q. At the time of your arrest, I do not know what the technical term is, I do not know whether you would be classed as a deserter or what, but undoubtedly you were away without leave?

A. Yes.

Q. At that time, how long had you been away without leave?

A. Approximately six weeks.

Q. I think the simplest way, my lord, from everybody's point of view is if he takes his statements and goes through them. Take your two statements. I am not going to ask you any questions about the first one; it did not contain the whole truth by any means?

A. No, it did not.

Q. The second statement, if you will just take that one alone, was made on 12th October. What time had you got up on that day?

A. Between five thirty and six o'clock in the morning.

Q. Had you any sleep during the day?

A. No, I did not.

Q. You have heard Mr Tarr tell us that the interview with Mr De Mott, when this statement was taken, started at a quarter to eight and finished at half past one in the morning. Is that correct?

A. Yes.

Q. If you would follow it: 'My name, rank, Army serial number and organisation are as shown above. I am 23 years of age, married and my home is in Boston Massachusetts. I was inducted into the Army 7th May 1942.' That is all true, is it?

A. 1943.*

*See note

Q. 'On Tuesday, 3rd October 1944, I first met Georgina Grayson, No 311 King Street Hammersmith. We met in a café on Queen Caroline Street, Hammersmith. I was introduced to her by a civilian known to me as Len Bexley. It was in the evening when I met her; I do not recall the exact time. When I left I arranged to meet her at half past eleven in front of the café. I was late and missed her. I was driving a two and a half ton United States Army truck 6x6 with ten wheels,' number so-and-so. 'I had stolen this truck in Reading on 28 or 29th September 1944.' Is all that true?

A. Yes.

Q. 'When I missed Georgina,' that means that you did not see her at the time and place, I suppose?

A. Yes.

Q. 'I drove down King Street looking for her. I met her walking down King Street. I stopped the truck and she got in. We started to go for a ride.' Do not bother about the statement for a minute. You know the expression that is used there about a 'gun moll'?

A. Yes.

Q. I want you to tell the jury what happened when you two met and how it developed about excitement and thrills and all the rest of it.

A. When I first met her on Queen Caroline Street at the café, or at the time when I met her when she entered the truck, I said - Do you want me to start from when I met her at the cafeteria?

Mr MAUDE: You can do it in exactly your own way. I want you to tell us…

Mr JUSTICE CHARLES: He only wants to know when to start. He says, 'Do you want me start from when I met her in the cafeteria, or the time when I got into the truck?'

Mr MAUDE: Start where you like; you start absolutely where you like, but show us how it developed about her wanting to do something exciting and so on; use your own words.

A. I had come into the cafeteria during the afternoon, close to the evening; I saw Len Bexley sitting there with a young lady. I took another seat, but he asked me to come over and join them, which I did. Then he introduced me to the young lady, Mrs Jones; I knew her at the time by the name of Miss Grayson, the name I was introduced to her by. We were talking there a while in the cafeteria and afterwards we all got up together and left together. Mrs Jones and I walked down towards the Broadway. I asked her if she would care to come out later on. I didn't know exactly the time so I said 11.30, the time I would be back. She agreed and then she left us. I told Bexley 'I don't believe she will turn up.' So he agreed with me there. And then Bexley and I were parted after a little while. Then later on I was going down after I left another young lady I was with that night. I came back in the truck and was driving down towards the Hammersmith Road, where I was supposed to meet her. She was not there, so I planned on going back to camp that night when I did not meet her there. So I started on my way down.

Q. Just pause. You were going back to camp; you were going to give yourself up? That means giving yourself up?

A. No I was going back to get some money from the fellows.

Q. To get what?

A. To get some money from the fellows back there.

Q. Borrow some money from somebody?

A. Yes. I did not see her there, so I started down King's Road on my way to the Great West Road towards my camp, when I thought I recognised her coming down the street. So I stopped the truck a little in front of her and called back to her. She answered and came and got up on the truck. She did not ask me where we were going. I started right out and we just started talking naturally and she brought up the subject about doing something dangerous.

Mr JUSTICE CHARLES: What did she say?

A. I just don't remember what it was we were talking about at the time.

Mr MAUDE: May I just say this? Don't stop but put it in your own words, because when my lord or any of us are in doubt about it we will ask. Just tell it in natural ordinary language like you would to another soldier. What happened?

A. Well, I told her I was a paratrooper and she said that was a dangerous profession to be in. I told her it was. Well, she said, 'I would like to do something dangerous like becoming a gun moll.'

Q. Did you know she had been in Canada?

A. No she told me after she had relatives there. She didn't say she had been in Canada.

Q. Did you know what she had been, what her professional life had been?

A. No.

Q. What did you think she was?

A. I didn't know what she was. I thought she was kidding at first, I didn't take her serious, but she did say she was serious about it.

Q. If you look at your statement, you told the police that you explained to her then, 'I then explained to her that we had a stolen truck.' You see that? It's in the same part. 'At first I thought she was kidding, but she told me that she was serious. I then explained to her that we had a stolen truck. We drove on towards Reading.'

A. Yes.

Q. Is that correct?

A. That is correct.

Q. Did you fill her up with any stories about yourself that were untrue?

A. No, I did not.

Q. What she told the police was – I am referring to her statement – that she told you that she would like to do something dangerous, 'meaning to go over Germany in a bomber.' Did she ever say anything like that?

A. No, she did not mention anything like that.

Q. When you told her you had got a stolen truck, you were dressed as an officer, were you?

A. No, I was not.

Q. You hadn't got the officer uniform then?

A. No.

Q. Hadn't you got it?

A. I had it but I was not wearing it.

Q. How were you dressed?

A. I was dressed in a leather jacket and pants.

Q. Would that show any badges?

A. No.

Q. It wouldn't show your rank?

A. No.

Q. What did she say when you told her you were in a stolen truck?

A. She did not make any comment to it at all.

Q. On the Wednesday night you saw her. 'I again saw Georgina, but we did not go out in the truck.' On that night, on the 3rd, where did you sleep? That is the first night you went out with her.

A. I slept in the truck.

Q. What you say I think, if I have got it in the right order, is, 'We then went back to Georgina's room where we stayed the night.' No; I'm sorry, I think that must be the 4th.

Mr JUSTICE CHARLES: 'Wednesday night I again saw Georgina, but we didn't go out in the truck.'

Mr MAUDE: Come to the next paragraph. 'I met Georgina at her room late Thursday afternoon, I do not recall the exact time. We went to a movie.' Is it true you did take her to the movies?

A. Yes.

Q. From the first to last, has the girl shown any fight?

A. No.

Q. Have you ever laid a hand on her?

A. No, I have not.

Q. What truth is there in the statement of you hitting her because she had gone downstairs to wash?

A. No truth at all. She often left me quite a few different times while I was in her room; she has been downstairs for a number of minutes.

Q. Was she under your domination in anyway?

A. No, she was not.

Q. Is there any truth in the stories that you had people to watch her?

A. No, there is not.

Q. Or that you always got people who informed first?

A. No, there is not.

Q. What is the truth about your sexual relationship?

A. I had no sexual relationship with her at all.

Q. Never?

A. Never.

Q. Was there any particular reason why that was so?

A. Yes. On the first night I stayed with her she told me she had a rash on her stomach and that she had to stop dancing on account of that. That put me cavy, because the Army is always telling us to watch out for things like that and stay away from that kind of thing.

Q. How many nights did you sleep in the room with her?

A. I believe it was three nights.

Q. Have you ever seen her cry?

A. No, sir I have never.

Q. Have you ever given her any money?

A. Yes, I did.

Q. How much?

A. Three one pound notes.

Q. When was that?

A. That was after the day George Heath met with the accident; that was that same morning.

Q. After Heath's death?

A. Yes.

Q. Where had that money come from?

A. That belonged to Heath.

Q. That was part of Heath's money?

A. Yes.

Q. Then we deal with Friday 6th October. You told the police, 'I remained in bed until 1500 hours. I gave Georgina the ticket for a B4 bag, which I had checked at the Metropolitan Tube Station in Hammersmith. She went down and got the bag for me.' Did she ever complain at all about being sent about by you, or being asked to go for anything for you?

A. No, she suggested herself that she should go down and get that bag for me.

Q. How long was she away?

A. Quite some time, I don't know the exact time of it.

Q. And although you may not have had any sexual relations with her, what were the relations between you? We know about the flowers; that is true is it – you got her some flowers?

A. Yes.

Q. How far did you go?

A. Well, almost the next thing to sexual intercourse.

Q. Oh, you did?

A. Yes.

Q. I will read on. 'After I changed clothes I left and went to visit my girlfriend Joyce Cook. We went to a movie and then returned to Joyce's house. I stayed at Joyce's until about 2300 hours.'

Mr JUSTICE CHARLES: That is eleven o'clock?

Mr MAUDE: Yes. People are getting so used to these hours now.

Mr JUSTICE CHARLES: Well I am not.

Mr MAUDE: 'When I left Joyce's house I went back to Georgina's house and whistled for her. She came down and met me out in front. We walked down the Hammersmith Broadway.' So far is that true?

A. Yes, it is.

Q. Look at the next sentence there; you see what it is? 'We had decided to stop a cab'; have you got that?

A. Yes.

Q. What did that mean? What were you two up to?

A. Well, when I met Mrs Jones I went up to her room after I had whistled for her. She brought me back up to the room and she then made some remark about going out at night and robbing a cab. I argued against her and she just kept on arguing with me and she told me to give her my gun and she was going to go out by herself. This I refused her.

Mr JUSTICE CHARLES: 'She said that we should go out and rob a cab. I argued against this. Then she asked me for my gun then she said she would go out herself'?

A. Yes, my lord. We dropped the subject there and I said, 'What do you say if we go and get something to eat?' which she agreed to.

Q. What?

A. I dropped the subject about the gun and I said, 'What about going out and getting something to eat?' which she agreed to and that is why we left the house and walked down the street from her place. That was closed. Then we walked down to another cafeteria, which was closed. She then said she knew of another place towards Knightsbridge and that is when we were on our way up there before we stopped in the doorway.

Mr MAUDE: That brought you into the doorway?

A. Yes.

Q. Was that the position between you at that moment?

A. Yes.

Q. Just look at it; you see it says, 'We had decided to stop a cab.'

A. Yes.

Q. You had decided to stop a cab, had you?

A. No.

Q. Not at that moment?

A. No.

Mr JUSTICE CHARLES: You had not? Are you sure of that?

A. These here words in this statement are not my own.

Q. You read it through and you signed each page of it?

A. Your Lordship, when this statement was taken, I did not read this through thoroughly.

Q. We have had a great deal of evidence that you read it through carefully and signed it.

A. I did not read it through carefully and sign it that way.

Q. 'We decided to stop a cab.' You go on, 'A cab went by and Georgina called "Taxi." I remained in the doorway. The car stopped.'

Mr MAUDE: My Lord, may I go on?

Mr JUSTICE CHARLES: Yes.

Mr MAUDE: 'A cab went by and Georgina called 'Taxi.' Is that true?

A. Yes.

Q. 'I remained in the doorway.' Is that true?

A. Yes.

Q. 'The car stopped. It was a grey Ford sedan, which I later learned to be driven by George Heath. I told Georgina to go and see how many people were in it.'

Mr JUSTICE CHARLES: Why?

Mr MAUDE: May I, my lord?

Mr JUSTICE CHARLES: As we go on we must know as we pass by these things.

Mr MAUDE: I know, if your Lordship would trust me just a little bit we are going to find out; but if I may take it in my own way, otherwise it is so tiring.

Mr JUSTICE CHARLES: Very well.

Mr MAUDE: 'I told Georgina to go and see how many people were in it. She went over and talked to the driver.' Why had you wanted to know how many people were in it?

A. After we were in the doorway we were arguing about stopping a cab and then we decided then…

Mr JUSTICE CHARLES: 'When in the doorway we decided.'

A. Yes.

Q. That is, to rob a cab?

A. Yes.

A FATAL PICKUP

Mr MAUDE: 'She came back and said that it was a private hire car and that only one person was in it, the driver. We both went over and got in the car.' Is that true?

A. Yes.

Q. 'I sat behind the driver and she sat on my left. I told the driver to turn around and go out King's Road.' That means King Street, does it?

A. Yes.

Q. 'He turned the car around and drove out of King's Road past Georgina's house. I told the driver that the place I wanted to go was just beyond the roundabout. It is the roundabout at this end of the Great West Road.' Is that, so far true?

A. Yes.

Q. 'When we got about twenty-five yards beyond the roundabout I told him that was the place.' Is that true?

A. Yes.

Q. Now you had a pistol, the automatic pistol?

A. Yes.

Q. Had you any ammunition for it? A. Yes.

Q. How long had you been carrying it about for? Ever since you were away without leave?

A. Close to that.

Q. It did not belong to you?

A. No.

Q. It is an American one?

A. Yes.

Q. Have you at any time intended or made up your mind to shoot somebody with it?

A. No, I never have.

Q. What were you doing, carrying it round loaded?

A. No particular reason at all. I just had it and the ammunition for it.

Q. Have you ever tried it at all?

A. Yes, I have.

Q. Where?

A. Just outside Reading, where I was shooting at a rabbit.

Q. How many shots before this night had been fired out of the pistol while it was in your possession?

A. About two.

Q. Had you been carrying it around the whole time loaded?

A. Yes.

Q. By loaded, I do not merely mean in the magazine, but in the breech, in the barrel of the thing?

A. No, there was none in it at the time.

Q. None in it at what time?

A. When I was carrying it around when I first had it.

Q. I am now talking about the night Heath met his death. As you came to the roundabout, to your knowledge then what was the state of the pistol so far as the ammunition was concerned?

A. I did not know it was loaded.

Q. Had you attempted to put it in a position to fire?

A. No, I did not.

Q. Where had you been carrying the thing?

A. Inside, between my belt and my body.

Q. Have you got the same sort of clothes on now, or not?

A. No, I have not.

Q. What is it can you explain to us, describe to us; what sort of jacket would you have?

A. I had a leather jacket on.

Q. Where is the belt? Does the jacket have a belt?

A. No, that is the pants belt.

Q. Does it go through things the leather belt goes through, straps on the pants, as you call them, on trousers?

A. Yes.

Q. So that pistol is stuck in between that belt and your pants?

A. No, that was on my body; it was on the inside of my pants.

Q. What side of you would you carry it?

A. I carried it on my right side.

Q. What was the idea in carrying it around?

A. I just had. There was no idea to it at all.

Mr JUSTICE CHARLES: Well, why?

A. I really don't know how to explain that, my lord.

Mr MAUDE: You had no address, had you?

A. No.

Q. Apart from the things you had got on you, you had no room, had you? Had you hired a room anywhere?

A. No, I did not.

Q. I think you told my lord and the jury that sometimes you slept in the truck. Was that right?

A. Yes.

Q. We know up to that time two nights you had slept with the girl Jones.

A. Yes.

Mr JUSTICE CHARLES: You could have left the pistol at her house, couldn't you?

A. I could have, yes.

Mr MAUDE: You evidently were not afraid to show it, because we have heard that you produced it at a restaurant?

A. I did not produce it at any restaurant.

Q. Just dealing with my point for the moment; we have heard a witness say that you did put it on a table openly. Were you afraid that anybody would see it or not?

A. Yes, I was.

Q. Had the girl said anything to you to try and prevent you doing this?

A. No, she had not.

Q. Any sort of indication?

A. None at all.

Q. That you ought not to, or that she did not want to?

A. No.

Q. And Heath was shot?

A. Yes.

Q. How did that come about?

A. After we got to the roundabout I told him where we wanted to stop. I had the gun in my lap because it had fallen out on the jaunting around of the car.

Mr JUSTICE CHARLES: 'I had my gun'; where?

A. In my right hand, between my legs and lap.

Q. 'In my right hand,' is that right?

A. Yes.

Q. 'It had jumped out from my belt.' Well, go on.

Mr MAUDE: Then he said it was in between his legs and his lap.

A. Yes, the driver of the cab stopped and as I was getting up, my arm, my right arm, was leaning on the armrest on the side of the car on the right side of the car. As he stopped he reached over the back to open the door and as he was reaching over the back to open the door, Miss Jones was up and I started to get up. At the same time my right sleeve caught on something on the right hand side of the door. What it was I don't know and as I went to go, the door just jerked me, and the gun went off at that time.

Q. In Jones's statement to the police there is nothing at all about a demand having been made to the taxi driver for his money before the shot was fired; but had there been any demand made of the taxi driver for his money before he was hit?

A. No, there had not.

Mr JUSTICE CHARLES: He was robbed after he was shot.

Mr MAUDE: Yes; I am much obliged. I wanted to make sure the point was clear. Then we know if we read on in the statement, that the man was taken and put in a place in the country, in a ditch or something. Had you spoken to him before you drove on?

A. Yes.

Q. What had you said to him?

A. His right leg was leaning over in the driver's part of the front of the car and I told him to move over, which he did and then I got in behind the wheel. That is all that was said to him.

Q. How was he taken from the car?

A. I had my arms under his armpits and I lifted his back and brought his feet across the seat. Mrs Jones got his bottom and his feet from the seat and helped me carry him and put him where he was put in the ditch there.

Q. Did she drive the car at any time?

A. No, she did not.

Q. I have dealt with one of those paragraphs and I am going now to this; 'I wish to state that, as we were driving to the ditch and Georgina was going through his pockets, I told her to look and see if he had a watch on. She looked and told me she had found a wristwatch on his arm.' So that all that, the taking of this man's watch, took place in the car on the way to the place he was eventually left?

A. Yes.

Q. 'As we were driving back after having disposed of the body Georgina gave me £4 in £1 notes, a long brown United States fountain pen, a silver pencil, a small leather cigarette lighter, a cigarette case and a watch. The watch which was just shown to me by Robert E De Mott is the watch she gave me.' That is all true?

A. Yes.

Q. 'As we were driving back Georgina threw all George Heath's pictures out of the car window. When we got back to

Hammersmith I parked the car in the old Gaumont car park where I used to park the truck. We took our handkerchiefs and wiped off the fingerprints from all parts of the car which we had touched.' I notice it says 'our fingerprints'; were you both wiping the car?

A. Yes.

Q. 'We stopped at a Black and White and got something to eat and then went home and went to bed.' Is there any truth in the story that you sat up all night unable to sleep, both of you?

A. No, there is not.

Q. Then we know you sold the watch to Mr Levene and the other articles, the pen and the pencil?

A. Yes.

Q. How does the girl come to know that you had only got nineteen shillings?

A. I think I had more than nineteen shillings on me.

Q. That is the same afternoon, is it, that you all went off to the greyhound racing?

A. Yes.

Q. Has she ever remonstrated with you over this death of Heath? What is the truth in the story about cold-blooded murder?

A. No truth at all.

Q. My lord will give me one moment; I have practically finished; I hope I have not taken very long. What is the last time before that revolver went off and resulted in Heath's death that you can remember attending to it; seeing what was in it, or what the state of it was?

A. I believe that was Friday morning, or Friday evening, close to Friday afternoon.

Q. Your evidence is inconsistent and contradictory to the statement you made to the police in respect of the actual firing of the gun. You know that, do you?

A. Yes.

Q. That is to say, you told the police in your second statement that you pulled the slide back and cocked the pistol as the car was coming to a stop; and when the car stopped you were holding your loaded and cocked pistol in front of your chest, when the car stopped. You looked over towards Jones and then, if I am right, the exact words are: 'As I was looking back towards the front again I pulled the trigger; just as I pulled the trigger the driver, who I later learn to be Heath, raised up and reached over the back seat to open the left rear door. He was reaching back with his left arm. When I pulled the trigger I intended to pull the trigger and fire the pistol. I intended to fire it through the car.' Had you ever had the intention of firing it through the car?

A. No.

Q. 'But I did not expect George Heath to raise up to open the door just as I did it.' I must ask you about that, those two stories being quite contradictory. How does it come that the story you told the police, or rather Mr De Mott, was not the truth?

A. When my statements were taken, Mr De Mott would ask me a question and I would give him an answer. Then he would turn round and say he would not take my answer for that, but he would say, 'Take it this way,' and start typing it out and he eventually put his own answer in.

Mr JUSTICE CHARLES: You know, other officers were there, watching. They say you were very calm, very collected and not in the least tired and that you read it quite carefully, you read each page through and signed each page. This is not a question of one sentence being wrong, it is a whole story, half the page. A whole complete story, which is totally different from the story you are telling now.

Mr MAUDE: My Lord, may I leave him for cross-examination by my learned friends.

Mr JUSTICE CHARLES: If you like.

Mr MAUDE: Hulten, you are not complaining of Mr De Mott, are you?

A. No, I am not complaining of him.

Q. Or the fairness of the British Police?

A. No.

Cross-examined by Mr CASSWELL defence for JONES.

Q. Hulten, were you trained as a paratrooper?

A. Yes

Q. How long were you trained?

A. About two months.

Q. I suppose you had other training as well?

A. Yes.

Q. Did you come over to this country to fight?

A. Yes.

Q. Did you do any fighting at all?

A. Very little.

Q. Did you go abroad at all?

A. No.

Q. Did you desert when your regiment went abroad?

A. No.

Q. How long before it went abroad did you desert?

A. I did not go absent without leave from the Army until after my outfit had gone.

Q. Then you did not go with them?

A. No.

Q. Why not?

A. Because I was left back to take charge of the motor pool while I was there.

Q. And having been left there to take charge of the car pool, apparently you deserted; is that right?

A. No.

Q. How long were you in charge before you deserted?

A. I was in charge quite some time. I had trouble with another American officer while I was there.

Q. Did you steal one of the cars of which you were in charge?

A. No.

Q. What made you desert?

A. As I told you a few minutes ago, I had an argument and trouble with another American officer.

Q. Another American officer? You are not an American officer?

A. No, but I put that term.

Q. Do you think that was a good excuse for deserting from the Army when your regiment was fighting abroad?

A FATAL PICKUP

A. If I may say so, I did not desert from the Army.

Q. What did you do then?

A. I went absent without leave.

Q. How does that differ?

A. It differs quite a lot.

Q. Tell me how.

A. If you are a deserter from the Army you have no intention of returning at all, but when you are absent without leave you come back.

Q. When did you intend to go back?

A. I went back to my camp quite a few different times.

Q. Did you ever report back?

A. Yes, I did.

Q. Do they take any steps in the American Army when a man has been absent without leave?

A. They do.

Q. Did they say anything to you about it?

A. Yes.

Q. Are you now telling us that you were absent without leave for six weeks, but that you went back from time to time?

A. I did.

Q. When did you go back?

A. I do not remember the exact dates. I went back there two or three different times. There is an American officer in the camp who will prove that to you, if you wish.

Q. Did you report to anybody when you went back?

A. No, I did not.

Q. How did they know you had come back?

A. Because I stayed there all night long with some friends of mine in the camp.

Q. Who did you report to anyone?

A. I reported to a First Sergeant there.

Q. Did anybody take your name?

A. They all knew my name; they did not have to take it.

Q. Your friends in the camp knew your name?

A. Yes.

Q. Did any officer know you had come back to the camp?

A. I was reported to another officer when I came back.

Q. Were any steps taken to deal with your offence?

A. I left right after that. The officer did not get there on time.

Q. Did that happen on several occasions?

A. Yes, it did.

Q. So that officer was never there in time to catch you?

A. No.

Q. Is that what you call reporting to your unit?

A. I do.

Q. Except when you slept at the camp with your friends, where did you sleep?

A. I slept in London.

Q. What?

A. I slept in London.

Q. There are American military policemen in London, are there not?

A. Yes, there are.

Q. I think you told us that you stole this big truck, did you?

A. I did.

Q. Where did that come from?

A. That came from Reading.

Q. What was the idea of stealing that?

A. I wanted to get up to London and I took that truck to go up there.

Q. Then you met Mrs Jones; you knew her as Georgina Grayson. How old did you think she was?

A. I was told what her age was; twenty-two years old.

Q. She doesn't look very old, does she?

A. She looked a lot older than she does now.

Q. Why did you want to go with Georgina Grayson? Did you want somewhere to sleep?

A. No.

Q. Why did you go with her?

A. I was introduced to her.

Q. Yes, I know; but because you are introduced to her it does not necessarily follow that you should take her out late at night?

A. I asked her to go out with me. She could have refused if she wished.

Q. Why did you?

A. I just asked her to go out with me.

Q. At the same time you were visiting another girl, Joyce Cook, were you not?

A. I had left there.

Q. You had left there?

A. I had left that house, was on my way down.

Q. Were you going back there again?

A. Not that night, no.

Q. Not that night. Then apparently this girl said to you that she wanted to do something desperate?

A. Not desperate; dangerous.

Q. Did you then show her your revolver?

A. I did not.

Q. Did you ever show her your revolver?

A. She saw it one night when I was up there with her.

Q. When?

A. I do not remember the exact date.

Mr JUSTICE CHARLES: There were only three nights, you know; which of them?

A. I think it was the second night when I was up there.

Q. That is the 4th, isn't it?

Mr CASSWELL: It would be the 5th I think, my lord. I don't want to make you say anything you don't want to say. Do you say the 5th was the first time she saw the revolver?

A. I think it was.

Q. Did you say anything to her at all about what you were when you first met her?

A. I told her I was a paratrooper.

Q. Did she ask you why you were not with your regiment?

A. She did.

Q. What did you tell her?

A. I told her my regiment was in Holland.

Q. Did she ask you why you were not in Holland?

A. No, she did not.

Q. Did you explain to her; give her any explanation?

A. I did not.

Q. Did you do anything to fire her imagination, if you understand if you know what I mean?

A. I am afraid I don't understand you.

Q. Did you say anything to make yourself a hero in her eyes?

A. I'm afraid not.

Q. Did you, in your own words, give yourself a build up?

A. No.

Mr JUSTICE CHARLES: Now, do think before you answer, you know.

A. I am quite sure I did not.

Mr CASSWELL: Will you look at your statement.

Mr JUSTICE CHARLES: Be careful; I am sure you will be careful.

A. He is talking about the 5th, isn't he my lord.

Q. Look at your statement, at the end of your statement. You make no complaint against Mr De Mott of any sort or description.

Mr CASSWELL: Do you see a sentence beginning, 'I did tell Georgina'? Two inches above where you say, 'I have read my statement and it is true.'

Mr JUSTICE CHARLES: The last page. 'I did tell Georgina.'

A. I am afraid it is not on the last page here.

Q. Haven't you got it?

A. No.

Q. Give it to me. (Handed to his Lordship) The last three words on that page and the next page, 'I did tell' (Handed back to the witness).

Mr CASSWELL: Just read those words out, will you?

Mr JUSTICE CHARLES: Read them yourself.

A. 'I did tell Georgina I had broken into a pub and that I had been running around with a mob in Chicago. This was not true. It was just a build-up for me.'

Mr CASSWELL: Did you tell Mr De Mott that?

A. Yes.

Q. Why did you say just now you had not?

A. I believed you were talking about the 5th.

Q. You thought I was talking about a different date?

A. Yes.

Q. Then how did you make her believe that you were a gangster running around with a mob in Chicago?

A. I told her that.

Q. Why?

A. It was just a build-up.

Q. A build-up? A. Yes.

Q. Does a build-up mean that you wanted to make yourself a bit of a he-man and a hero with her?

A. No.

Q. What does it mean, this build-up?

A. I really don't know.

Q. You were telling her a gross untruth, weren't you?

A. Yes, I was.

Q. I want to know why. Can't you explain why? I suggest you were making yourself out to be a very fine man, one of the adventurous spirits who does not care what he does; is that what you were doing?

A. No.

Q. Did you go further and say you were the sort of man who shot on sight?

A. I did not.

Q. Did you tell her that you shot anybody who told about you?

A. I did not.

Q. All that then is untrue?

A. That is untrue.

Q. Did you simply stop at that and say, 'I have been running around with a mob in Chicago'? Is that what you said?

A. Yes.

Q. Nothing about what you did with the mob?

A. No.

Q. Nothing more to help you with the build-up, as you say?

A. No.

Q. You thought that was enough?

A. Yes.

Q. That was a lie. You also told her a lie when you said that you were a lieutenant, didn't you?

A. I did.

Q. And you gave her a false name?

A. I did.

Q. What was the idea in deceiving her like this?

A. Hardly anyone in Hammersmith knew my name. There was only two or three different people who knew my true name. No one else did.

Q. Did you show her how the revolver worked?

A. When?

Mr JUSTICE CHARLES: At any time?

Mr CASSWELL: When you first showed it to her, which you have told us was on the 5th.

A. No, I did not.

Mr JUSTICE CHARLES: Did you at any time?

A. Yes, I did.

Mr CASSWELL: When was that?

A. I believe that was the day I was cleaning up, Friday morning or close to Friday afternoon.

Q. After the death of Heath?

A. No, that was before the death of Heath.

Q. This afternoon you told us that, before you went out that night, she asked you to hand her the revolver; is that so?

A. That is so.

Q. Do you suggest that she was going with the revolver, to hold up a taxi?

A. She wanted that revolver and I did not give it to her.

Mr JUSTICE CHARLES: What for?

A. She just said, 'Give me the revolver. I will go out by myself.'

Q. To do what?

A. She did not say what.

Mr CASSWELL: Have you ever told anybody that before this afternoon?

A. I have.

Q. You notice that it was not put to her when she was in the box?

A. I noticed that.

Q. Was your idea was that you would make her into a 'moll', as it is called?

A. No.

Q. When you went out that night – is it not true, I understand you went out deciding to stop a taxi or a cab, or is it?

A. It was not.

Q. Had you made up your mind when you went out to stop a cab?

A. No.

Q. When did you decide to stop a cab?

A. When we stopped in the doorway.

Q. And you sent her out into the road, I understand, to stop a cab. Did you see her speak to the driver?

A. No.

Q. Did she go out?

A. She did go out, yes.

Q. Wasn't that because you told her to?

A. No, she called from the doorway. She didn't go out into the road.

Q. Then, after that, she went out into the road, I understand. She says you told her to; is that so?

A. No.

Mr JUSTICE CHARLES: To go and see how many people there were in the car?

A. I did not tell her that. She came back and I asked her then.

Q. How many people were in the car?

A. Yes.

Q. Why did you want to know that?

A. As I said before, we had decided to rob a cab.

Mr CASSWELL: Why did you stay in the doorway?

A. Because it was windy out.

Q. So the girl could go out into the wind, but the soldier must stay in cover?

A. She was in the doorway. She had left that doorway before I knew she had gone out there.

Q. You did not mean her to go out?

A. No.

A FATAL PICKUP

Q. Do you mean that?

A. I do.

Q. Then as I understand, all the way during that journey you did not mean to use the revolver; is that so?

A. That is true.

Q. Did you ever tell her that you were going to use the revolver?

A. No, I did not.

Q. When did it slip out under your belt and get into your lap?

A. Just a little after the car turned around.

Q. Just when it went round?

A. Just a little after the car turned around and was going down the street.

Q. It had turned round before it started up King Street, had it?

A. Yes.

Q. All that time your revolver was on your lap, was it?

A. No, it was not; it was in my belt until then.

Q. That was before you started to drive, or just when you started to drive?

A. It was in there all that time before then.

Q. I understand you said the car turned round and you started towards King's Street?

A. That is true.

Q. And it was then that the revolver fell into your lap?

A. It did not fall into my lap. It fell on my right side.

Q. Did it move then, or what?

A. It fell out. It had moved; it had worked itself up during the jaunting of the cab.

Q. Did you realise it had moved its way up?

A. No, I did not.

Q. When did you first realise your revolver was loose?

A. When it took and slipped back.

Q. When was that?

A. That was when we were going along the road.

Q. Before or after you passed her house?

A. I think it was a little before her house.

Q. Did you tell her that it had fallen out?

A. No, I did not.

Mr JUSTICE CHARLES: You were sitting next to her, weren't you?

A. The back seat is…

Q. She was sitting next to you, wasn't she?

A. Over in the corner, and I was then in the other corner.

Mr CASSWELL: She did not know you had got it there at all in your hands, did she?

A. No, she did not.

Q. I think I heard you say that there was no cartridge in the barrel that morning, is that so?

A. Yes.

Q. How did it get there?

A. When I took and threw the bolt back, any cartridge that was in the barrel would come out.

A FATAL PICKUP

Q. Just let me have the revolver. Just tell if I am right. That is where the magazine goes in, isn't it?

A. That's right.

Q. With seven cartridges in it, if it is full?

A. That's right.

Q. Is it quite safe if I put the magazine in there; nothing can happen, can it?

A. That's right.

Q. I have first got to pull the trigger back, haven't I?

A. No, you do not.

Q. Do you mean you can pull that without pulling the trigger back?

A. Yes, I think you can.

Q. You have got to do that before the cartridge goes into the barrel?

A. You do.

Q. When did you do that?

A. I did that Friday morning, or Friday afternoon, whatever you call it. It was close around noontime when I was fooling with the gun.

Q. What for?

A. I did that to make sure there was nothing in the chamber.

Q. That very action put something into the chamber?

A. It does.

Q. You did not realise it?

A. No, I did not.

Mr JUSTICE CHARLES: Do you mean to say you did not know, when you did that, you were putting a cartridge into the chamber?

A. Before I took and pulled the bolt back I took and pushed the little clip there and the magazine came down and caught my little finger. That extracted the bullet and the magazine was not down far enough and at that time it threw another bullet into the barrel.

Mr CASSWELL: She said as she was sitting beside you she heard a click. Were you doing that?

A. No, I was not.

Q. Was there any click?

A. Not that I could have heard.

Q. Why was the hammer back? So that it would fire?

A. That had probably been back all day long for all I knew.

Q. You did not pull it back at that moment?

A. No, I did not.

Mr JUSTICE CHARLES: Do you mean you were wandering about with the hammer up all the day?

A. As far as I know I was.

Mr CASSWELL: So you did not even mean it to go off?

A. No, I did not.

Q. It did go off; and it must have made a very loud noise in that car, didn't it?

A. Yes.

Q. Then you found that a man had been very grievously injured?

A. I did not know how bad he was hurt.

Q. Did you look to see?

A. No.

Mr JUSTICE CHARLES: Didn't you?

A. No.

Q. A man in a cab who has been shot with your pistol, as you say, by pure accident and you never looked to see how badly he was shot, whether he was dead or alive?

A. No, I did not. I knew he was shot and I got frightened.

Mr CASSWELL: You got frightened, yes. The next thing was you asked this girl to take the things out of his pockets, didn't you?

A. I asked her to find out who he was.

Mr JUSTICE CHARLES: That is not the question.

Mr CASSWELL: Did you ask her to take the things out of his pockets?

A. I did not.

Q. You asked her to put her hands in the pockets of a badly wounded man to find, you say, his wallet?

A. No, I did not say that.

Q. To find out who he was, did you think that was the right thing to do, the right request to make to a young woman?

A. I asked her to find out who he was. I did not say to take his wallet or anything else.

Q. Did you ask her where his watch was, whether he had a watch?

A. No, I did not.

Q. Did she hand over to you various things, cigarette case, a watch and a lighter?

A. She handed me four pounds. The rest of the things she put in her pocket until she was back in her room.

Q. She says you told her to put them in her pocket and hand them to you after; is that right?

A. No.

Mr JUSTICE CHARLES: But she did?

A. She did have them.

Mr CASSWELL: I see in your statement you say, 'I got in under the wheel. I told Georgina to look him over for his wallet.' Is that right?

A. I did not.

Q. Another mistake that Mr De Mott made then, in taking down your statement?

A. Yes, it is.

Q. Do you ask the members of the jury to believe that you are telling the truth now?

A. I certainly do.

Q. You have told an untruth many times haven't you?

A. I didn't hear.

Q. You didn't hear me?

A. No.

Q. I said, you have told untruths many times, but now you ask the jury to believe that you are telling the truth?

A. I am here under oath.

Q. You were under oath when you made the last statement to Mr De Mott, were you not?

A. I was.

Mr JUSTICE CHARLES: Members of the jury, I am sure it is unnecessary to tell a jury of Central Criminal Court not to talk about this case to anybody. It is very difficult not to. I know it is even difficult for a judge, but it is more difficult, perhaps for jurors; but don't talk about it.

(Adjourned till Monday next at 11 o'clock.)

CHAPTER TEN

THE TRIAL - FIFTH DAY

MONDAY 22ND JANUARY 1945

Mr CASSWELL: My Lord, there was one question I ought to have asked Hulten. I don't know whether I might ask it now?

Mr JUSTICE CHARLES: Certainly.

KARL GUSTAV HULTEN, Recalled.

Further cross-examined by Mr CASSWELL.

Q. Hulten, as a paratrooper are you issued with a knife?

A. We are.

Q. Is that something which looks like or might be mistaken for a dagger?

A. No.

Q. It is a long knife isn't it?

A. No.

Q. For use as a dagger?

A. No.

Q. What is it for use as?

A. For cutting your lines.

Q. What does that mean?

A. If you are hooked up any place you use it to cut yourself out.

Q. Did you show that knife?

A. No.

Q. Never?

A. No.

Q. She says you showed her two?

A. Those were bought in London.

Q. Did you have such a knife on you? You had two knives on you, had you?

A. No, I did not have any knives at all on me.

Q. Where were they?

A. They were in a bag, a B4 bag.

Q. The valise which she got from the station?

A. Yes.

Mr MAUDE: There is one matter which I should be obliged if your Lordship would allow me to mention?

Mr JUSTICE CHARLES: Certainly.

Mr MAUDE: Your Lordship remembers Mr Casswell quite properly making the point that certain questions had never been put to the woman in respect of her having urged him to go out with the gun. Does your Lordship remember that?

Mr JUSTICE CHARLES: I do.

Mr MAUDE: I sat in silence, but the position was this; I saw Hulten on the Saturday before this trial started and when I had finished I told the solicitor's clerk that I wished him to have his statements signed, as your Lordship can imagine in such a serious case. An addition was then made to the statement the same as he swore in the box, but that addition was brought to my notice verbally, was not incorporated in my proof. Does your Lordship remember when I bent over my papers to see if I got anything else and not being there, it entirely escaped my mind. It might, I suppose, fairly be called an afterthought; he had added after the proof had originally been taken, but he had in fact, instructed us. That is the position.

Mr JUSTICE CHARLES: I quite understand.

Mr MAUDE: I thought I ought to say that it is not his fault, but we now know the whole facts.

Cross-examined by Mr BYRNE for the Prosecution.

Q. Hulten, you have been absent from the Army, you say, for six weeks?

A. Yes.

Q. During that time, you had been drawing no Army pay?

A. No.

Q. Had you been spending the greater part of your time in and around London?

A. Yes.

Q. The pistol we have seen in this case, how long had you had that in your possession?

A. I could not say for sure.

Q. Well, was it a matter of days or weeks?

A. A matter of weeks.

Q. How long had you had the ammunition that was found on you when you were arrested?

A. Just a few days.

Q. When you first came into possession of the pistol, did you at the same time come into possession of ammunition for it as well?

A. No.

Q. Did you acquire the ammunition that was found on you when you were arrested, at some time after you first got possession of the pistol?

A. Yes.

Q. Was it a pistol that you had been taught how to use in the Army?

A. Yes.

Q. On Friday 6th October, were you hard up?

A. No, sir.

Q. How much money had you?

A. I had a little over £2.

Q. A little over £2?

A. Yes.

Q. Had you a little over £2 when you called at Jones's room that night?

A. I believe I did.

Q. Are you quite sure of that?

A. I am quite sure.

Q. You know Jones has said that you had 19 shillings that night?

A. I had a little over £2.

Q. How much had she?

A. I don't know.

Q. If you wanted any more money you would, would you not, either have to steal it or borrow it?

A. I could have borrowed it.

Q. You could have borrowed it, could you? Do you mean from friends of yours in the Army?

A. Yes.

Q. You hadn't very much prospect of repaying it, had you?

A. It was money that they owed me.

Q. It is quite true is it not, that night you and Jones decided to rob a taxi cab driver?

A. Yes.

Q. That is quite true; and when you and she got into that cab you got into it, did you, with the intention of robbing the driver of that cab?

A. Yes.

Q. You never intended to pay him a fare for driving you anywhere, did you?

A. No.

Q. If she had not wanted to get into that cab with you, was there anything on earth to prevent her from walking away?

A. No sir, there was not.

Q. She says she got into that cab on your orders. Is there a word of truth in that?

A. No sir, there is not.

Q. When you got into that cab with Jones you had the pistol with you?

A. Yes.

Q. Was it loaded?

A. I did not know at the time.

Q. There is no doubt about it that in fact it must have been?

A. Yes.

Q. There is no doubt about it, is there, not only it must have been loaded but its magazine was in such a position that all you had to do was to pull the trigger in order to fire the shot?

A. Yes.

Q. When you were arrested on Monday 9th October that pistol was in precisely the same condition of readiness then, was it not?

A. No.

Q. Are you sure?

A. Yes, I handed that pistol over to the officers.

Q. Well, you heard the evidence of the police officer, didn't you, when he gave it in the witness box?

A. Yes.

Q. Did you hear him say that the pistol was cocked?

A. Yes, I did.

Q. The safety catch was in a position when it could be fired by merely pressing the trigger?

A. Yes.

Q. Was he right or wrong when he said that?

A. He was wrong.

Q. How were you and Jones proposing to rob the driver of this car; what was your method to be?

A. After he stopped it to get out and then confront him at his side door.

Mr BYRNE: I am going to ask you to be good enough to repeat that because I don't think any of us on this side of the court quite heard that.

Mr JUSTICE CHARLES: The method of the robbery that you proposed to carry out was what?

A. After the door was open, to get out and go round to his side.

Mr BYRNE: What were you going to do when you got there?

A. When I got there, just to leave him.

Q. What?

A. To go back our own way.

Q. No, no; we had got to this point: you say you were to get out of the car and go round to his side door. What were you going to do when you got there?

A. Demand the money from him.

Q. By what means?

A. By showing him the pistol.

Q. Had you decided what you would do if he did not yield?

A. No, I had not.

Q. Would you have fired in order to frighten him?

A. I don't think I would have.

Mr JUSTICE CHARLES: Might you have?

A. No, sir.

Mr BYRNE: Just let us see. You see, if you had gone round to his side door, presented the pistol at him, called upon him to hand over his money and he had refused to do so, if you had taken no further step in the matter, presumably he would have gone away, wouldn't he?

A. Yes.

Q. And you would have gone away without effecting your purpose?

A. That's right, sir.

Q. And he would have seen you?

A. Yes.

Q. And would be able to put the police on your track?

A. Yes.

Q. Had those thoughts occurred to you?

A. No.

Q. Do you really tell the jury that?

A. Yes.

Q. Didn't you look to your weapon before you embarked on this exploit?

A. No, I did not.

Q. Where was the pistol when you got into the car?

A. It was tucked in on my right side between my shirt and pants on the right side.

Q. Were you wearing an overcoat?

A. No, I was not.

Mr JUSTICE CHARLES: It was between what?

A. My shirt and my pants.

Mr BYRNE: According to the story that you have told the jury, when the pistol was tucked into your pants it was cocked, the safety catch was in the ready position so that it could be fired if the trigger was pressed; is that right?

A. That is right.

Q. Were you content to walk about with a pistol in that condition of readiness tucked into the top of your trousers?

A. I didn't know that it was in that position.

Q. You didn't know it was in that position?

A. No.

Q. Do you really seriously tell the jury that?

A. I am serious about that.

Q. You are used to handling firearms in the Army, are you?

A. Yes.

Q. You have been taught ever since you have been in the Army that a weapon must be rendered safe if you are going to carry it about?

A. Yes.

Q. That is an elementary precaution isn't it?

A. Yes.

Q. Are you seriously telling the jury that you stuck that thing in the top of your trousers without troubling to see whether it was in a position in which it would be fired by merely pressing the trigger?

A. I am.

Q. When you got into the car you sat behind the driver, did you?

A. I did.

Q. And this woman in the dock sat in the other corner of the back seat?

A. On my left.

Q. As you sat down, was your pistol firmly tucked into the top of your pants?

A. When I sat down the pistol came out.

Q. As soon as you sat down?

A. Yes.

Q. When you gave evidence on Friday afternoon you were cross-examined by Mr Casswell. Did you say that the revolver fell out of your belt when you were passing Jones's house in this car?

A. I did.

Mr JUSTICE CHARLES: I think he said with the jaunting of the car. It jumped out with the jaunting of the car as he was passing Jones's house.

Mr BYRNE: What are we to understand? Did it fall out twice then?

A. Yes, it did.

Q. Why didn't you tell the jury that?

A. You did not ask me.

Mr JUSTICE CHARLES: And even then it was cocked and the safety catch was at danger, so that you only had to pull the trigger for it to go off?

A. It was dark in the vehicle; you couldn't see.

Mr BYRNE: It is possible, is it not, to feel whether the hammer is back and the safety catch is up or down without looking at it?

A. It is.

Q. Did you take those elementary precautions?

A. No, I did not.

Q. Have you got a hip pocket in your pants?

A. Yes, I have.

Q. Big enough to hold a pistol?

A. Yes.

Q. When it first fell out of your pocket as soon as you got in, did it occur to you that evidently the top of your pants was not a very good place to keep it?

A. Yes.

Q. Why didn't you put it in the hip pocket?

A. It would not fit in when I was sitting down.

Q. When you were sitting down? You told me a minute ago the hip pocket would take the pistol?

A. If you are standing up it will take it.

Q. But sitting down it won't?

A. No.

Q. So back you tucked it into the top of your pants?

A. Yes.

Q. Without troubling to find out the position of the safety catch or the hammer?

A. Yes.

Q. Or indeed, whether the thing was loaded?

A. That's right.

Q. And then, as the car bounced, it came out again?

A. It did.

Q. What happened? Did it fall down onto the floor, or what became of it?

A. It just slipped out to my rear.

Q. Onto the seat?

A. Yes.

Q. Then, according to the story you told the jury, you decided that you would nurse it after that keep in in your hand?

A. I just held onto it.

Q. That is what I mean, you kept it in your hand?

A. Yes.

Q. Did you find out whether it was in a safe condition?

A. I did not look to see.

Q. Did you feel to see?

A. No.

Q. Then you arrived at the spot that you had selected for the robbery?

A. Yes.

Q. That was the roundabout on the Great West Road?

A. Yes.

Q. That was the moment, was it not, when the pistol was going to be used?

A. Yes.

Q. That was the moment when it was going to be presented at the driver?

A. Yes.

Q. Here you were sitting behind the man whom you intended to rob nursing a pistol which in fact was loaded with your finger on its trigger; that is the position, isn't it?

A. Yes.

Q. Are you asking the jury to say that, because your sleeve caught in something, the pistol went off by accident?

A. It certainly did.

Q. When the driver had been shot, you and this woman robbed him, didn't you, after he had received the bullet?

A. Yes.

Q. Did you by any chance say to the driver after he had been shot, 'Move over, or I will give you another dose of the same thing'?

A. No, I did not.

Q. You heard her say that?

A. Yes, I did.

Q. The position then was this, was it not, that by pure accident the driver had now received a shot in his body from behind, so that you and this woman were able to carry out quite easily the very purpose for which you had got into his cab, namely to rob him? Is that the position?

A. It is.

Q. A most extraordinary coincidence isn't it?

A. It is.

A FATAL PICKUP

Q. Now I am going to suggest to you in the plainest possible terms that the story that I have now been investigating is a pack of lies. You understand that?

A. I understand.

Q. Do you realise that the version of what happened in the cab, according to your statement, bears no resemblance to your evidence in the witness box? Do you realise that?

A. No, I do not.

Q. Take your second statement in your hand will you? I will hand it to you, as I think you will find it more convenient, a typed copy of your statement; it is easier to read and it is paged the same as ours so that one can refer you to particular pages.

A. This is the statement that Lieutenant De Mott took. These are not my own words.

Q. Pardon?

A. This is the statement Lieutenant De Mott has taken; they are not my words.

Q. Don't think for one moment that I am not going to deal with that aspect of the matter; I know what you said about it. Mr De Mott would ask you a question - I can find your actual words in one moment: 'I would answer the question. Mr De Mott would say: 'Isn't it this way?' and then write down another version'?

A. Yes.

Q. That is what you say about it, is it?

A. Yes, I certainly do.

Q. Don't think for one moment I am overlooking that; I am going to deal with that. When you had completed this statement, what happened? Did you read it yourself, or was it read over to you?

A. I did not read it and it was not read over to me.

Q. You know it has been said by Mr De Mott that you read it yourself?

A. I know he said I read it. I glanced through it and that was all.

Mr JUSTICE CHARLES: And by Inspector Tarr and Inspector Tansill.

Mr BYRNE: Yes it was said by Mr De Mott and the two inspectors Tarr and Tansill that you read it over. Did you sign each page of it?

A. I did.

Mr JUSTICE CHARLES: Let me have the original. Do you say, 'I did not read this statement'?

A. That's right.

Q. You really mean that? Turn round to the jury. Do you really mean that?

A. I most certainly do.

Q. You made alterations even in the spelling and initialled the alterations.

A. I was asked to do that. I did not see those alterations myself; Lieutenant De Mott showed me where they were and I took and initialled them.

Mr BYRNE: Tell me this. When that statement was being made, did you realise that you were in a very serious position?

A. I did not.

Q. Let me see what your knowledge amounted to. You had been arrested when you were actually getting into the car in which Heath had been shot? Is that right?

A FATAL PICKUP

A. That's right.

Q. Shot accidentally by you?

A. Yes.

Q. And robbed by you?

A. He was not robbed by me.

Q. What do you mean by that answer?

A. I didn't take anything out of his pockets or off him.

Q. Do you think that, if you did not take anything out of his pockets, you are not guilty then of robbery?

A. If you are in possession of them afterwards you are equally guilty.

Q. Let us understand the position. You told me - tell me if you want to alter it - that you and that woman in the dock got into that cab with the intention of robbing the driver?

A. That is true.

Q. And she took things out of his pockets as part of that common plan that you both had?

A. Yes.

Q. Well, then did you mean by your answer that you yourself did not take anything out of the man's pockets?

A. I did.

Q. I see; I will not pursue that. Well, I had got as far as that you knew you had been arrested when you were getting into the very car that in which that man had met his death. You knew that when you were making this statement, didn't you?

A. I did not know that the man was dead when I was arrested.

Q. What?

A. I did not know the man was dead when I got into the car.

Mr JUSTICE CHARLES: You did not know the man was dead when you were arrested?

A. No, sir I did not.

Q. On 9th October?

A. Yes.

Mr BYRNE: You are seriously telling that to the jury, are you?

A. I certainly am.

Q. You really mean that?

A. I do. I asked Lieutenant De Mott what charge I was on and he refused to tell me for quite some time.

Q. Let us just pursue that for a minute or two. After the driver had been shot you drove the car, did you not?

A. I did.

Q. He was slumped on the seat by the side of you?

A. I could not say he was slumped.

Q. What was he doing; was he talking?

A. He was, yes.

Q. Talking, was he? What did he say?

A. I could not understand him.

Q. When did he cease to talk?

A. I don't remember.

Q. Was he talking still when you dumped him in the ditch?

A. No, he was not.

Q. Did you see blood from the bullet wound on him?

A. No, I did not.

Q. Did you mean you did not trouble to look?

A. No.

Q. Did you trouble to look when, by accident, you had shot the man?

A. I did not.

Q. Did you care whether in fact he was dead or alive?

A. I really don't know.

Q. Don't you? Just think about it.

Mr JUSTICE CHARLES: Just a minute; let me take that down. 'I do not know whether I cared if he was dead or alive.'

Mr BYRNE: Just think about it.

A. It all depends on how you mean that, sir.

Q. Well, you see, you had according to your statement to the jury, accidentally shot that man and you had put his body in or near a ditch on some lonely part of the Great West Road. That is right, isn't it?

A. Yes.

Q. And left him there?

A. Yes.

Q. Did you know when you left him whether he was dead or alive?

A. No, I did not.

Q. Did you care whether he was dead or alive?

A. I didn't look.

Q. Did you care whether he was dead or alive?

A. I am sorry, but I can't answer that. I don't know what you mean by it.

Mr JUSTICE CHARLES: It is a simple question.

A. But it carries a lot of meanings, sir.

Q. It is a simple question. You dumped this man in the ditch and left him. Did you know whether he was dead or alive when you dumped him there?

A. I did not know.

Mr BYRNE: Now let us return to the statement. When you were making that statement to Mr De Mott, you knew that a man had been shot by you accidentally and that he was lying, whether dead or alive, in some ditch by the Great West Road. You knew that, didn't you?

A. Yes.

Q. And you knew, moreover, that he had been robbed, didn't you?

A. I did, sir.

Q. Are you telling the jury that, when you made this statement, you did not realise what a serious position you were in?

A. I don't think I did.

Q. You what?

A. I don't think I did.

Q. You don't think you did?

A. No.

Q. Well, what did you think about the position that you were in? What did you think about it?

A. I didn't think.

Q. You didn't think?

A. No.

Q. Just look at the statement, will you? You will find the pages numbered at the bottom. Will you just look at page eleven? Do you see at the top of that page: 'After I changed clothes I left and went to visit my girlfriend Joyce Cook'? You are dealing then with the 6th October, do you follow? Have you found that passage?

A. Yes, I have.

Q. 'We went to a movie and then returned to Joyce's house. I stayed at Joyce's until about eleven o'clock. When I left Joyce's house I went back to Georgina's house and whistled for her. She came down and met me out in front.' Is all that accurate so far?

A. Yes.

Q. You didn't make any mistake about that?

A. No.

Q. 'We walked down to Hammersmith Broadway and on towards Knightsbridge.'

A. Yes.

Q. You didn't make any mistake about that?

A. That is right.

Q. 'It was windy and we stopped in a doorway.' Is that correct?

A. That is correct.

Q. 'We had decided to stop a cab.'

A. Yes.

Q. So that so far he has got down accurately what you said with regard to this night?

A. That's right.

Q. Now let us go on. 'A cab went by and Georgina called "Taxi".'

A. Yes.

Q. 'I remained in the doorway.'

A. Yes.

Q. 'The car stopped.'

A. Yes.

Q. 'It was a grey Ford sedan, which I later learned to be driven by George Heath.'

A. Yes.

Q. 'I told Georgina to go and see how many people were in it.'

A. Yes.

Q. 'She went over to talk to the driver.'

A. Yes.

Q. 'She came back and said it was a private hire car and that only the driver was in it.' Is that correct?

A. Yes.

Q. 'We both went over and got into the car.'

A. Yes.

Q. ' I sat behind the driver.' Correct?

A. Yes.

Q. 'I told the driver to turn around and go up King's Road.'

A. Yes.

Q. 'He turned the car around and drove up King's Road past Georgina's house.'

A FATAL PICKUP

A. Yes.

Q. 'I told the driver that the place I wanted to go was just beyond the roundabout.'

A. Correct.

Q. 'It is the roundabout at the end of the Great West Road.'

A. Yes.

Q. Then the first two paragraphs of this he has got down quite accurately, has he?

A. Yes.

Q. Now let us go on. 'When we got about twenty-five yards beyond the roundabout I told him that was the place.'

A. Correct.

Q. 'When we got to the roundabout I took my pistol from my right hip pocket.' Is that correct?

A. No, sir.

Q. Now what had you told him, do you allege, which caused him to write down, 'When we got to the roundabout I took my pistol from my right hip pocket'?

A. I don't remember the words I said at the time, but I know it was not those.

Q. You see, your version of it in the witness box is nothing like this at all, is it?

A. I know that.

Q. Nothing like it. What is it you say about it then? Are you saying that by some mischance a version of what happened in that cab was written down which was quite contrary to the version that you told him?

A. Yes.

Q. Are you telling the jury that you told him that the pistol was tucked into the top of your pants and that it fell out?

A. It certainly did.

Q. And instead of that, what he gets down to is that you took the pistol from your right hip pocket?

A. I believe there are similar words to that in Jones's statement.

Mr JUSTICE CHARLES: A great deal of this he could not have gathered from Jones's statement at all; so that will not do.

Mr BYRNE: Did you tell him that you did not know whether the pistol was cocked and ready for action?

A. I did.

Q. And he wrote down, did he, if you look at the next sentence, 'Just as the car was coming to a stop I pulled the slide back and cocked the pistol'? That is what appears there, isn't it?

A. I see that. I really read this statement over the first time my solicitor brought it to me and I mentioned those facts to him at the same time.

Q. You see at the end of that page, the very last line: 'When the car stopped I was holding my loaded and cocked pistol in front of my chest.' Do you see that?

A. I do.

Q. You never said a word like that, did you?

A. That is approximately the place it was held, but I did not say it was loaded and cocked.

Q. You were holding it in front of your chest, were you?

A. Yes, I was.

Q. Pick it up and let us see what you mean.

A. I was holding it like this and my arm was resting on the armrest there; it was just dangling in front of me.

Q. It was not pointing at the driver at all?

A. No.

Q. 'When the car stopped I looked over towards Georgina. As I was looking back towards the front again I pulled the trigger. Just as I pulled the trigger the driver, who I later learned to be George Heath, raised up and reached over the back seat to open the left rear door. He was reaching back with his left arm.' Did you say anything like that?

A. Yes, but I did not say I pulled the trigger. I described how George Heath was reaching over to open the back door.

Q. 'When I pulled the trigger I intended to pull the trigger and fire the pistol. I intended to fire it through the car, but I did not expect George Heath to raise up to open the back door just as I did it.' Did you say nothing at all from which he would have written that down by mistake?

A. I said that the gun went off as I was getting up. He was in approximately that position when he was hit.

Q. Yes, but did you say, 'When I pulled the trigger I intended to pull the trigger and fire the pistol'? Did you say that?

A. No, I did not.

Q. 'I intended to fire it through the car.' Did you say that?

A. No, I did not.

Q. 'But I did not expect George Heath to raise up to open the door just as I did it.' Did you say that?

A. No.

Mr JUSTICE CHARLES: You say that he got in the way of the bullet; you did not mean to fire at him. You meant, I suppose, to fire to frighten him across the car and he moved just at that moment and the bullet went into him. Do you say Lieutenant De Mott invented all that?

A. Those are not my words.

Q. Never mind about your words; do you say he has invented that story?

A. That is his version of it.

Q. It is not a question of version; has he invented that story?

A. I don't know whether he has invented it.

Q. Oh, well he must have.

A. It is his version of the thing.

Q. Did you say anything like it at all?

A. I said something approximately like it, but I did not say those things.

Mr BYRNE: Are you telling the jury that you told Mr De Mott the story that you have told in that witness box?

A. I believe I did.

Mr JUSTICE CHARLES: Now think carefully. Don't say, 'I believe.' You know whether you did or did not.

A. I say I believe I did.

Q. And, having put all the rest of it down correctly, he suddenly started inventing and putting down a totally different story?

A. He put down what I said up to the fact of walking up to the doorway at Hammersmith Broadway towards Knightsbridge.

Mr BYRNE: Oh yes, the earlier part you told me you agreed with; but the vital part in this case, you say, is entirely different from what you told him; is that correct?

A. Yes.

Q. When you were telling him something quite different from what he wrote down all that was being done in the presence of two other people was it?

A. I imagine it was.

Q. Don't 'imagine'; you were there. Just use your intelligence.

A. I believe there was more than two other people there.

Q. That may well be, I think there was an Agent Riddle; Agent Riddle and Mr De Mott and two Scotland Yard Officers, Inspectors Tarr and Tansill: is that correct?

A. That is correct.

Q. And in spite of the fact that Mr De Mott had, in addition to you, three other people present listening to what was taking place, he was there writing down a version completely different from the version you were telling him?

A. That is true.

Q. I just want to go on a little further. You see the next sentence: 'When I fired the shot I knew that I had hit him as I heard him say 'Oh'.' Is that right; did you say that?

A. I did not say, 'When I fired the shot.'

Q. 'As I started to get out of the car I said, 'Move over', he did not move. When I opened the front door Heath was leaning against the left door with his head down, his chin resting sort of on his chest.' Did you say that?

A. Yes, I think I did.

Q. You know, it might have been an expression you did not understand, in which case one will make every allowance, but what I suggested to you not very long ago: When you got into the driving seat this man was sitting slumped in the seat beside you and you said, 'No, he was not.'

A. No, he was not. It doesn't say here he was slumped in his seat.

Q. No, I may not have exactly indicated the attitude he was in but is it right to say, is it: 'With his head down, his chin resting sort of on his chest'?

A. I would say so. Yes.

Q. Obviously a man who was on the point of death?

A. No, his head was just down like this; no more.

Q. You knew perfectly well the bullet had gone through his body?

A. I did not know where, though I knew he was hit; yes.

Q. 'His body was sort of across the car with his right foot under the clutch. When I got into the car he moved his right leg out of the way and mumbled something to me which I didn't understand.' Did you tell Mr De Mott that?

A. Yes, I did.

Q. Then did you go onto say: 'I got in under the wheel. I told Georgina to look him over for his wallet.' Is that right?

A. No, I asked her to look him over for identification.

Q. For identification?

A. Yes.

Q. What did it matter to you who he was?

A. That is just something I did.

Mr JUSTICE CHARLES: What did it matter to you who he was? Why did you tell her to look for his identification?

Mr BYRNE: What you wanted was money, wasn't it?

A. Yes.

Q. It didn't matter who the person was, as long as you relieved that person of money, did it? (The witness did not answer) Well, what is the answer to that question?

A. Just what I said: I asked her to look for his identification.

Mr JUSTICE CHARLES: Why? Why did it matter who he was if he had got anything on him and you could get his money? That is what you were out for. Why?

A. I don't know as I can answer that sir.

Mr BYRNE: Let us go on. Did you say, 'As we were driving along I told Georgina to take everything out of his pockets'? Did you tell Mr De Mott that?

A. No, I did not.

Q. Did you tell her to take everything out of his pockets?

A. No, I did not.

Q. Did she take everything out of his pockets?

A. I don't know.

Q. Did you take anything out of his pockets?

A. No, I did not.

Q. So whatever was taken out of his pockets must have been taken out by her; is that what you say?

A. Yes.

Q. So you did not tell Mr De Mott that, according to you?

A. No, I did not.

Q. 'I drove onto Staines and turned left at the police station.' Is that correct?

A. Yes.

Q. 'About a mile past the police station I turned off the road to the left and followed a dirt road of to the left.' Is that correct?

A. I didn't say a mile past because I didn't know the distance beyond it.

Q. Did you say about a mile?

A. I could have, yes.

Q. 'A short distance down this road and drove over to the left and stopped the car. I got out and walked around the rear of the car.' Is that right?

A. Yes.

Q. 'Georgina got out the right side of the car and walked around the front of the car.' Is that accurate?

A. Yes.

Q. 'I opened the left front door and put my arms through his armpits. I raised him up and pulled him out of the car.' Is that correct?

A. Yes.

Q. 'His feet dropped to the ground. Georgina picked up his feet and we carried him to a ditch which was about three feet from the car.' Is that right?

A. Yes.

Q. 'We returned to the car. I turned around and started back. I wish to state that, as we were driving to the ditch Georgina was going through his pockets, I told her to look and see if he had a watch on.' Is that correct?

A. Yes.

Q. Is that what happened?

A. Yes.

Q. 'She looked and told me she had found a wrist watch on his arm.' Has Mr De Mott got that right; did you tell him that?

A. Yes.

Q. Is it true?

A. Yes.

Q. 'As we were driving back after having disposed of the body Georgina gave me £4 in one pound notes.' Is that right?

A. No.

Q. Do you mean he has not got down accurately what you said?

A. No, it was not on the way back, it was in the time at her room when I got those notes.

Q. 'A long brown US fountain pen, a silver pencil, a small silver cigarette lighter, a cigarette case and a watch.' Is that accurate?

A. All these things were given to me when we got back to her room.

Q. In her room?

A. Yes.

Mr JUSTICE CHARLES: That is all correct?

Mr BYRNE: 'As we were driving back, Georgina threw all of George Heath's pictures out of the car window.' Has Mr De Mott got that down accurately?

A. No, he did not.

Q. Well, what do you say you told him?

A. I threw those pictures out.

Q. 'When we got back to Hammersmith I parked the car in the Old Gaumont car park where I used to park the truck.' Is that correct?

A. Yes.

Q. 'We took our handkerchiefs and wiped off the fingerprints from all parts of the car we had touched.' Is that right?

A. Yes.

Q. You said that, did you? 'We stopped at the Black and White and got something to eat and then went home to bed.' Has he got that down accurately?

A. Yes. There is one part: 'We took our handkerchiefs and wiped the fingerprints off all parts of the car which we had touched.' Well, I didn't say that; I said we wiped off the handle and the steering wheel, that was all.

Mr JUSTICE CHARLES: Wiped off what?

A. The handle of the car on the door and the steering wheel that I had touched.

Mr BYRNE: You wiped the door handle and the steering wheel of the car, was that in order to remove fingerprints, do you mean?

A. Yes.

Mr JUSTICE CHARLES: Yes, there is nothing in that.

Mr BYRNE: No. Before you made that statement were you cautioned by Mr De Mott? Just look at the front page of that statement, will you? Do you see your signature just after the first paragraph?

A. I do.

Q. Did you sign that?

A. No, not until the statement was complete, that is when I signed it.

Q. Was that caution administered to you before you made the statement?

A. Yes, it was put this way: 'I want a statement from you now, the whole truth about the case.' Then he cautioned me after that.

Q. Then he cautioned you after that?

A. Yes.

Q. Did he use these words: 'Private Karl Gustav Hulten, it is my duty to inform you of your rights at this time. It is your privilege to remain silent. Anything you say may be used either for or against you in the event that this investigation results in a trial. Do you thoroughly understand your rights?' Did he use those words?

A. I couldn't say for sure.

Q. Did you reply, ' I do'?

A. Yes.

Q. Are you telling the jury that you did not know you were in a very serious position when you were making that statement?

A. I myself didn't think it was very serious: no.

Re-examined by Mr MAUDE defence for HULTEN.

Q. Only one question in re-examination. Hulten, before you leave the box is there anything in what Mr Byrne has asked you, or what Mr Casswell has asked you, that you would like to explain further?

A. Sir, I think my solicitor has the letter that I received from Mrs Jones. That would explain quite a bit. It was one of those letters that I gave to Mr Trussell [Hulten's solicitor]. I believe it was the first letter I received.

Mr JUSTICE CHARLES: What is this?

Mr MAUDE: My lord, that puts me in a very difficult position.

Mr JUSTICE CHARLES: Well, he is your client.

Mr MAUDE: I know, but nevertheless it is a very difficult position. My lord, I think it should be explained to him. Of course, if in fact any letter is used I shall lose the last word on your behalf, Hulten.

The witness: You see sir, this young lady is saying she was frightened of me.

Mr JUSTICE CHARLES: Don't say what she says!

A. I am not saying what was in the letter.

Q. Deal with what your counsel is dealing with.

A. You see the letter proves that she was not.

Mr MAUDE: Just tell me this, indicate this to me…

Mr JUSTICE CHARLES: You mustn't say the contents of the letter, but he has, you know. Although he was told not to, it slipped in. He said, 'It proves that she was not in fear.' That is what you said, wasn't it?

A. Yes.

Mr JUSTICE CHARLES: You see, he slipped it in, and that won't do. The letter must either be produced or not referred to at all.

A. My lord, I did not know your laws here to that extent.

Mr JUSTICE CHARLES: No, I quite understand.

Mr MAUDE: My lord, I propose to leave it. I have thought about it and I propose to leave it; it is my responsibility.

Mr BYRNE: Let me make it quite plain on behalf of the prosecution. If my learned friend is in any difficulty about that letter, or something of that kind, he need not anticipate I am going to take advantage of any technical situation.

Mr JUSTICE CHARLES: Well, Mr Maude, that is clear and fair enough isn't it?

Mr MAUDE: My lord, I propose to leave it.

Mr JUSTICE CHARLES: I just want to ask one question. (To the witness) It is no good pulling the trigger unless a cartridge is in the breech. Just show the jury how you get it into the breech; go through the action.

A. You draw the bolt back and let it come forward.

Q. That makes a click, doesn't it?

A. Yes.

Q. You had that pistol for about a week?

A. Yes.

Q. There was a cartridge in the breech?

A. Yes.

Q. Who put it there?

A. I might have put it there myself for all I know.

Q. But could have anyone else have? It had been in your possession all the time.

A. Well, I left it in the room while I have been out; I take it could have been put in that way, or I might have done it myself; I don't know. It is something I can't explain.

Q. It could not have got in by accident?

A. No, it did not.

Q. The trigger could not have been pulled back by accident?

A. Yes.

Q. Could the slide have been put at the unsafe condition by accident? Just think what you are saying!

A. This is the slide.

Q. I know.

A. What do you mean?

Q. The safety catch on the side?

A. That could come down by accident; it could go up by accident.

Q. So there would be two accidents and one can understand the third, the introduction of the cartridge, which can only be put in by making that click?

A. Yes.

Mr JUSTICE CHARLES: Thank you, that will do.

FINAL SPEECHES

Mr BYRNE for the Prosecution: May it please your Lordship; members of the jury you have now heard the whole of the evidence and you are at last within measurable distance of the end of this case – which you may think is a sordid and deplorable story – which you have been listening to since Tuesday 16th January 1945. He described in outline the facts of the case, referring to the shooting scene as 'Journey's End on the Great West Road.' Now, in any case there are certain functions which a jury has to perform and certain functions which my lord performs and we at the Bar, no matter which side we are upon, prosecuting or defending – it is our business to give whatever assistance we can give for the proper elucidation of the matters that have to be determined. The plea for double conviction is based on the law. If two persons conspire to commit a felony, and if one of them performs a dangerous act in committing it, then both are guilty and responsible for the consequences. My lord will direct you with regard to the law in this case; you will take the law from him, as we, of course accept the law from him. You yourselves, on the other hand, will find the facts, you are the sole judges of all questions of fact and having found the facts and ascertained those facts, you will then apply those facts as my lord lays it down and in that way you will arrive at your verdict I hope that is quite clear.

Mr CASSWELL defence for JONES.

Your Lordship will recollect that during the re-examination of Hulten, he referred to a certain letter and before he could be stopped, he said quite clearly that it would show that there were no threats by him.

Mr JUSTICE CHARLES: That was a very unfortunate thing; it slipped out, because Mr Maude did not desire that to slip out, but it did.

Mr CASSWELL: By the courtesy of the Prosecution I have seen a copy of that letter and in my submission it does not bear that out at all and I should like your Lordship to see it, to see whether I ought not to have permission to put it in.

Mr JUSTICE CHARLES: I will look at it now. I know Mr Byrne will not have any objection.

Mr BYRNE: Oh no, my lord.

Mr JUSTICE CHARLES: Nor, indeed would Mr Maude. It is no good the jury labouring under a misapprehension, if misapprehension there be. (Letter handed to his Lordship.) This is a letter from the prisoner Jones. Mr Maude, have you any objection to it being read? You see, a totally false impression has been given by your client, a totally false impression, because so far from saying that she was not in any way in fear of him this letter, if I can read plain English, reiterates that what she did she did in fear.

Mr MAUDE: One moment; before your Lordship says that, surely we must decide what should be done about it?

Mr JUSTICE CHARLES: Well, look at it.

Mr MAUDE: I have seen it.

Mr JUSTICE CHARLES: Have you any objection to it going in?

Mr MAUDE: I don't think there could possibly be any objection.

Mr JUSTICE CHARLES: Well, it will be put in and Mr Casswell, you can read it. It has been produced by me by agreement with Mr Maude, representing the prisoner Hulten, and it shall be put in and read.

Mr CASSWELL: Perhaps I may read it now, my lord.

Mr JUSTICE CHARLES: Mr Casswell, I think it ought to be shown to Hulten for him to identify it as the letter. (To the prisoner Hulten) Is that the letter you referred to?

The Prisoner Hulten: I am just going to read it through to find out whether it is right. (After reading the letter) Yes.

Mr JUSTICE CHARLES: It has been identified by Hulten as the letter to which he refers. Mr Casswell, you may now read it at the appropriate point in your speech.

Mr CASSWELL: My lord, I think perhaps I ought to read it now, if your Lordship would not mind.

Mr JUSTICE CHARLES: If you will.

Mr CASSWELL: Members of the jury, this is a letter written from Holloway Prison on 9th December 1944, which says:

'Dear Ricky, I arrived back to Holloway about 7 pm on Monday night. My people were in court and I was talking to them after court was over. They are so very worried, Mum was breaking her heart over me. If I get sent to prison - convicted - it will kill her, so you see, Ricky why you must tell the truth, if I lost my mother, I would go mad. You must tell the truth, Ricky. Don't you think I've suffered enough being in Holloway on remand only? You promised me in court you would tell the whole truth, do not go back on your word Ricky. What the police have against me is going through the man's pockets. Had you not ordered me to do so, I could never have done it. But as my own life was in danger, I did so. I could not believe you had done it, Ricky. You know the condition I was in for hours afterwards. I was dazed and you still threatened me, even when you knew I was too scared to go to the police.

'And there is another thing, you must tell the police as you promised the truth about the body. I did not help you to carry him to the ditch. You know that. Ricky, for God's sake tell the truth. You and God are the only two who know of my innocence. Half this case is fresh to me. The gun for instance - I did not know it was stolen. I did not know your real name, your age or your rank. You were posing as an officer. I did not know you were married and had a child. I did not know you had deserted the Army.

'Why did you do it Ricky? And why have you got me into this? You are making me pay for a nightmare, which I can't believe has really happened. I beg of you to tell the truth Ricky. If you have any respect and honour, or pride, you will speak the truth, Ricky. Sincerely, Georgie.'

MR CASSWELL defence for JONES.

If your Lordship pleases and members of the jury, at one time I was tempted sorely to take a course which I doubt has ever been taken before, and that was to make a speech to you at all, because, you know in my respectful submission no reasonable jury could convict that girl of murder.

(With his hand flung out towards the figure of Jones huddled in her chair)

'He said he was not going to make 'an emotional plea to play on your sympathies. Such tactics would not go down with a hard-headed London jury - but, he asked earnestly, 'does she look like a gunman's moll?'

He then went over the evidence, stressing his client's case of terrorisation.

'If you believe she is guilty - convict her. There is one conclusion you must have reached: that you would not hang a dog on Hulten's evidence.

'Members of the jury, your responsibility is very heavy; so is mine. However often one may appear in this position, one never fails to feel the great responsibility that falls upon one. Members of the jury, she is in your hands and I ask you to find her not guilty.'

(Adjourned to tomorrow morning at eleven o'clock)

CHAPTER ELEVEN

THE TRIAL - SIXTH DAY

TUESDAY 23RD JANUARY 1945

Final speeches continued
Mr MAUDE defence for HULTEN.

Maude rose to make his address to the jury. It was obvious that there was something wrong with him. He was unsteady on his feet, his face drawn with pain.

'May it please your Lordship and members of the jury', Mr Maude began very quietly, his voice low, 'I confess I have never done it before – I confess to a degree of tiredness. Whether it is the war and other matters I do not know. The sixth day of a trial. The sixth day of a long and anxious trial where I now reach culminating point. The Bar knows what it means. The Bench know and you know what it means too.'

Mr Maude then took a bold step, a daring attempt to nullify the natural indignation involved in a case of this nature by emphasising it and turning it upon itself.

'Do not misunderstand my purpose, for was this not a filthy thing, a fearful plot to rob a dying man? This ghoulish account of attendance at a place of public entertainment and the dog races on the same night might take the breath away in its abominableness. Am I not expressing the view of every man and woman? I am going to make the supreme appeal to you. May I remind you of your oath you would not have taken, had you not believed that it meant everything.'

Maude then dealt with Elizabeth Jones, describing her as 'the accuser of someone else as well as the defender of herself.'

'That letter she wrote from Holloway Prison to Hulten on December 9th, it is not a foolish letter as you may think, but a very clever one. Whether certain matters had been explained to her by December, one does not know. But it is abundantly clear she is able to lie, just as Hulten is able to lie. I do not disguise that they both made most ingenious first statements - most ingenious. To get her convicted of murder would be an appalling thought, and quite useless to Hulten, but to show her to be absolutely unreliable does invite you to weigh the scales of justice and do right.'

Maude then asked the jury to make certain that they had no doubts to what actually did happen in that hire car. He then played on the possibilities of an accident and made his plea - for manslaughter on behalf of Hulten. He concluded:' I have nothing more to say, my task is over; your task remains.'

Mr JUSTICE CHARLES - SUMMING UP

Mr Justice Charles took an hour and thirty-five minutes to instruct the jury. He began by defining murder.

'If this shot was fired during and in the forwarding of the felony of robbery and did cause death - that is murder. That is so even if the shot was fired in the midst of a commission of a felony and in order to frighten. That still would be murder. Mr Maude has invited a verdict of manslaughter. Unfortunately he said that with the absolute disregard of the evidence of his own client.

'Although I am not going to exclude consideration of manslaughter, my rule is that if you believe that story told by Hulten as to his total lack of knowledge then he would not be guilty - of anything.'

The judge then traced the movements of Hulten and Jones until they reached the place which Hulten had judged to be suitable for the robbery.

'The pistol was resting on his sleeve, the hammer was back, the safety catch was off and a cartridge was in the breech. It could only have been introduced by that movement, and as the driver bent over he was shot in the middle of the back. There ensued a scene which was almost incredible in its cold-blooded brutality. He did not know whether Heath was alive or dead. Neither knew or cared. Then, quite deliberately - quite deliberately after this affair you are asked to believe was a pure accident - the car was driven off the road, over the grass near a ditch. The body was dragged out. He was asked 'Did you know whether he was alive or dead?' and he said 'No'. He did not seem to take very much interest. He said he did not know the hammer was back and a cartridge in the breech. Can you believe a word of it?' (The judge shook his head.)

'You are entitled to acquit the woman if you believe she was forced into the matter against her will, for she would not then be an accomplice in law. I would remind you here that her landlady said that Jones did not seem to be frightened of Hulten. Jones has stated that she wanted to be thrilled; I can only say that she had found someone who gave her a bigger thrill then she ever expected.

'I now come to the letter read near the close of yesterday's proceedings. It was introduced under somewhat unusual circumstances. I will not read it again, because I do not want you to attach too much importance to it. If you consider that there is some doubt, that her story is true, you can acquit her. If you are satisfied that she was under the domination of that man, you can also acquit her. You can bring in a verdict of guilty or not guilty against either or both of the prisoners.

'Members of the jury, will you consider your verdict and tell me which way you find? Do you find Hulten guilty or not guilty of murder? Do you find Jones guilty or not guilty of murder? If you think it was a pure mischance, such as might have happened, as I say, on a seat in the park – I am afraid there is not much evidence of that, except his own evidence which I commented on – you could find that it was a pure accident, in which case you would find them both not guilty.'

THE FOREMAN OF THE JURY: May we retire my lord, to consider the matter?

Mr JUSTICE CHARLES: Yes, if you like. I have dealt with the question of manslaughter and you understand what I said.

(The jury retired to consider their verdict at 2.45 pm and returned into court at 4.30 pm)

CHAPTER TWELVE

THE VERDICT

THE CLERK OF THE COURT: Members of the jury, are you agreed upon your verdict?

THE FOREMAN OF THE JURY: We are.

THE CLERK OF THE COURT: Do you find the prisoner Elizabeth Marina Jones guilty or not guilty of murder?

THE FOREMAN OF THE JURY: Guilty, with a recommendation to mercy.

THE CLERK OF THE COURT: Do you find the prisoner Karl Gustav Hulten guilty or not guilty of murder?

THE FOREMAN OF THE JURY: Guilty.

THE CLERK OF THE COURT: You find both prisoners guilty of murder, and that is the verdict of you all?

THE FOREMAN OF THE JURY: That is the verdict of us all.

THE CLERK OF THE COURT: Prisoners at the Bar, you severally stand convicted of murder. Have you, or either of you, anything to say why the court should not give you judgement of death according to law?

THE SENTENCES

Mr JUSTICE CHARLES: Elizabeth Marina Jones and Karl Gustav Hulten, you have been found guilty after a long and patient trial by a jury of your fellow men of a most brutal murder. There is only one sentence which the law of this country allows me to pass upon you and upon each of you.

(Formal sentence of death was then passed.)

The Chaplain: Amen.

(The prisoners were removed from the dock.)

Those solemn words were spoken above the condemned woman's sobs and screams as she was dragged away under the court, until the slamming of a door cut off all sounds. Hulten followed, his face blank.

Mr JUSTICE CHARLES: Members of the jury, a very distinguished judge took the course that I think perhaps, for your satisfaction, I ought to take now. You have heard that there was a very long statement taken from Hulten and a very long statement from Jones; you have heard that they made journeys to Reading. I think you should know that the statements of both of them show that those two people had been engaged in murderous or near murderous assaults on other people on those expeditions and that upon one occasion Hulten with a revolver held up another car, but finding that an American officer was in it, desisted from his attempt to stop it. I thought that perhaps it would interest you to know that which by the rules of law in this country, it was impossible to disclose to you at an earlier time.

Members of the jury, I need hardly say that the recommendation that you thought proper to add to your verdict against Jones will forwarded to the proper authority.

★ ★ ★

A FATAL PICKUP

The trial was over, but the story of Karl Gustav Hulten and Elizabeth Marina Jones was to remain in the public eye through many more frantic days. It was announced that both Hulten and Jones were to appeal against the death sentence. With the extremely detailed newspaper revelations of the condemned couple's past, public opinion had swung completely over; sympathy for the eighteen-year-old girl had overnight turned into an overwhelming demand that she should be made to pay.

Jones's parents were allowed to see her in a special room at Holloway Prison reserved for interviews with condemned persons. Her parents tried to calm her, but she refused to talk to them, and they eventually left and went back home to Neath.

Hulten, in Wormwood Scrubs Prison, was living a quiet life, hoping that the United States Government would intervene on his behalf. His wife Rita and his mother Signe Hulten appealed first to the State Department, then to the President of the United States himself.

The date for the appeal was announced: Tuesday 20th February 1945 at the Royal Courts Of Justice. Jones, from refusing to believe that her appeal could fail, would suddenly be plunged into panic for days on end; from ever more frequent bouts of religious fervour, she would unexpectedly launch into a venomous outburst against the jury which had found her guilty. Here is an extract from one of her many letters:

'God - what a jury! I hate the London people. I hate that jury. Everything pointed to my innocence and they found me guilty.'

Hulten wrote very few letters. He was guarded night and day by two members of the so-called 'Death Watch.' One of the wardens' hardest tasks was to persuade him to take exercise in the yard; he preferred to lie on his bed for hours at a time, just staring into space. Karl Gustav Hulten asked no favours from the prison staff.

Tuesday 20th February 1945 was the day of Hulten's and Jones' appeals, to be heard in Court of Appeal No 2.

Before: - Mr JUSTICE MACNAGHTEN.
Mr JUSTICE WROTTESLEY.
Mr JUSTICE CROOM-JOHNSON.

The Strand outside the Law Courts was packed with people trying to get in. Every seat inside the court was filled, including the press seats. The door at the back of the curtained dock high up to the left to the bench opened and the pallid face of Hulten was seen looking round into the court. He was wearing his Army greatcoat. Mrs Jones followed, wearing a dark-coloured sweater under a grey coat. She looked tired and ill and very unsteady on her feet. The curtain protected them from all but the bench counsel and the press box.

Mr Maude rose to open his appeal on behalf of Hulten. He started by saying that the learned Judge had omitted to direct the jury adequately upon the law relating to manslaughter and that he had wrongly admitted in evidence statements made by Hulten. He also said that in his summing up, he had not put the defence adequately to the jury.

His Lordship said to the jury that there was a suggestion by counsel that on the evidence that they might find a verdict of manslaughter. He gave no direction of the nature of the evidence on which a verdict of manslaughter might have been found.

Mr Maude continued, criticising the admission of Hulten's statements as evidence. He asserted that Mr Justice Charles had acted upon a wrong principle.

If ever there was a case, Maude said, where a voluntary statement was followed by questions clearly suggesting the answers, it was this one. He was not suggesting anything against Mr De Mott, but the nature of some of the answers indicated that Hulten had been led. The Lieutenant had given a most careful caution to Hulten, but it was abundantly clear that the statements had been taken in a way their Lordships would never tolerate for one minute. He went on to submit that in Mr Justice Charles's summing up there was nothing inviting the jury to consider that Hulten's defence might possibly be true.

Mr Maude then sat down; his appeal had lasted about one hour. The Court then adjourned for lunch.

When the court resumed, Mr Casswell rose and began his appeal on behalf of Jones. He submitted that Mr Justice Charles had gone out of his way to attack his client's character. He then went on to say that he supported Mr Maude's argument that there was evidence to support a verdict of manslaughter. Hulten's story was that he had intended to frighten Heath, and the jury were entitled to say that what happened was an accident, occurring in the course of proceedings which were not intended to result in violence. In Casswell's submission, to render anyone liable for murder in these circumstances the test was not whether he did something in the course of carrying out an unlawful design. The evidence was all in favour of the fact that the mode of robbery was putting Heath in fear and not by violence.

Mr Casswell was quickly pulled up on this point, two of the judges pointing out that there was no appreciable difference between physical violence and mental violence. Mr Casswell argued, but he had to give way.

He continued to support Hulten's case to the utmost, when Mr Justice Macnaghten calmly reminded him: 'I seem to remember, Mr Casswell, that during the trial you suggested to the jury that they would not hang a dog on Hulten's evidence, am I correct?' Mr Casswell's face reddened slightly and there was suppressed laughter in the court.

At the end of the day it was apparent that Mr Maude's and Mr Casswell's appeals to the three judges were getting nowhere.

The Court was adjourned until the following morning, Wednesday 21st.

On the Wednesday, Mr Casswell returned to his attack with the allegation that Mrs Jones had entered upon the expedition with no foreknowledge of the violence that was to take place.

Mr Justice Macnaghten: 'But there is no doubt that she knew what Hulten meant when he said 'Get a taxi.' It meant go and rob a taxi driver.'

Mr Casswell replied, 'But what sort of design was she a party to? Was it one involving violence? No'. Before Mr Casswell could get away from this subject he was twice reminded by Mr Justice Macnaghten that Mrs Jones had selected the victim.

Mr Casswell then went on to his final comments. 'I approached this part of my case with the greatest reluctance, but it is my duty to draw attention to one or two matters. It is not desirable that any remarks should come from the Bench in the way of criticism during the evidence of the accused. She was defending her life. She was never known to have committed or taken part in the commission of any act of violence before she met this man. She knew that even if acquitted of this charge, there were others hanging over her in respect of those three days.

It is undesirable for criticism to be made from the Bench - especially criticism implying that her previous life had not been what it should. It was especially important in this case because of her age, the circumstances of the case and the tremendous amount of press publicity, during the giving of her evidence. His Lordship interposed: 'You did live with other men.' That was not put in the nature of a question, but as a statement of fact.

Mr Justice Macnaghten: 'But did you not yourself introduce the question of her past?'

Mr Casswell: 'Yes, your Lordship, I did, because of the unfortunate stories that had appeared in the newspapers that Mrs Jones had been a prostitute.'

Mr Casswell did not continue long after that and the appeals were concluded. At 12.30 pm Mr Justice Macnaghten conferred with his fellow Justices and the court was adjourned until two o'clock that same day.

At two o'clock the three judges resumed their places on the Bench. There were several United States Admirals present and also Elizabeth Jones' parents. There were hordes of press reporters ready to report the news of the verdict. Hulten and Jones were brought in. Hulten looked quite relaxed and composed, but Jones was a pitiful sight. They both stood in the dock for some time, waiting to hear the result of their appeal.

Mr Justice Macnaghten spoke slowly but quite plainly: Hulten's statements were rightly admitted, for they were taken in accordance with the custom prevailing in his own country, but not in this country. Concerning the other grounds, which came under the heading of inadequate direction on the law of manslaughter, in the opinion of the Court, by the common law of England, Hulten had committed murder. His appeal was therefore dismissed.

There was no reaction from Hulten. As for Jones, on hearing this she swayed on her feet and the three wardresses had to hold her up.

Mr Justice Macnaghten went on to crush the grounds of Jones's appeal. He said that she knew quite well the violence Hulten intended to use in the robbery, furthermore she knew he was in possession of a deadly weapon, which was used to shoot Heath. This made her guilty of murder, although it could be second degree murder. Her defence was that she was in fear of Hulten throughout and there was nothing to support this but her word only. The Judges concluded that she was a willing actor in the matter and she had rightly been convicted of murder. Her appeal was dismissed.

The girl's parents just stared at the bench and did not once look at their daughter, who was carried out screaming. Both Hulten and Jones were driven back to their prison and preparations began for their execution, which was to take place on March 8th 1945, just two weeks away.

CHAPTER THIRTEEN

THE AFTERMATH

Immediately after the appeal, Commander Locker-Lampson, Conservative MP for Handsworth, put down a question to Herbert Morrison, the Home Secretary in the House of Commons asking for a reprieve for Jones on the grounds of her youth. For Hulten there was no sympathy – yet, though naturally his relations in America were doing their best to save him. Rita, his wife, and his mother, Signe Hulten, engaged a lawyer who contacted Mr Maude asking what measures could be taken to ask the Home Secretary for clemency. Sadly Mr Maude had to reply there was nothing that could be done. It was now the Home Secretary's responsibility whether Hulten lived or died.

As the March days passed and the date of execution approached, Herbert Morrison faced great public pressure. Jones' parents even wrote a letter to the King and Queen pleading for their daughter's life. Mr John Winant, the American Ambassador in London, was cabled from Washington to be told that an appeal to Herbert Morrison was on its way from Hulten's home state of Massachusetts. Rita Hulten made several unsuccessful attempts to telephone her husband, but on each occasion she was refused permission. Many were convinced that Hulten was being victimised, especially when he was not allowed to speak to his wife on the phone before he died on the British gallows. Yet Jones's parents were allowed to visit her in a special room reserved for condemned prisoners.

With all this controversy spreading around the country Mrs Winifred Ivy Heath, widow of the murdered man, was doing domestic work. She was earning nine shillings a week to help with her widow's pension of eighteen shillings. She also received a public assistance grant of twenty-four shillings and sixpence. There was a contribution of 100 guineas from the *News Of The World* newspaper to help her and her two sons, George Anthony, aged eight, and Arthur Barry, aged five. Later a fund was opened for the education of the two boys.

At midnight on Tuesday March 6th, two days before the pair were due to be hanged, the Governor of Holloway Prison, Doctor Mathieson, went to Jones's cell to inform her that the Home Secretary had granted her reprieve. She broke down and started sobbing. After a few minutes she asked for a pencil and paper to write to her mother to ask her to bring her best clothes to the prison and prepare for a home-coming party. But the Governor quite sternly told her that a reprieve did not mean she was going free. She would have to come to terms with the fact that she could face a prison term of between 12 to 15 years. With this she became hysterical, and was removed to the prison hospital.

During this time in Wormwood Scrubs Prison, Hulten was told that the Home Secretary did not feel justified in interfering with his sentence. Later Hulten wrote to Mr Maude thanking him for his efforts in trying to save him. The same night the news was flashed across to America; reactions were mixed. Mrs Rita Hulten commented: 'Karl was certainly never the type that this girl was. All I can do now is pray for my husband'.

Senator Charles Guinness said that by sparing Jones and not Hulten the British Government was laying itself open to charges of discrimination against an American soldier.

On Wednesday March 7th the country learned that Jones was to live and Hulten was to die. Reaction was overwhelming. Herbert

Morrison had not fully foreseen the cries of protest that went across the country. Why should she be saved and not him, was the cry. Telegrams by the hundred began to arrive at the Home Office demanding that Jones should hang, and abusing Morrison for his decision. Workers all over England and Scotland drew up joint protests and sent them to the Home Office. Newspaper officers in Fleet Street were besieged by telephone calls from angry women.

In Jones's home town of Neath, slogans were appearing on walls reading 'She should hang' with a crude drawing of a figure dangling from a scaffold.

The day before the hanging was to take place, Rita Hulten tried once more to speak to her husband on the phone. The Prison Governor at Wormwood Scrubs stated that direct contact was impossible, but he would pass on any message to Hulten. A United States spokesman in London said they would give Rita Hulten a seat on a plane across the Atlantic, but they were told it was a matter for the British authorities to grant permission for her to see him. A radioed photograph of Hulten's wife and mother together appeared in the London evening papers. It would seem that Rita Hulten was unable either to speak to her husband or see him before his execution.

On the afternoon of the 7th March Hulten was taken to Pentonville Prison, where the execution was to take place at 9 am the next morning. That night, before Hulten retired to bed, he wrote a last letter to his wife and mother.

The next morning, March the 8th 1945, a crowd was beginning to gather outside Pentonville Prison and by 8 am there were over 500 hundred people round the gates. Special police squads had been posted and were watching very carefully as the mass of demonstrators gathered. A scene was obviously anticipated.

At 9 am an American car drove up and went into the prison; it was carrying two high-ranking United States Army officers. A chaplain followed a few minutes later. A third car drove straight up to the gates of the prison, and out stepped the figure of Mrs Violet Van Der Elst. This lady was a wealthy campaigner for the abolition of the death penalty. She pushed her way through the crowd and tried to open the prison gates. Police officers tried to stop her, but she went on to try and open the gate. The crowd began to shout and followed this woman, shouting out 'You let the girl off but you are hanging this young man, is this British justice?'

Extra police were called to guard the prison gates, while others struggled to control the jostling, shouting crowd. Mrs Van Der Elst climbed into the cab of a commercial lorry which was parked in a side street. The young man behind the wheel started the engine up and made an attempt to ram the prison gates. The intervention of two police cars managed to stop them. Four policemen tried to escort them away, but men and women were pushing and shoving calling for the police to let them go. It was mayhem. It seemed that the police had lost all control over this angry crowd.

At 7 am Hulten was given prison clothes, without a collar or tie. The United States Army authorities would not allow him to wear his uniform. Hulten was offered breakfast, but refused it. He was calm and relaxed, and being a Roman Catholic he was ready to receive the Last Sacraments from the Prison Chaplain, who then stayed with him. At a few minutes to 9 am the Prison Governor, the executioner, his assistant, a medical officer and the prison engineer went into Hulten's cell and told him the time had come.

As he was being walked to the death chamber, Hulten asked about Elizabeth Jones. When told she had been reprieved, he said: 'I wish her luck, I do not bear her any malice but if I had never met her I wouldn't be here today'.

He was given a tot of brandy and then the executioner's assistant pinioned his arms behind his back above the elbow. Before the white cap was placed over his head he said to the Chaplain, 'Thank you padre for saying with me'. Then two guards walked him into the execution chamber and he was guided to a chalk mark on the trap. The white cap was placed over his head, the noose adjusted, the executioner stepped back - and the life of Karl Gustav Hulten was finished.

Doctor H P Young, the prison Medical Officer, went down into the pit below the execution chamber and pronounced that Hulten was dead. At 10 am his body was drawn up and taken to the mortuary. After the Prison Governor had identified the body, a verdict of 'death by judicial hanging' was returned. Karl Gustav Hulten's body was then buried in the prison grounds.

★ ★ ★

When the American GIs had arrived in Britain in preparation for D-Day, Elizabeth Maude Jones, like so many young girls, was gripped with excitement. One may wonder if the six days she spent in the company of Karl Gustav Hulten and his death on the British gallows ever returned to haunt her.

Never again in this country, one may hope, will a would-be 'gun moll' come together with a real potential gunman to cause the death of an innocent man. What possessed this 22-year-old man to go down the road to destruction after arriving in England in 1944 will never be known. From the moment he left his army base armed with an automatic pistol and stole a ten-wheel Army truck, Hulten's destiny was surely sealed.

On the evening of 3rd October 1944 he had walked into a café in Hammersmith and been introduced to eighteen-year-old Elizabeth Maude Jones, a young woman who from her early childhood had been beyond her parents' control and had ended up in an approved school. Her marriage to a soldier at the tender age of sixteen was never consummated. While she was still sixteen she had arrived in London, the place of her dreams, in the hope of becoming a striptease dancer, a job she knew nothing about.

The meeting of these two young people was to lead to carnage. First, on a lonely country road, an innocent girl cycled into the path of Hulten's truck and was deliberately knocked off her bicycle while Hulten and Jones robbed her and left her dazed and helpless on the roadside. Then Hulten attacked another young woman, Violet Hodge, striking her over the head with a block of wood and attacking her with his fists while Jones looked on. She helped Hulten to go through her belongings, taking a few shillings in cash, while Jones took the girl's coat off her before her apparently lifeless body was thrown into the Thames River. It was a miracle that she survived such an ordeal. Violet was barred from several public houses and cafés, simply because of her connection with this case.

And then we come to the night of Friday 6th October 1944, when George Heath picked up Hulten and Jones in his hire car - truly a fatal pickup.

The day after this brutal murder, Jones told Hulten she had always wanted a fur coat, and she knew where it was possible to get one. They drove in the dead man's car to the side entrance of the Berkeley Hotel in London and waited until a woman appeared in a white ermine fur coat, whereupon Hulten rushed over to the woman and pulled the coat off. The robbery was prevented only because the woman's screams attracted the attention of a nearby policeman.

Jones's trumped-up story of being afraid of Hulten was her only line of defence, and she well knew it. This woman could have walked away from Hulten more than a dozen times, but she had not.

When Heath's body was found and the police came knocking on her door, Jones knew there was no hiding place. All she could do was repeat one of her many pathetic cries of innocence: 'Hulten shot Heath, not me, and everything I did he ordered me to do or he would use the gun on me'. Yet this woman still went back to Hulten each time for more.

★ ★ ★

In that last letter written by Hulten to his mother and wife, he said 'Everyone makes a mistake in their lives and this one was mine'. As the letter was being read, his wife wept and clung to their baby daughter Jean. 'Please don't feel too badly about this and try in your hearts to forgive me' the letter went on. 'I am very lonely without you, mother and Rita and I wish I could start my life over again. So to end this letter I send lots of kisses for each mile that this letter must travel to reach you.'

Hulten's mother, Signe Maria Hulten, is believed to have died on the 21st February 1991 at the age of 96 years, outliving her errant son by more than 45 years. Her last place of residence was believed to be 16 Westland Avenue, Boston, Massachusetts. Before her death she tried to have her son's remains brought back to America. Whether she was successful or not, my research did not reveal; it remains unknown.

Hulten's wife, Rita M Hulten, was reported to have returned to her parent's home at 22 Prince Street, Cambridge Massachusetts.

During the trial it was reported that a man sitting at the back of the court was Hulten's father, but his name was not disclosed.

President Franklin D Roosevelt said Hulten was an embarrassment to the United States Government and the case should serve as a warning to English girls against hobnobbing with flashy yanks.

As Jones was under twenty-one years of age, she began what was supposed to be a life sentence in a Borstal institution at Aylesbury, Buckinghamshire. She continued to write to her solicitor asking him to intervene with successive Home Secretaries for her release, and eventually, after serving only nine years of her sentence, she was released on licence in May 1954. There are conflicting reports as to what became of her when she was released, one indicating that she changed her name, remarried and went to live in the country, while another says there was no trace of her after she was released. Some British and American newspapers reported that she died in 1984; if this were true she would have been 58 years old.

When she was released, much to her parent's disapproval, she gave a story to an Australian newspaper about her six weeks in a condemned cell. It was printed in the newspaper in five parts from 12th October to the 18th October 1954.

Mrs Violet Van Der Elst was a vigorous campaigner against the death penalty, and she gained publicity from her vocal campaigns against the death penalty. At one time she had been a washerwoman, but that all changed when she married a wealthy Belgium painter, Jean Van Der Elst. On his death she was left a fortune, but over the years she squandered away all the money and died penniless in 1966.

Both Hulten and Jones denied having sex. However, according a statement by Jones's landlady, Mrs Edris May Evans, whilst cleaning her room one day, she found a used rubber contraceptive under the carpet. This was not mentioned in the trial.

George Heath's Ford V8 saloon was bought by a London second-hand car dealer who later put it on display with images of Heath, Hulten and Jones.

★ ★ ★

The following are extracts from the Court Martial in America of Private Karl Gustav Hulten, Serial No. 31357916.

From the War Department Washington, dated 20th February 1945:

Memorandum for the Judge Advocate General: The Under Secretary Of War has directed me to transmit to you for study and retention in your file, the following papers received from the Commanding General UK Base CZ, ETO. Letters involved on Hulten's case and the Transcript of the record of the trial of Hulten.

Signed Robert Cutler Colonel G.S.C. Office of the Secretary of War.

C.M. Form 4 Forwarding Endorsements.

Name of accused: Hulten Karl G. Aged 22 years seven months.

Character of service (prior to this offence): Satisfactory.

Previous Convictions: One.

In my opinion he should be eliminated from the service. I recommend trial by General Court Martial.

Signed Arthur W. Coapman Captain Signal Corps. Investigating Officers.

Walter F. Graham Colonel CE Commanding. I also recommend trial by General Court Martial.

Headquarters United Kingdom Base: Communications Zone European. Theatre of Operations: APO 413 U.S. Army c/o Postmaster New York NY.

Dated 23rd February 1945

Herewith for your information is a copy of the decision of the Court of Criminal Appeal dismissing the appeal of Private Karl Gustav Hulten. The date of execution has been set 8th March 1945.

Signed for the Commanding General Peter Perters Lt. Col. Adjutant General.

To the Under Secretary of War: Washington 25, D.C.
Pursuant to cable No EX 97147 from ETOUSA signed Eisenhower to AGWAR dated 12th February 1945 copy of which is enclosed herewith.

Report of investigation and allied papers: In the case of Private Karl Gustav Hulten. Signed Peter Peters Lt. Col. Adjutant General.